THE SONG OF
THE NIBELUNGS

THE SONG OF THE NIBELUNGS

A Verse translation from the Middle High German
Nibelungenlied

by Frank G. Ryder

Indiana University

Detroit   *Wayne State University Press*   *1962*

TO SHIRLEY

✠ TRANSLATOR'S PREFACE

This translation tries to reproduce the *Nibelungenlied* according to the principal characteristics of its style and language and in a verse form approximating that of the original.

The basic unit of the poem is a quatrain resembling (though not necessarily derived from) the typical strophe of one of the earliest German troubadours or *Minnesänger*. This lyric strophe, called the *Kürenberger,* after its creator, was set to music and sung. Recent studies have suggested that the *Nibelungenlied* was at first chanted, in a sort of recitative, so that the use of a musically oriented verse form would not be surprising. (Unlike the lyric, the epic strophe can scarcely have had an independent melody, as the most patient audience would not have stood for over 2,000 repetitions of even the most popular tune.) In later years, the poem was certainly what the Germans call a *Leseepos,* an epic to be read.

The most obvious feature of the stanza is its long last line. It is attained, in terms of the usual prosodic analysis, by the regular filling of a metrical foot which is invariably empty in the first three lines. The latter have a pattern of four stresses (´or `) before a caesura and three, plus a pause, after it. In the fourth line the pause is replaced by a syllable with stress. The first stanza therefore scans

uns	íst in álten mǽrèn	/		wúnders víl giséit (Pause)
von	hélden lóbebǽrèn,	/	von	grózer árebéit, (Pause)
von	fröúden, hóchgezítèn,	/	von	wéinen únd von klágen, (Pause)
von	küéner récken strítèn	/ muget	ír nu wúnder hǿren ságen.

The word *klagen* (with short vowel in open syllable plus in-flectional *-en*) is considered the equivalent of a monosyllable (metrically = *-seit*), and the strophe thus incorporates the two common types of rhyme word. The caesural rhyme is rare. (Only this and strophe 17 carry it through the quatrain.) In other quatrains there are end-rhymes like *wíldè:schíldè*, and even trisyllabic ones. Sometimes one finds no unstressed syllable between stresses—sometimes two or three instead of the usual one.

Rhyme is strongly repetitive (*man* appears as rhyme word 512 times; the rhyme pair *líp:wíp* 175 times). It is also predominantly pure. Some exceptions, for example the frequent rhyming of long *a* with short, doubtless reflect the dialect area involved. There are cases where exact judgment is impossible, but rhymes like *Hagene* with *degene* (or with *gademe, menege*) and *frum: sun* are certainly what we should call slant rhymes or off-rhymes.

Any translator who takes up the challenge of working in verse has several crucial decisions to make. The first concerns line length. There is one older version which chooses octameter, but given the relative morphological compactness of English (compared to Middle High German) and the original poet's addiction to padding, the result is sheer verbosity. Even hexameter, the usual solution, makes intolerable demands for expansion of the content. The present version uses a five-beat line —pentameter will say all that is needed, and it is basically more congenial to English. I have taken considerable liberty with unaccented syllables, though actually less than would be warranted by the precedent of the original.

All but one of the previous translators eliminate the long last line. I feel that it is the most distinctive feature of the strophe, a hallmark of the poem; I have therefore kept it. Now of course it becomes a six-foot line.

The name "Nibelung" is vexatious. It is used for Sigfrid's knights and then, astonishingly, for the Burgundians in Part II.

I saw no other choice than to leave it so. There are two possible explanations for the duplication. One is that "Nibelung" must have been a very old designation for Burgundians (appearing in the prototype of Part II), and that the repetition is therefore striking but coincidental. This would seem to accord best with the genealogical view of the poem's origins. The other is that the name went with whoever had the treasure, and I chose (e.g., strophe 1523) to follow this explanation because it seems at least to make sense within the story.

There are three principal manuscripts of the *Nibelungenlied*. B, the one used as the basis for most editions and for this translation, is in the *Stiftsbibliothek* in St. Gall, Switzerland. A slightly shorter version appears in manuscript A in Munich. C, in Donaueschingen (in Southwest Germany), is sufficiently lengthened and altered to constitute in effect what the most recent editor of the epic, Helmut de Boor, calls "a second, revised edition." A much more recent manuscript, **d**, has made possible a good deal of textual improvement. Beyond these there are many copies and fragments. The Nibelungen story was obviously one of the most popular works of the Middle Ages.

The text and dictionary of Karl Bartsch, and the reworking thereof in the text and annotations of de Boor, constitute the immediate basis of this translation. The writer of manuscript C, beside adding substantially to the text, was often aware of inconsistency or awkwardness in it, which he took pains to eliminate. In two cases his ideas result in passages so much improved that I have incorporated them, with due footnoting. There is good precedent for this. Through the years, scribes of other manuscript traditions borrowed freely from C.

I have not hesitated to use more run-on lines (though not many more run-on strophes) than the original. There are two reasons for this. Not only is it more in keeping with modern taste but it helps to avoid at least partially the obtrusiveness of the rhyme. For the same purpose, I have increased the number of off-rhymes.

There are other areas of language, less tangible but more significant, in which the translator must take a stand. In level of diction the *Nibelungenlied* is closer to natural speech than to an elaborate or elevated style. To be sure, there are many repeated epithets in the poem, and many sentence fillers (the latter due especially to the quatrain form). Without violence to the poem one can remove some of this excess, especially in the narrative passages, where it is most frequent. The speech of the characters in this very "dramatic" epic is surprisingly natural, and most of the narration is clear and uncomplicated. This should, I feel, be the prevailing tone of a new version.

The *Nibelungenlied* was largely free of conscious archaizing, and the poet certainly did not create his own Homeric dialect or lexicon. An older form occasionally appears, but it is relatively rare. Maintaining this predominant naturalness of vocabulary I take as a mandate. (In all the previous versions, prose as well as verse, there is scarcely a line free of conspicuous archaisms. Here, as in archaizing translations from the classics, one is left with the impression that, in T. F. Higham's words, "one dead language is burying another.")

Morphologically, the *Nibelungenlied* is largely chaste and unadorned, which outlaws *hath* and *doth* and their numerous kin. In this respect too, the poem cooperates with the translator in search of naturalness.

Unfortunately, not all the problems are so easily resolved. The *Nibelungenlied* has certain shortcomings which press hard on the translator. It is somewhat prolix, and the quatrain form forces a noticeable juggling of content. If there is a choice between cliché and freshness the singer of the Nibelung story too often chooses the cliché, in rhyme and imagery as well as in general expression. Where the greatest epic poets soar, he remains on the ground, a posture which has some advantages but many disadvantages. Yet the form at its weakest never completely vitiates the story. At its best it is an essential participant in the excellence of the whole—witness many passages where the heroic is presented with stark directness or beauty described with moving economy. One must not make too much of the shortcomings. Any translator will have enough of his own.

A few details need explanation. I have tried to use modern names for places (and persons) where these are known or reasonably surmised. For Middle High German *Etzel* I have used the original name *Attila* and have tried to write so that it may be read with either stress. For *Îslant* I decided to say *Iceland,* because this is what it would be phonetically, and as such it looks interesting or at least familiar. I realize the poet did not have any place clearly in mind. For the name of the hero of Part I, which appears with some variation in the poem to begin with, I chose to write Sigfrid, though with less—or entirely—unfamiliar names I stayed closer to the Middle High German orthography.

The poet had a considerable attachment to the indefinite pronoun subject. Some reduction is possible, but I am afraid unidentified "they" still appears rather often.

I have not even raised the question: Why a verse translation? Taste and preference suggest the answer. The poem has its own definite, characteristic form, and one's first reaction is that the modern reader should encounter the work in something approximating that form. In contemplating any other course, I recall what Robert Frost said about writing without rhyme: It is like playing tennis with the net down. Besides, other verse translations are either inaccurate, archaic, or out of print.

F. G. R.

Dartmouth College
Hanover, N. H.

✠ CONTENTS

Part II

✟ INTRODUCTION

Around the year 1200 an unknown Middle High German poet, probably an Austrian knight-cleric, composed an epic which ranks as the most impressive single work of medieval German literature and stands in the small company of great national epics, with the *Iliad,* the *Aeneid,* the *Roland,* and the *Cid.* In mastery of poetic form and in certain aspects of structure the author was no rival for Homer or Vergil. His parity with his French and Spanish counterparts may even be debated. In every other way—in the pure art of story, in the creation of epic figures, in vigor and directness of characterization, in monumental scope and power—his work can bear comparison with any of the great epics. Like them, it is a true work of world literature, faithful to its time but not bound by it, comprehensible and of significance to an audience centuries removed.

The present English translation, the first in over forty years, is an attempt to make the text of the poem more readily available to the modern reader. The purpose of the succeeding prefatory remarks is to introduce and briefly explain certain features of the poem to the same modern reader, primarily—in the spirit of current criticism—through the poem itself.

In the largest view the work is bipartite. Two great complexes of epic action are joined together: in the first part the life and death of Sigfrid, his glory, fault, and betrayal; in the second the massive destruction of those who betrayed him, engineered by Kriemhild his wife and in the end engulfing her.

The great human emotion which dominates the entire action

is the drive for retribution—"overweening pride . . . and awful vengeance" (strophe 1003). The mood is that of fated tragedy, but the pathos of inevitable loss is countered by the valor, excellence, and "loyal commitment" (*triuwe*) of chivalry. The theme, struck so often in the lines of the poem, is the inexorable connection of *liebe* and *leide,* of happiness, that is, and what it must end in: suffering and grief: *als ie diu liebe leide z'aller jungeste gít* (strophe 2378)—the almost literal counterpart of Chaucer's *For evere the latter ende of joye is wo* (*NPT 385*).

The Course of Action

In Part I, against a backdrop of courtly rituals, journeys, wars, and hunts, there unfolds an inexorable sequence of tragic events proceeding from the encounter of fixed elements of character and situation, and dominated by a sense of hostile fate and impending doom. Overconfidence and rash intervention (the shadow sides of excellence and generosity) lead to entanglement, misunderstanding, and insult. Insult demands revenge, jealousy and rivalry encourage it, and revenge is taken. The crying need for counterrevenge stands at the end like a gulf into which the events and persons of the second part must be drawn, completing the fatal progression toward complete disaster.

The note of fate is struck in the first "Adventure": Kriemhild's dream of the falcon (her husband) destroyed by two eagles (Hagen and Gunther), and the somber motto "Pain is the price of pleasure" (17). Even the introduction of the two main characters (Adventures 1, 2, and much of 3) has its augury of trouble—Kriemhild's vow to shun love, and, in the midst of the introduction of Sigfrid as a perfect knight, the ominous note of overbearing pride ("What can't be got from them on a friendly tack / I'll take with the strength of my hand"; 55), which his father significantly regrets even as he accedes to his son's plan.

The encounter, then, is prepared in a context of ill omen on the one hand, arrogant pride on the other. The chivalric world was of course not averse to well-founded pride, and verbal humility was not one of its virtues, hence we must be wary of modern character judgments on Sigfrid—yet incautious pride remains a flaw not unrelated to ancient *hybris*.

The interlude of the Saxon War serves much the same purpose as the Homeric *aristeia*: a witness of greatness. It also offers the first instance of Gunther's dependence on Sigfrid, and thus anticipates the action to follow. Basically it remains—and not in a paradoxical sense—an idyll of martial prowess, just as the next Adventure (5) is, in the meeting of Sigfrid and Kriemhild, an idyll of courtly love. This is the poet's technique. Before each "descending action" he places a moment of fruition, splendor, or serenity. So it is here. Then the concentrated action of the plot begins in earnest and with little delay (Adventure 6). The source of the terrible chain of consequences is not hard to specify. It lies in the pattern of deception to which Gunther (in his weakness and overambitious desire) and Sigfrid (in thoughtless overconfidence) agree. Gunther gets into trouble because he is willing to accept the help of another to accomplish what he should either manage himself or abandon, Sigfrid because he lends his vast powers, not thinking at all of the possible result. Each man does this in order to win himself a wife. On either a medieval plane or a modern one, their approaches are wrong, though perhaps for differing reasons. The importance of this pattern of deception is underscored and imaged in the next vital step of the progression: the masquerading of Sigfrid as Gunther's vassal.

The actual winning of Brunhild proceeds entirely according to plan. From a realistic view—and this is an astonishingly realistic work—there is weakness in the supernatural quality of these curious "track and field events," somewhat made up for by the excellent touches of Gunther's momentary anxiety and Sigfrid's ruse of surprised pleasure at the end.

The next step in the grim development of the principal plot comes after long interludes of adventures, journeys, and ceremonies. It is again realistic and logical. Sigfrid having secured his betrothal to Kriemhild, the two sit in a place of honor totally out of keeping with the role of a vassal. This causes in Brunhild an immediate reaction of shock and grief. (More subtle reasons for her distress can be found between the lines.) "I'm sick at heart for your sister! Here at the side / Of your own vassal she sits; I must weep / At seeing her degraded thus and sunk so deep" (620). The consoling words of Gunther merely postpone the crisis. The complex of deception must be renewed after the terrible travesty of Gunther's wedding night. Each step is again an inevitable extension of previous involvement, and there is, as always in the *Nibelungenlied,* no possibility of return. Sigfrid has to conquer Brunhild for Gunther again. This time it happens in what would seem to be even more humiliating circumstances, though the question is only briefly raised. (A comic quality attaches to the episode, but it can be overestimated.)

To the ill-considered loan of his prowess, Sigfrid now adds a gesture of stupefying rashness—literally an act of "souveniring" in a context of considerable delicacy. He takes Brunhild's ring and sash (the author says "I cannot say if being overbold / Made him do this") and, even more wildly irresponsible, hands the souvenirs of this struggle to his wife. These articles become instruments as fatal as Desdemona's handkerchief.

The pattern of deception augmented by impetuosity leaves in the hearts of both queens a precipitate of angry suspicion. Clearly Brunhild's umbrage at the sight of Kriemhild wedded to her "vassal," and at Sigfrid's proud and independent life, rankles for a long time before it produces that invitation with malice aforethought which renews the forward motion of the plot.

"Gunther's wife kept thinking all the while. . . ." "This she held in silence in her heart, / Embittered. . . ." (724-725). If the *Nibelungenlied* were a modern psychological novel (which it is in Edith Simon's *Twelve Pictures,* but with a background precluding the question about to be raised) there is scarcely any doubt that the presence of another thorn in the sensitive flesh of Brunhild would receive even fuller attention: suspicion that all was not in order with her double defeat, and that Sigfrid is somehow connected with the discrepancy. As it is, only the external affronts to the courtly pattern are explicitly noted by Brunhild: Kriemhild's "mismarriage" and Sigfrid's "nonfeasance." But several earlier occurrences point at least to confused jealousy and frustration (though not to any previous love): She thinks Sigfrid must be the one who will try to win her; her welcome and her later astonishment are accordingly portrayed; she is not truly convinced of her own defeat; she "cuts" Sigfrid after Gunther has told her to greet him; at Worms her tears are not allayed even when Gunther says Sigfrid *is* a king.

By contrast, the reader is left entirely to his own speculations as to the effect upon Kriemhild of the humiliating evidence now in her hands—and even her words in the quarrel do not fully enlighten us.

The argument of the two queens is the final disruption of the uneasy equilibrium and the unleashing of the machinery of vengeance. It is also another exhibit in the spiraling of evil, and the impelling role therein of the irrevocable taunt. The quarrel begins—with unsurpassed logic and effect—when Kriemhild strikes at the very core of Brunhild's irritation and vastly intensifies it. If Brunhild had hoped to achieve anything by bringing Kriemhild and Sigfrid here it was to put them in their places, for the sake not merely of vanity but of the sanctity of the feudal order. Now Kriemhild flatly asserts the absolute reverse of Brunhild's premise: "My husband's hand / Should rightly rule

5

the width and breadth of all this land" (815). The fatal argument is joined. There is no point in following its course—a masterful piece of dramatic writing made more effective by two ironic interruptions (both connected with church-going). Kriemhild has an ultimate weapon in this encounter, but no modern reader can avoid the feeling that it is a two-edged sword, for as she "proves" that Brunhild is a vassal's harlot, she also reveals what must *ipso facto* be Sigfrid's infidelity. Exactly how much this meant to the medieval reader is hard to say.

Sigfrid's cavalier abjuring of the boast and his equally cavalier remarks about women's tongues are immediately succeeded by much more serious business, as Hagen makes to his injured and insulted lady the pledge upon which the future action rests— vengeance against Sigfrid. The ulterior considerations raised by Hagen (the wealth that would fall to them on Sigfrid's death), and the feelings behind Gunther's reaction ("troubled and sad") help to characterize the two men. The morass of indecision, jealousy, inferiority, and ambition which is Gunther's mind contrasts directly with Hagen's unblanching and remorseless subordination of means to the end.

All that is really left is the unfolding of Hagen's ingenious and savage plot, the cruel ruse by which he gets Kriemhild to reveal the secret of her own husband's vulnerability, the careful machinery of the hunt, the brutal murder. Added to the irony of Kriemhild's contribution to Sigfrid's death is the illusory relief of the hunt and the terrible symbolic reversal of roles: Sigfrid becomes the hunted animal. The final irony: it is Sigfrid's very courtesy, that prized chivalric virtue, which leaves him open to attack, as he lets Gunther and Hagen drink from the spring first.

The work of vengeance is symbolically capped in the cruel delivery of Sigfrid's corpse to Kriemhild's door. It is a tribute both to the artistic responsiveness of the poet and to his assessment of the Germanic ethos of retribution that he took upon himself the necessary continuation of this awful chain of events into the story of countervengeance which occupies the second part. With the decrescendo that succeeds the bloody climax he secures the leisure to regroup his forces and consolidate his motivational patterns (Adventures 17, 18, 19): Kriemhild's logical rejection of the pressure for immediate avenging bloodshed; her decision, doubtless valid in the pattern of familiar ties, but a bit of a strain on the author nonetheless, to remain at Worms; the false reconciliation; the final and crowning insult of the sequestering of the treasure which is rightfully Kriemhild's. This latter is a new area of motivation certainly far from inappropriate to the plot. Germane enough in a society where both prestige and allegiance depended so heavily on largess, the treasure still derives its real force from its symbolic value: It stands for Sigfrid. The stage is set for individual revenge to be raised to the power and level of totality.

The cast of the second half is in large part new. The only major figures who carry over are Kriemhild, Hagen, and Gunther, and they, but especially Kriemhild and Hagen, bear the burden of the action. The other Burgundians (Gernot and Giselher, the kings, and Dankwart among their highest vassals) continue their roles but in neither greater nor lesser scope except as war itself makes them more prominent. The new figures of the second part are new because the scene shifts. The author has not merely patched together, he has knit carefully, and if the seams show at all, they do so, as far as characters are concerned, only in the great new prominence of Folker (and the curious inconsistency in Dankwart). Gunther's return to grace and excellence is a natural development.

Kriemhild and Hagen thus become the polar figures of the new pattern of retribution, and they determine the fate of all the others, Burgundians and Huns, the old figures and the new ones (Attila, Ruedeger, etc.).

7

The pace of the second part is notably and logically different from that of the first. There the poet had room and time for atmospheric digressions. Even after the engines of revenge are turning, there are long interludes of chivalric life, so many as to make the *Nibelungenlied* a better source book of courtly life than the best of the so-called courtly epics. Here there are in effect only the interludes at Pöchlarn, underscoring the courtesy, generosity and high-mindedness of the great Ruedeger, plus the brief but fascinating description of the exotic international court of Attila. The reason is close at hand. Vengeance is here more urgent and the time span more restricted. There is no developmental suspense; the forces at work are known and clear.

In the preceding section, the pattern of revenge was worked out among individuals, against the backdrop of courtly society in jousts and journeys and ceremonies. Here the scale is so extended that the whole society is involved because whole peoples are caught in the work of revenge that once was personal. The "group" can no longer be background, just as armed conflict can no longer be merely a game of jousting because it has become war. Thus the pace is now virtually unrelieved. The dominant currents of motivation nonetheless remain personal, and interest centers on the figures who work out the pattern of vengeance.

Ineluctability is again the essential quality of the action, but the plane of awareness is different. Sigfrid remains a complete stranger to his fate. For Kriemhild the inevitable end was at first only adumbrated in dreams and foreshadowings, and finally revealed to her in the terrible realization of her own unwitting complicity. Hagen alone operates in full clarity and knowledge. In the second part we follow an equally inescapable but transparent progression toward a specific and certain disaster. Kriemhild is deluded only as to its extent; Ruedeger—briefly—as to its bearing on him. Attila's unique unawareness is the measure of his total remove from the other characters. For all but Attila, the cards are on the table, and human beings are the willing agents and defiant victims of fate. The last veil of uncertainty is torn away, in what amounts to a conscious drive to know the worst, when Hagen tests the water-maidens' prophecy, and informs everyone of the result.

Not only does the journey to Austria bring explicit confirmation of their fate, it anticipates thematically the events at Attila's court—another demonstration of the structural invention of which this anonymous poet was capable. Here, in transit so to speak, are the motifs of desperate but wanton homicide leading to retribution (Else, like Ortlieb), violent assault not really approved by the kings (on the chaplain as on the knights at the banquet), pitched battle arising from individual violence, rational but unavailing warning (Eckewart's, like Theoderich's).

The crossing of the river becomes not only a mysterious act (surrounded by some of the few—and certainly the most concentrated—supernatural elements of this section) but also a symbolic one, the crossing with no return.

Before this, of course, the whole stage has been set for disaster. As earlier, the action begins with the anticipation of courtship and marriage. In keeping with the rapid pace of the second part—and since love is not so much the issue—less time is spent on courtly "atmosphere." Attila remains aloof from the actual proposal to Kriemhild. The immediate involvement of Ruedeger acts as the dramatic catalyst, and also lays the foundation for one of the most moving and perfectly devised conflicts in literature. Consistent with his earlier role, Hagen is the prime force opposing the marriage. His function as a major link between the two parts is thus obvious and logical.

The evolution of Kriemhild's position from dissent to acceptance is psychologically true and profoundly ominous. The crucial point is carefully framed: "Their pleading did no good, till Ruedeger / Assured the queen, in trust alone with her: / Whatever wrongs she suffered he'd requite." Kriemhild: "Swear me an oath, whatever is done to me, / That you will be the first to avenge my hurt." The inner dialog reveals her true mind: "What if my lord's dear life should be avenged some day?" (1255, 1257, 1259).

We know that this possibility of revenge will be utilized and, if we are willing to credit the poet with the structural sophistication he has a right to claim, we know how the possibility will be realized: through an invitation with malice aforethought, the same courtly ceremonial used for similar covert purposes by Brunhild. Now, in keeping with the overt nature of the second half in general, there is no shadow of doubt about Kriemhild's design.

When the invitation comes, Hagen, devoid of sentiment and with no need to dissemble, advises against it as he had advised against the marriage. His role as counselor is once again so compounded of foresight and evil that perhaps its very consistency militates against the acceptance of his advice. (And Hagen himself can be moved to ignore his own advice, by the twin forces of duty and pride.) Gunther is still incapable of undiluted self-interest, as he is incapable of undiluted sincerity or loyalty, and on the ambiguity of these character traits rests his muddled decision to go—a right and proper thing to do and a gesture of reconciliation—but only given a clear conscience. Here it is a decision taken on sentimental grounds and a fatal one. With this we are back to the crucial journey.

Immediately comes the visit with Ruedeger. The central geographical location of his court images his pivotal position in the plot—innocently caught between two factions hostile to the death. Here, in the hospitality he tenders the Burgundians, in the exchange of gifts and friendship, in the bond of betrothal, the geometry of conflict is completed.

The rapidity of pace in this half of the poem is nowhere

clearer than in the arrival at the court of Attila. What in the first part would have been the occasion for an elaborate setting of chivalric proprieties and display is here an occasion of unalleviated tension. Kriemhild's welcome is openly invidious. She immediately challenges Hagen, and he her. The court is tense and irritable. Theoderich is defiant. The whole scene of meeting, so central to courtly form, disintegrates literally in minutes. The poet is entirely capable of subordinating the demands of courtly form to those of plot, indeed of doing this to heighten effect. Kriemhild has begun to rouse the Huns, and Hagen has defiantly proclaimed his ancient guilt, before the Burgundians are formally welcomed by the king of the land!

From now on, as was the case at a similar point in Part I, the development is linear and predictable. The pattern is that of increasing involvement and mutual annihilation, until "all those whose fate it was to lose their life / Lay slain" (2377). Its zenith, poetically, is the summoning of Ruedeger, his conflict and tragic resolve, a canto in which the author's resources of tragedy, pathos, and irony are expended to the full.

The Unity of the Poem

Since, in the most common view, the two stories which serve as the principal bases for Part I and Part II come from two different traditions of the Germanic epic, and since, approximated in their "original" form they would offer one major and several minor points of contradiction, it has long been the fashion to emphasize the points of internal inconsistency in the *Nibelungenlied* and to dwell at length on the separateness of its sections. This has been doubly true because of the tendency, only recently being reversed, to regard the genesis of the poem as rather more interesting and worthy of critical study than its finished state.

If we look at the *Nibelungenlied* as a complete work we certainly find it to be bipartite, but we also find that elements of repetition, explicit harmony, and correspondence are a major feature of the structural design of the poem. It is written, as it were, in two books or parts, but this is accepted and by and large turned to artistic advantage, not fumbled with or glossed over. The roster of evidence is extensive, and it ranges from structural features to details of seemingly coincidental mirroring. We can only allude to them here.

On the broadest thematic level, of course, we have already noted that vengeance is at the heart of both I and II. In each part there is also vengeance for a lady-liege wronged (Brunhild in I, Kriemhild in II), and in each part Hagen is, for the lady-liege in I, for the victims of the lady in II, the towering agent of revenge.

The complex of consultation, courtship, and marriage occupies a patently important position in both parts of the poem. Structurally—quite aside from *Kulturgeschichte*—the two aspects of the complex are closely related. The initial impulse for the bringing together of the two geographically removed participants is in each part a scene of "marriage counseling"—Sigfrid and his parents discussing the courting of Kriemhild, Attila being advised to marry the widow of Sigfrid. (With the quadripartite diagram of I, the theme is repeated in Gunther's plan to seek the hand of Brunhild—and the debate which follows. In II there is a similar subplot of different structure in Giselher's betrothal to Ruedeger's daughter.) In each of the major instances and one of the subthemes, the journey of courtship caps the initial impulse of the action, completing the conjunction of the two great forces involved. In I, Sigfrid goes to Burgundy himself—and the whole process is more extended and encrusted with "atmosphere." In II, Ruedeger comes to court Kriemhild in Attila's stead. Remember however that the "John Alden" motif is present prominently though in a singular way in I also.

Sigfrid performs an indispensable part in the wooing of Brunhild!

Of extreme importance in the development of both plots and of parallel ironic effect on a grand scale—the proper forms of courtly life in distorted service of base intent—is the motif of the dissembling invitation. The degree of intensity differs but the centrality is undeniable. The renewal of the tragic action in I hinges on the invitation of the Nibelungs to Worms by the affronted and suspicious Brunhild who maneuvers her vacillating husband into doing what is chivalrically right but pragmatically disastrous. The downfall of the Burgundians is engineered out of their invitation to Attila's court, secured by the disingenuous Kriemhild in the delusion of her courteous husband. Gunther also repeats his pattern of taking the wrong step for the right reasons.

We have already alluded to the importance of another motif; initiative seized by a vassal precipitates involvement, reluctant or otherwise, of master and man alike (Hagen and the treasure, Hagen and Folker starting the fight in the hall, Wolfhart drawing Hildebrand into the battle against the Burgundians, the latter both in II).

Among the many lesser parallels which serve to bind the two parts together are: the importance of omens (dreams and mermaids); the identification of strangers by Hagen (Sigfrid in I, Ruedeger in II); Hagen's awful gifts of death to Kriemhild (the corpse of her husband, the head of her son), the tears of an injured liege-lady as incitement to action (Brunhild's before Hagen, Kriemhild's before the Huns); the manifestation of highest nobility just before death (Sigfrid and Ruedeger).

Certain correspondences are doubtless of less significance because they stem from the paraphernalia of the court poet (e.g., the pressing of the white hand of the beloved) or the inevitable etiquette of the courts (the surrender of armor, acceded to in I at Brunhild's, refused in II at Attila's court).

The cohesive impact of all such motifs is only strengthened by the similar use *within* one part or the other of equally striking parallels. One has already been noted. The device thus becomes a central unifying aspect of the poem. To mention only one more: The two instances, ironic in their contrast, of Kriemhild entrusting a loved-one to the care of another knight, her brother Gunther to Sigfrid in Adventure 6, Sigfrid to Hagen in 15.

True, if Homer nods, this poet occasionally falls asleep. Dankwart's protestation of innocence in the whole business of the plot against Sigfrid—"I was merely / A youth . . . when Sigfrid lost his life" (1924)—is either duplicity in dire straits, which is highly unlikely and out of character, or evidence of the writer's forgetfulness. Those who emphasize sources see it as an oversight in combining two epic traditions or models. There are other inconsistencies which should not, granted, elude the critic but which should also not be blown up beyond their due. By no means all the contradictions and structural flaws represent defective bridges between Parts I and II. Does Kriemhild know who killed her husband or not? (1008, 1010, 1012, 1024, 1033; also 1093 after 1046!) Whatever became of Brunhild?

In sympathetic defense of Homeric lapses it was long ago pointed out that Vergil seems to forget from one part of his poem to the other just what wood the Trojan horse was made of, and that Cervantes in the space of a few pages has Sancho riding on a donkey he had just lost. And these oversights are not urged as demonstration that *Don Quixote* was written by two or more hands or that the *Aeneid* is an obvious composite.

Characters

The rare power of the *Nibelungenlied* stems not only from the relentless sweep of its action, but also—perhaps more—from its extraordinary *dramatis personae*. In range and in intense individuality they entirely transcend the courtly epic in the narrower sense (Hartmann von Aue, Heinrich von Veldeke) and are fully the equals of Wolfram's Parzival and Gottfried's Tristan and Isolde. They are, I think, far superior as characters in literature and in "life" to Roland and Olivier. The poet exhibits his mastery and range of portrayal, his transcending of stereotype (a disease endemic to medieval literature) in two principal ways. He does it in the creation of individual characters of fascinating variety and complexity, like Kriemhild, Gunther, and Hagen, and he does it in his displaying of that ideal figure to which any great narrative artist of this time must inevitably turn: the perfect knight. The recent and laudable trend toward more internal criticism of the *Nibelungenlied* has led to a wise emphasis upon the courtly background of the poem and the identification of Sigfrid as an exemplar of knighthood. It is important to realize however that by the explicit testimony of the poet there are two perfect knights in this poem (along with many who receive *de rigueur* praise, and Hagen whose final encomium is from Attila: "The finest thane / Who ever carried shield or went to war"; 2374). Sigfrid receives superlative praise in life. His death is an apotheosis. Yet it can hardly be denied that the ultimate tribute is rendered to Ruedeger, by those he fought against as well as by his other friends—Ruedeger had no foes except in battle. Fierce Hagen praises only Ruedeger in all the poem: "There'll never be one like you anywhere. . . . May the good Lord grant your virtues live forever" (2199). Every other person who speaks of him speaks in similar terms. The poet has his own summation: "The model of chivalry" (2202).

How different are these men, and how different the ideals they represent. The pattern of values by which medieval courtly life was ultimately guided and illuminated, during the brief span of its flourishing, is a strangely monolithic structure, a vertical scale of merit and prerogatives. By virtue of birth and accomplishment every man had his place on it. The value words of Middle High German are like points on this scale, unlike their modern cognates which imply moral judgments. Thus *êre* (modern *Ehre* "honor") was a complex of ideas in which "superiority" and "excellence" were the central notions, with a peripheral area of what we should perhaps call "honors," the tribute one got for high position and merit. (The difficulties for the translator are apparent.) The historical and sociological genesis of this value system, in the age of the Crusades, is well and succinctly described in one of the few recent treatments in English of the German aspect of this pattern, Martin Joos and F. R. Whitesell's *Middle High German Courtly Reader* (Madison, 1951), an excellent general introduction to the narrative literature of the period.

Recent revaluation of the *Nibelungenlied* has, as we have noted, led to closer identification of the poem with the courtly tradition, and perhaps inevitably to the consideration of Sigfrid and other figures as typically courtly personages. This involves a certain reaction against the earlier dichotomy of courtly epic and heroic or popular epic. In the terms of the latter, the *Nibelungenlied* and its actors are on the old Germanic level of warrior ethics where valor and strength are utterly paramount, fierce loyalty in combat is the prime virtue, pride and good name transcend even the bond between father and son, strife is normal and an early death virtually guaranteed, where women function largely as a source of feuding and men carry on their shoulders a chip of mythic proportions.

Germanic heroism, being part of its ancestry, is not incompatible with the chivalric ideal. Both can serve as references in our examination of the figures of Sigfrid and Ruedeger. But Sigfrid and Ruedeger do not exist as abstractions, and further, the greater a work of literature, the more its characters are apt to resist classification by cultural and historical clichés. Our recourse is to the text.

It is amply clear that Sigfrid *is* set up as a chivalric paragon, and his personality and his actions accord reasonably well with the courtly pattern. He is brave, strong, handsome (in that order of frequency in adjectival modifiers, by the way). His "courtesy" is a source of praise, and he is represented as a master in paying court to noble ladies. His initial gentleness and modesty vis-à-vis Kriemhild are noteworthy. Equally essential: In his proud assumption of the rights accruing to sheer strength and prowess, in his acknowledged surpassing of other men in all arts of war, actual or feigned, indeed in all his conscious and unconscious hauteur he is a medieval knight on the grand scale. He acts unthinkingly, and this is right because it proceeds from both inborn and cultivated excellence. All this is true and valid, but not exclusively so. Germanic heroes were brave and strong, and they were certainly full of pride. If they reflected about anything it was about fate. There are also limits to the courtly interpretation itself.

Comparison of Sigfrid with any good Arthurian hero in Chrétien or Hartmann will show that there is in Sigfrid a strong element of the fated Germanic hero, perhaps even of the doomed demigod (here largely humanized). He is also a character from the world of Achilles, with whom he shares not only valor and strength and magic invulnerability, but also headstrong will, pride, lack of foresight, stubbornness, and childlike naïveté. (Unlike Achilles he does not *choose* glory and a short life over a long undistinguished one—nor of course does he sulk.) In these terms his death is the inevitable working of that same law which in the *Iliad* determines the finite limit of human greatness—a sort of positive correlation between transcending excellence and early tragedy.

The one-line standard of chivalric merit is not entirely valid in its own terms. The handiest fault of a true courtly hero is temporary failure to live up to the code, or some misapprehension of what the code is, a tendency for example to take things too easily and not go out on the required adventures (Hartmann's Erec). Sigfrid certainly does all the required things, yet he gets into definitive trouble. It is clear that his initial fault is not a failure to live up to the monolithic standard. Rather it is to some degree a flaw of a sort that is familiar in the traditional analysis of tragedy from Aristotle on. His overbearing self-confidence is recognized and stated by his own wife when she unwittingly reveals his secret vulnerability to his foe Hagen: "I should never fear . . . Had he not this rash and headstrong will" (896). It is the same characteristic that worries his parents when he announces he will conquer what he wants with his own hands. This trait leads him to his original and seminal misstep, his agreement to do Gunther's courting for him—with the chain of misfortunes to which that casual agreement led. His proud confidence—a right and natural thing for the true courtly hero—starts him on the road to his downfall.

It is only fair to say that this character trait is activated, so to speak, by a clear and overriding purpose: "Not so much for love of you I take / This step, as for your lovely sister's sake, . . . that she should be my wife" (388).

Similarly, it is his very sense of propriety and courtesy which, in the decision to go on the hunt and in his waiting to drink at the spring, guarantees the success of the base plot against him. The picture is obviously a subtle and perhaps in part an ambiguous one. On the one hand he is a paragon of merit, and his death is at the hands of evil men. There are many passages which make this explicit. On the other hand his downfall is in some degree "his own fault" and thus not the reduction of a wholly good man to utter misfortune which Aristotle warned us is not right for tragedy. A certain tension between these two views of Sigfrid cannot, in my opinion, be erased from the lines of the *Nibelungenlied*. It is right to say that his very heroic excellence leads to his downfall but not to deny absolutely the presence of guilt (cf. N. Dürrenmatt, *Das Nibelungenlied . . .* [Bern, 1945], p. 253). It is not right to call him entirely a courtly hero or entirely a fated Germanic warrior, nor even a sum of these and no more. He is rather a character of independent psychological interest and some complexity, viewed by a writer with reliable insight and a mixed ethical viewpoint.

There is another kind of tension in the poet's view of all this, and it lifts him well above the "Arthurians." For him the world and life are not totally subsumed under the courtly ethos. That ethos and the world can be in mortal conflict. The way of the Arthurian knight is beset by magicians and dragons, Sigfrid's by human beings and human destiny.

A further indication that the author of the *Nibelungenlied* did not subscribe entirely to nor create his figures in the light of the chivalric code lies in the figure of Ruedeger. Critics and readers have viewed Ruedeger in a variety of lights but to all of them he remains one of the magnificent figures of the medieval epic—of the whole breadth of epic narration—not simply for his moving nobility, but for the artistic perfection with which his role is created and executed. He is the "best" character in the poem—his standing adjective is *guot* "good, noble, excellent, kind"—and his suffering is, among all the woes of this somber tale, the most acute, the most inevitable, and the least deserved.

The central variance at which critics find themselves concerns the nature of the decision forced on Ruedeger during the battle at the court of the Huns. G. F. Jones, in "Rüdiger's Dilemma" (*Studies in Philology*, LVII, No. 1 [1960]) makes eminently clear the danger of interpreting his dilemma in terms of modern equivalents of old value words. We have already seen that *êre,* which is explicitly at issue in Ruedeger's mind, is not the moral term which it has become in modern *Ehre,* that it means "honors," "honored fame" (and is so translated here), that is, what Falstaff and Norfolk mean by "honor." Jones feels that Ruedeger has, essentially, his good name at stake, not any inner moral principle (a post-Kantian notion) that he "decides in favor of his worldly reputation," (p. 19) identifying "God" at most with his obligation of safe-conduct, though even here his good name was at stake as well. He therefore is disposed to question any reading based on "grave spiritual conflict" (Panzer, de Boor) or "conflict of two duties" (Ehrismann). In Jones' own words Ruedeger is "other-directed," and his dilemma (not conflict) is not a precisely even balance of equally compelling obligations. (Jones does agree that "Rüdiger's abstract words already had strong moral overtones" but he feels they must be kept in their Germanic context.)

I prefer the essentially different, more internally oriented interpretation. The reader must decide for himself how he feels, always remembering to accord full weight to the historical considerations which buttress the opposite stand. The modern reader will after all tend to ignore the "medieval" view in proportion as he is unfamiliar with it. It is my feeling that the author of the *Nibelungenlied* transcended the medieval view himself and was thus quite capable of creating a modern—or timeless—internal conflict.

Ruedeger is both a high noble and a vassal. His allegiance to Attila is a given quantity. His commitment to Kriemhild takes on the force and weight of that allegiance in the very process of her marriage to Attila. But that marriage would not have come about except for the additional personal pledge of loyalty which he gives her, not just to persuade her, though it does so, but to give expression to the full but still conventional extent of a great vassal's loyalty to his lady-liege. From Kriemhild's point of view the stages of Ruedeger's commitment can be and are viewed in an ulterior light. For Ruedeger it is only the unfolding in words of the same loyalty which we (not Ruedeger) must remember as the driving force and justification behind the revenge of Hagen for the wrong done to Brunhild. When Ruedeger says "If you had among the Huns no one but me, / . . . A man would pay for any harm he did to you" (1256), he means it in one way, and Kriemhild takes it in another. What Ruedeger did, he did in complete good faith and innocence, and the structure and geography of the *Nibelungenlied* is such that no accusation of "contrivance" can be leveled. One obligation, sacred in the structure of feudalism but perfectly familiar in some form to any Western society, is now established. The other will be set up with equal care and logic.

Each visit at Ruedeger's court cements further the bond between him and the Burgundians, and the culmination of them is the whole complex of the last sojourn of the Burgundians at Pöchlarn; hospitality, exchange of gifts, pledge of loyalty, betrothal of Giselher and his daughter—all of which we have noted. In terms equally sacred, with all the formal sanction of tradition and custom that supported the other bond, Ruedeger is now friend and kinsman of the Burgundian lords. In absolutely equal degree he is bound to the two poles of a mortal conflict. It is one of those perfect situations of inner conflict which are among the highest manifestations of tragedy in Western literature—the one great level to which the Greeks gave little consideration, for where but in the figure of Neoptolemus in Sophocles' *Philoctetes* is such a carefully balanced internal conflict presented? And that play, perhaps significantly, ends not as a "regular" tragedy but in resolution and reconciliation.

With the beginning of hostilities at Attila's court a terrible chasm opens between the two allegiances on which Ruedeger's existence is concentrated. The revelation of Ruedeger's reaction is accomplished with fine psychological realism. He tries to effect a reconciliation, but disintegration has proceeded too far. He knows what the end must be: "Alas that no one has the power to turn / This evil aside" (2136). His grief and immobilization misinterpreted as cowardice, Ruedeger turns in the fury of frustration and anger upon the man who voiced the accusation and fells him with one blow—adding as the poet says "one more grave misfortune" to the woes of his king, Attila. When Kriemhild recalls his pledge and in her anguish and desperation demands his loyalty, when even Attila falls to his knees before him, Ruedeger states his dilemma with utter clarity. It is one of the great situations of spiritual crisis in literature:

> "Unhappy man, that I should live to see
> My honors forfeit, my inner loyalty
> And the decent breeding God enjoins—surrendered!
> This, oh Lord in Heaven, I wish my death had
>   hindered!
>
> Whichever course before me I reject,
> To do the other, I've done a cursed act.
> If I do neither, I face the people's wrath
> And their reproach. Counsel me now, who gave
>   me breath!"   (2153-2154)

He first attempts to gain release from the obligation to Attila and Kriemhild by surrendering the symbols of that obligation. With this he might have purchased the right to abstain from fighting. (Jones' treatment here is detailed and excellent.) This is fruitless. Attila turns the offer back with promise of outright gift. The issue is settled and Ruedeger makes his decision to fight for Kriemhild and Attila—perhaps only because it is the more ancient loyalty. "Today the cost is paid with Ruedeger's life. / The kindness you and my lord have done to me— / I now must die for that" (2163).

22

One critic has said that Ruedeger obeys the queen even though he knows it will mean his death. He could equally well have said "because he knew it." Ruedeger is cognizant of the necessity of tragic choice but no less so of the atonement in the light of which alone it can be made. What remains is the full development by the poet of all the pathos latent in the tragic situation, and it is done with perfection.

To my mind the only place where the purely medieval, chivalric (or Germanic) ethos plays a role is in the words "If I do neither . . ." Even this however is not essential.

I take it that if the basic question of interpretation is ever to be decided it must be decided on the grounds of the text. Not only Ruedeger's reputation is at stake, as might be the case in a purely Germanic *or* "courtly" reading, but explicitly his eternal soul. "I swore to risk for you both honors and life, / But not to lose my soul" (2150). I consider it of great significance that he is willing to risk *ére*—the very concept we were talking about, but not another and higher thing, his soul. It is in this light that I prefer to view the two strophes above, a tragic choice, either path ending in soul-damaging guilt, not a dilemma, either horn entailing loss of good name (*ére*). His ascription of his "decent breeding" to God, his cry for divine counsel, seem also to comport better with a mind divided by two equal inner loyalties. The most striking image in which his dilemma is couched reinforces the notion of equal allegiances. "He placed upon the balance soul and life" (2166). (This could perhaps be read merely as a stereotyped expression for "risk.")

It is also my understanding of Ogier, the possible source or parallel of Ruedeger, that he and other heroes of *Les quatre fils Aymon* are not (cf. Jones, p. 14) "motivated largely by concern for their good names," rather that the poem implies a very strong inner, ideal sense of right action. Probably Ogier and almost certainly Ruedeger should be seen as men who transcend the strict system of externally oriented standards.

One more moot point and we are through. The reader will have to decide what he thinks of Panzer's suggestion (*Das Nibelungenlied* [Stuttgart, 1955], pp. 260-261) that the secrecy and the extent of Ruedeger's promise to Kriemhild constitute a degree of tragic error. The relation of this to the conflict is obvious.

The figures of Sigfrid and Ruedeger are each restricted to one section of the poem. They serve to unite the poem only on the ideological level, as it were, each constituting an exemplar of knighthood. Yet the ideal pictures of which they are the realized prototypes are themselves highly divergent. If anything, Sigfrid and Ruedeger function to emphasize the division of the epic into two great actions.

The uniting characters, the ones who by their presence in both actions give continuity to the poem are Kriemhild, Hagen, and Gunther. The greatest of these is Kriemhild. Out of the terrible injury done her in the first part grows the fury of vengeance which dominates the second. She is, in a way, a one-dimensional figure, any subtleties of inner tension must remain hypothetical. Even the playing of the terrible trump card in the quarrel with Brunhild cannot be proved to be ironic. On the other hand—partly because of her nature and partly through the structure of her role and the architecture of the poem—she is the clear reference or triangulation point for even the physically most remote segments of the plot. Sigfrid goes to court Brunhild in order to gain Kriemhild's hand, just as he fought in the Saxon War in order to establish his merit in her eyes and her brothers'. She is the point at issue in the debate over the visit to Attila, and it is her invitation which draws the whole Burgundian nation from Worms to Vienna.

In the course of developing action, seen across the whole content of the epic, it is necessary for Kriemhild to move from a person only wronged to one who carries a just cause to punishable excess, and finally to a raging Medea who must be destroyed. (Similarly the Burgundians and Hagen must evolve from conniving murderers to proud defiers of a just fate, and then to heroic victims of unwarranted evil.) It is easy to view the changes as if they were made within Part II or in the interval before it. Actually, if Panzer and others are right, there is a very early doubt cast upon the unmitigated praiseworthiness of Kriemhild's character. Not only does she seem unusually eager to secure her full share of wealth and vassals before she leaves for Xanten as Sigfrid's wife, she also displeases Sigfrid by urging such demands and, further, makes the extraordinary, almost insulting selection of Hagen and Ortwin as the chief vassals to accompany her. The first two might be subsumed under the normal exchanges of courtly form, though even here there is legitimate doubt. The last is a clear affront and is so regarded by Hagen. In her attack on Brunhild she is certainly not blameless. Sigfrid takes her to task—we find out later how vigorously and crudely—for her irresponsible tongue. Whatever weight be given to these reservations, the overwhelming fact of the first part is that vastly more than condign revenge is taken upon Sigfrid and Kriemhild and that she is the rightful object of pity.

The figure of Kriemhild becomes more problematical in the period after the cruel return of Sigfrid's corpse. That she feels a wild desire for vengeance is scarcely out of character with the Germanic heroic tradition which, here as elsewhere, breaks through the courtly. Mixed with her blind grief, however, is cautious foresight. She keeps Sigmund from starting a battle because she knows his forces are too few. But she also says "Wait until some better time, / My lord, and you and I shall avenge this crime / Against my husband" (1033). The central objects of her hate are Hagen and Brunhild (1010), Gunther and Hagen (1046).

The poet takes advantage of this limited association to motivate in part one of the most difficult of all his scenes: Kriemhild's decision to remain at Worms. A great deal has been written in theoretical justification of this decision (the ancient Germanic priority of family over marriage, etc.), yet the fact remains that her first reaction is horror, that she stays with murderers, that she must leave her son to the care of his grandfather. When her mother and her innocent brothers rightly urge her to stay, when she removes herself from all contact with Hagen and Gunther, the situation regains some of its psychological validity.

Out of her decision to remain, and out of her second cruel deluding proceeds the new element in the motivation of revenge, the treasure. First its loss functions as a further motivation for— or reawakening of—the plan of revenge. In the second part it helps, by the growing emphasis placed on it, to cast a harsher and more sinister light on the queen. There is really no other new external factor to be taken into account. Why then is her vengeance not just? Why must she too be destroyed?

Quite apart from what the author may be trying to tell us about the logical conclusion of the philosophy of "an eye for an eye," there are several reasons. Her revenge, originally directed against Hagen (plus, at most, Gunther and Brunhild), extends like an awful malignancy to the whole race of Burgundians. To reply that this was necessary because the original on which Part II is based has as its theme the destruction of the Burgundians is to strip the poet of every vestige of skill and his plot of verisimilitude. Further, as Hagen notes more than once, her thoughts of vengeance are abnormally long. For well over a dozen years she has cherished them. Her very scheming is inordinate: not only her deception of guileless Attila, nor her seeking of mercenary help, but such devices as the malicious separation of pages and squires from knights. (The treatment of strophe 1912 leaves us of course in a quandary about the most horrifying addendum of Kriemhild's guilt: Did she or did she not voluntarily sacrifice her own son in order to start the fight?) Her extension of revenge (and refusal of mercy) even to Giselher, who was loyal to her, is a crucial point. And the poet gets the fullest effect from the frantic and calumnious suspicion with which she greets the silence that ensues upon the death of good Ruedeger. Her final enormities in the treatment of Gunther and Hagen raise the crescendo to its final, deafening intensity, and she becomes what Hagen calls her, a fiend of hell.

Hagen stands in fascinating contrast to Sigfrid (and Ruedeger) on the one hand, to Gunther on the other. The reader may do his own analysis of this monumental epic figure (the only one in all the poem, by the way, whose physical appearance is described: 1734). His is the most terrifyingly consistent personality in the whole epic. In this he is the antithesis of Gunther, whose character, Panzer said, is that he has no character. (Perhaps better balanced is the assessment of Gunther as the man of pathetic indecisiveness and troubled but ineffective conscience—still psychological worlds apart from Hagen.)

Hagen shares with Sigfrid and Ruedeger the attributes of bravery, strength, loyalty, and courtesy, but also an astonishing considerateness (summed in 1526: "a help and solace"), in seeming contrast to his savage temper but manifesting itself time and again, in every solicitude a good officer shows for his men.

He also shares Sigfrid's wide knowledge of lands, routes, and people, but in all other ways is his opposite. He exhibits in every possible context a total and often savage awareness. His own motives and duties are clear to him and he scorns concealment, once the deed is done. Before the deed he will use every resource of cunning and deception to secure his goal. He lives in the conviction that the end—it is either loyalty (so violent and absolute as to be Germanic rather than chivalric in flavor) or vengeance or both—justifies all means. Even the poet is appalled at his own creation: "the false and faithless man" (911), "I doubt if ever knight will do such deed / Of treachery . . ." (906).

The poet's fine sense of ironic fate makes this man the very one through whom Sigfrid is brought closer to the Burgundians—in the Saxon War, in the journey to "Iceland," and in getting Kriemhild to prepare the fine clothes for that journey.

The creation of the few characters treated here—and of so many others, major and minor—is a literary achievement of high order, particularly in a period which tends more to types than to individuals, to Byzantine profiles rather than to portraits. It reminds us again that this is a work centered on character, not merely event. The emphasis is achieved not by psychological analysis (no medieval specialty) but, as Bert Nagel (*Zeitschrift für deutsche Philologie,* LXXVI [1956], pp. 268-305) has well said, by the marshaling of actions and words to reveal inner states.

The Ideological World of the Poem

The reliability and superiority of the *Nibelungenlied* as a source book for courtly life has already been alluded to. The reader will scarcely have any trouble finding and, if he wishes, categorizing the passages. Remarkably enough, this job was not completely done—and the logical conclusions drawn therefrom—until 1945, when Nelly Dürrenmatt's book *Das Nibelungenlied im Kreis der höfischen Dichtung* appeared. The author's thesis is well sustained and balanced. The *Nibelungenlied* is closer to the courtly epics than scholars have thought. The author is courtly where he can be. He treats generously the major aspects of the knight's career, from his chivalric upbringing to his funeral rites. External qualities and gestures mirror inner worth and bearing, and so on.

The relationship of the personalities in the poem to the value system of chivalry has been considered in the treatment of Sigfrid and Ruedeger.

There are substantial exceptions to this harmony of epic and ethos (or custom). The ideal of loyal allegiance (*triuwe*), so central to the poem, is not merely courtly. It is also a cardinal virtue of the early Germanic tribal code, and the closest tie between that ethos and the feudal. And it is also in part the personal construct of the author.

In many features, large and small, the work is noncourtly (even anticourtly). Brunhild in "Iceland" is certainly no lady. Wolfhart and Hagen are something more than Arthurian knights when it comes to combat or the antecedent exchange of insults. Chivalric moderation and control (*mâze*) is about as prominent in this poem as "nothing in excess" is in the *Iliad*. Passions in general are wilder, more "Germanic." And above all Dame Fortune does not stand as presiding genius over this work, rather Moira and Nemesis, as Dürrenmatt says.

One is tempted to add another basic distinction, made especially clear by Joos and Whitesell (pp. 245-246):

"[The] epic hero [courtly variety] is essentially a social climber. . . ." Words describing behavior and attitudes are not used "for differentiating and individualizing . . . characters" but "for praising or for dispraising, in various degrees, persons who were all theoretically of the same stamp." In our poem we deal with a "society of island personalities," somewhat like sovereign nations, "where each party is only partly known to or understandable by each other; where compromise is the only basis for stability, and stability may at any moment explode into catastrophe." Here "the diversity of persons" is the "source of its motivations (that is to say, . . . dramatic conflict and psychologically autonomous drives rather than decorum and convention . . . motivate social acts)."

The Germanic heroic tradition and chivalric culture were not the only transcendent systems of thought available to a poet in the year 1200. What of the relation of the *Nibelungenlied* to the ordering of reality and life represented by medieval Christianity?

The question is not easily answered. The vocabulary of Karl Bartsch's edition has over 100 entries under *got,* but this means little enough, since an equal list might be compiled, for example, from a highly profane modern. The world in which the characters move is one at least externally and formally Christian. Yet there is really only one genuine prayer in the whole epic: Ruedeger's at the time of his spiritual crisis.

The poem abounds in the *realia* of religion: churches, sacred precincts, the mass, the duties of religion, priests and monks, baptisms, funerals. The issue of religion is specifically raised in the contemplated marriage of Kriemhild to Attila—both by Attila (1145) who worries lest Kriemhild object because he is a pagan, and by Kriemhild, who does object—though not without such thorny inconsistencies in the presentation that one is strongly tempted to regard the whole business as an afterthought.

Ruedeger, of course, meets her objection with the encouraging idea that Attila, who has already a number of Christian courtiers, might be converted. Nothing comes of this.

Significantly, there is an almost total absence of heaven as the basis of immortality. The body seems *in toto* doomed to finality, good name and fame are what is undying. This is voiced by Hagen, in a striking phrase: "May the good Lord grant your virtues live forever" (2199). God is not asked to grant personal immortality, and there is no speculation in the poem about the rewards of the afterlife.

Attila's court is a monument of tolerant coexistence, specifically and it would seem nostalgically praised: "Under his rule (but scarcely any more) / Men lived by Christian faith or pagan lore, / As they might choose" (1335). (If the poet was indeed associated with the cathedral chapter of Passau, he lived in a society not entirely unlike this, where in addition to bishop, priests, and monks there were—not pagans perhaps—but secular nobility of several ranks and members of the middle and lower classes.)

The Christian elements in the *Nibelungenlied* are thus usually taken as superficial or *pro forma*. The work has been called a "purely secular poem." The one substantial area of doubt centers in the figure of Ruedeger, but his kindness to all men is usually interpreted as an extension of a chivalric virtue and hence religiously ambiguous. There are at least two passages which are, for this view, somewhat disquieting. Ruedeger, as we know, clearly regards his decency and good breeding as enjoined by God (2153), and it is not only his life and good name he risks but, of explicitly greater import, his soul (2150, 2166). (He is the only character in the poem who seems to be aware of having one. Without exception, all other substantial references to "soul" occur in connection with the ministrations of Kriemhild and the priests to the spirit of the slain Sigfrid, and they could all be *pro forma*. But Ruedeger's soul is important to him—and to us.)

The epilogue added to Part I by the writer of manuscript C— in which Kriemhild uses much of her treasure to found a cloister —cannot be urged in support of a strong religious direction in the poem. At most it indicates either that this writer found in the material as it came to him nothing incompatible with his religious sense—or, in substantial contrast, that he felt the action needed to be capped and balanced by a more churchly conclusion—a sort of implied moral, as it were.

Nagel, who sees a substantial Christian element in the poem, rests his case not only on Ruedeger but also on the incontestable reduction, compared to known sources, in the importance of magic and mythic features. He also considers the saving of the chaplain through God's hand to be a piece of positive evidence.

Considerations of this nature make one uneasy about the labels "religiously superficial," "purely secular." It may be quite impossible to prove, hence perhaps useless to speculate, that the poet not only introduced Christian motifs and reduced non-Christian ones, but in general told a story by whose characters and events he was fascinated and moved but also in a quiet way profoundly appalled. Both old Germanic valor and the pride of chivalry come to the same violent end. That tragic end was traditional for the ancient hero, but *not* for the knight, in his typical literary manifestation. The poet thus writes counter to the tradition of his own contemporaries. Did he intend that his readers look upon the story, shake their heads, and perhaps take warning? The same question, with the same difficulties, has been raised about Homer's attitude toward war.

If we do not feel this, we may be subtly forced to another reading: that the first part shows us how it is the will of fate and the nature of man for greatness to be brought low, and that this is triumphant and somehow right. For the second part a reading of this sort has more drastic implications, for then we may be faced with more than a glimpse of that most harrowing of combinations, a mystique of violence, the raising of force, terror, suffering and destruction into a splendid *Götterdämmerung,* a submerged desire not only to do rightful vengeance or to counter fatedness with defiance, but to move as it were one step ahead of fate and plunge into the maelstrom in a glorious act of annihilation.

Another area of medieval culture whose prominence in the *Nibelungenlied* has recently received greater attention is courtly love, the service of *minne,* which we know largely from the troubadours. We have alluded to this in treating of Sigfrid's relation to Kriemhild, and a substantial part of their story is in the true *minne* spirit: the eager longing for the remote beloved, the refining influence of her sweet gentleness, the long wait and the proof of loyalty—all the "apprenticeship in love." But the dual nature of the poem is apparent here, too; there is no lack of frank sensual pleasure and the culmination of love is not neglected.*

Genesis of the Plot

The search for the sources of the *Nibelungenlied* is an interesting study and a complex one. It is also the beneficiary of by far the largest share of the critical effort expended on the work.† Neither for the modern critic, however, nor for the general reader can this balance prevail. If we are interested in things outside the epic itself, it is apt to be more in the relation of the actions and attitudes there depicted to the courtly ethos of the late 1100's, for example, or to the Germanic-heroic heritage, less in textual development. Presentation of the latter in its broadest outlines is, however, of some inherent interest, and it may add positively to the picture of the poet's task and his mastering of it.

* While this book was in press, there appeared what is virtually the first full length study in English of the poem itself. Werner Mueller's *The Nibelungenlied Today* (Chapel Hill, 1962) raises—with great care and thought, but not always clearly—almost all the important questions of plot, character, and meaning. Among the few articles in English: J. Bostock, "The Message of the 'N.'," *Modern Language Review*, LV (1960), 200-212; H. Wilson, "Blood and Wounds in the 'N.'," *Ibid.*, LV (1960), 40-50, and "Concord and Discord . . . ," *Medium Aevum*, XXVIII (1959), 153-156; A. Price, "Characterization in the N.," *Monatshefte*, LI (1959), 341-350; M. Thorp, "The Unity of the N.," *Journal of English and Germanic Philology*, XXXVI (1937), 475-480. D. Mowatt, "Studies toward an Interpretation of the N.," *German Life and Letters*, XIV (1961), 257-270; H. Sacker, "On Irony and Symbolism in the N.," *Ibid.*, 271-281.

† The early history of textual scholarship is available to the English reader in Margaret Thorp's *The Study of the Nibelungenlied* (Oxford, 1940). Andreas Heusler's *Nibelungensage und Nibelungenlied* (3rd ed., Dortmund, 1929) dominated subsequent scholarship, which consists largely of amplifications and modifications of his basic ("genealogical") approach. The largest study since Thorp is represented by D. v. Kralik's *Die Sigfridtrilogie* (Halle, 1941). The major opposition to the genealogical or accretional view is eloquently argued by F. Panzer in *Das Nibelungenlied* and elsewhere. Perhaps the most convincing and closely argued extension of the genetic approach is K. Wais, *Frühe Epik Westeuropas . . .* , Tübingen, 1953 (*Zeitschrift für romanische Philologie, Beiheft* 95).

A salient fact, remarkably easy to forget, is this: There is no existing German Nibelung story in any form before the *Nibelungenlied*. This is not to say that there may not have been heroic songs, now lost, which deal with parts of the story. Nor is it to say that individual figures or motifs are never mentioned in existing works. It does mean, however, that much of the elaborate edifice of ancestry provided for our poem is reconstruction, however careful.

In the main, there are two fundamental approaches to the problem. The first—based on Heusler, and the dominant one, at least until Panzer—is literally genealogical. The ancestry of the poem is viewed as a sort of family tree. The immediate progenitors are two fairly well defined stories from two different traditions, corresponding to Parts I and II of the *Nibelungenlied*. The stages, chronologically far apart though they may sometimes be, are compositionally very close. Virtually all of them are Germanic. The development is in a word evolutionary, and the final author is just that: the last in a series of stages. He expands and rearranges with great imagination, but his creation of new material is limited. (A related view deals with a simultaneous accumulation of still separate lays, rather than with such a progressive melding. It constitutes a sort of middle ground.)

Through comparison of the *Nibelungenlied* with other German works (the *Klage,* the *Hürnen Seyfried*) but principally with works of Norse literature (*Thidrekssaga, Elder Edda, Völsungasaga, Younger Edda**), it is possible, said Heusler, to reach a reasonable picture of the two heroic lays which are the ultimate ancestors of the *Nibelungenlied*.

This, in outline, is the story of the fall of the Burgundians as it is supposed to have been recited in the sixth and seventh cen-

---

* The most famous works in the modern lineage of the Nibelungs, Richard Wagner's *Ring* operas, are based largely on these Norse sources rather than on the *Nibelungenlied* directly.

turies: Attila has married the sister (Grimhild?) of the Burgundian kings and now devises a plot to get the treasure which constitutes their wealth and power. He invites them to his court, the queen (their sister) tries in vain to warn them, battle ensues upon their refusal to hand over the treasure to Attila, and all those who knew of the location of the treasure are destroyed, except for one—in this case Gunther. He remains defiant, and Attila has him killed. In awful vengeance Kriemhild serves Attila the hearts of his murdered sons, kills the king, burns the hall and the Huns in it, and throws herself in the fire.

This, similarly, is said to be the story of Sigfrid: A warrior of shadowy, semimagic past, Sigfrid visits the Burgundian kings, joins them as blood brother, marries their sister Grimhild, helps Gunther win Brunhild, but has (in disguise) to reconquer her, taking as a souvenir of the struggle her ring. A quarrel over upstream priority in hair-washing results in Grimhild's revelation of the secret. Brunhild cries that Sigfrid or Gunther or she must die. Hagen, with Gunther's complicity, kills Sigfrid. Brunhild, in whom revenge fights with suppressed love for Sigfrid, commits suicide.

The two stories were different in plot (diametrically so, for example, in the role of the Burgundians). They differed in source and general orientation. For the Sigfrid story there is no substantial historical foundation. The Burgundians, on the other hand, were actually destroyed by the Huns in a decisive battle in 437 A.D., in which a king Gundaharius (Gunther) was killed, and as far as the Burgundians are concerned historical reality could easily be distilled and intensified into an exemplary tale of heroic fortitude in the face of doom. Attila actually died in 453, having in one evening progressed spectacularly from a drunken banquet to a rendezvous with a captive German girl, and a violent hemorrhage. Poetic (and historical) imagination led naturally to the invention that the girl murdered her would-be lover in familial vengeance—for which Burgundian brothers provided a handy tie to the other historical source.

Knowing the *Nibelungenlied,* we know the one change which was necessary to release, in a sort of literary catalysis, the epic power inherent in the combination of the two major sources. It is of course the change of Kriemhild in the Burgundian story from friend of her brothers to implacable foe, from warner to destroyer. Credit for it must, whatever theory one accepts, be denied the author of the *Nibelungenlied.* Danish sources speak of the existence in the year 1131 of a Saxon lay telling *notissimam Grimaldae erga fratres perfidiam,* "Grimild's notorious betrayal of her brothers." Most followers of Heusler believe that the tale thus reflected was only the Burgundian story, revised but not yet joined with the Sigfrid story.

Many would deprive the final poet of even more. They posit the existence around 1160 of a combined epic of smaller extent (especially in the Sigfrid story), an immediate progenitor of the *Nibelungenlied,* called the *ältere Nôt.* Others deny its likelihood, pointing to the total absence of fragments or fragmentary mention of what, in its posited scope, would have been one of the greatest and surely most popular works of its time.

Between the separate lays and the finished epic there lie, in this view, vital and extensive changes—to whosoever honor they fall: a new orientation not only toward courtly standards and values, but toward the love patterns of the troubadours and the forms of Christianity (however restricted), a great increase in tourneys, battles, and single encounters, a wealth of courtly background in ceremonial and ritual. In the first part: a development of Sigfrid toward stature as an ideal knight and a proportional reduction of his supernatural elements (though the latter is far from complete and the former does not preclude frequent outcroppings of traditional Germanic furor in taunts, arrogant threats, and wife-beating); motifs created to parallel those of the second part, for example Brunhild's engineering of the invitation to court. In the second part: besides new major figures like Ruedeger and lesser but still important ones like Iring, the whole interlude at Pöchlarn, its idyllic quality and its terrible ironic consequences, along with Dankwart's role in the opening of hostilities, and episodes like the casting out of the corpses.

Along its way of independent development the Sigfrid story is assumed to have been subjected to processes of growth or attrition which leave us with certain inconsistencies or mysteries, all staples of *Nibelungenlied* scholarship. Why does Brunhild clearly recognize Sigfrid when he first comes to her land? Are her tears at the sight of Kriemhild and Sigfrid together adequately motivated? What actual part did she have in the plot against Sigfrid (1010)? (It is only fair to remind ourselves that these questions take on quite different proportion and significance depending on whether we approach the poem as analytical historians of the text or as critical readers of the finished work.)

Completely opposite is the approach of Friedrich Panzer, who starts with the *Nibelungenlied* itself, and taking its "adventures" seriatim, shows the poet's dependence on or use of a great variety of sources available to any highly-read person of the time. The existence of two basic works as "parents" of the present poem finds no favor with Panzer. He denies the existence especially of the so-called *ältere Nôt,* a high-point of Heusler's theory. The Norse *Thidrekssaga,* in this view, borrows from the German epic, not the other way around. By contrast, themes from French literature abound in the *Nibelungenlied*. The genesis of the poem, in a word, is contemporary, and our emphasis should be on the wide-ranging selectivity (and creativity) of the unknown author.

In the first part alone, beside the two separate and independent narratives which are basic to it, these works have left substantial traces of their influence: the epics of the courtly poets Heinrich von Veldeke and Hartmann von Aue, a number of Provençal works, *King Rother,* the Alexander story, several fairy tales, *Les quatre fils Aymon* and the *Aiol,* Russian tales of the Czar who wins his love through another's help, the German-Latin *Ruodlieb,* Scandinavian stories, the *Chanson de Roland,* and the *Aeneid.* To these, says Panzer, we may add at least two or three specific events of contemporary history. In spite of the tenacious appeal of Heusler's reconstruction, Panzer's approach is, I feel, methodologically more defensible and certainly kinder to the *Nibelungenlied* as a work of literature.

Wais, in his genetic study, extends the area of extant and reconstructed sources far beyond the range of Heusler (whose neat stemma is too simplified). Drawing on all works in which various Nibelungen figures and themes appear, he places the *Nibelungenlied* as one of the principal end-points in a far-flung Western European literary tradition—including substantial Celtic and Hungarian sources, for example, and even a cuneiform epic of the second millennium B.C.

Without arriving at any real consensus, the body of scholarship devoted to the tracing of sources and influences has reached massive proportions, far beyond all that is hinted at here. It has at the same time reached the point of diminishing return, since most of what can now be added to the picture is a rearrangement of hypotheses. This has happened concurrently with a shift in the direction and emphasis of literary criticism, toward intrinsic rather than extrinsic concerns. Exclusively historical or genetic criticism left the *Nibelungenlied* a fascinating agglomeration of fragments. It was hard to see the whole work for the parts, hard even to say what artistic or structural merit it possessed. As a literary phenomenon at least the *Nibelungenlied* has already gained much from the change.

The Poet

Barring a discovery as dramatic as the recovered parchments of Menander, we are likely never to know the exact identity of the author of the *Nibelungenlied*. With certain substantial reservations we can be somewhat more positive about where he came from. Scholarly hypothesis has tended to crystallize about the town of Passau in Bavaria, on the border between Germany and Austria, at the confluence of the Inn and the Danube.

Even the reader of the text in translation can follow the steps which lead to this hypothesis, for there are virtually no pieces of external evidence. There are only half a dozen principal scenes of action in the *Nibelungenlied*: Worms, Xanten, "Iceland," and the Vosges in I; Pöchlarn, the route from Worms to Vienna, and the area of Vienna and Gran in II. The poet knows and says very little about any of the places in I, and he makes one sizeable geographical error (placing the Vosges on the opposite shore of the Rhine from Worms). The route to Vienna—specifically that portion of it from Passau on—he knows, and he describes it as fully as a medieval writer is apt to. Interestingly enough it is not Pöchlarn, the most important stop on that fateful route, nor its destination (Vienna) which he describes in greatest geographical detail, but Passau. This geographical "disproportion" is matched by the pleasant but gratuitous introduction of the bishop Pilgrim, brother of Queen Uta. In point of fact, there was a Bishop Pilgerim of Passau in the tenth century, and his prominence in the poem *may* be connected with the destruction of the cathedral of Passau in the great fire of 1181, and the subsequent opening of his grave, with attendant miracles. We may thus be dealing with a consciously anachronistic tribute.

Scholars have tended to speculate almost as widely and freely about the poet of the *Nibelungenlied* as they have about the genesis of the poem, with the result that it is extremely difficult to sort out facts from fancies. There has nonetheless been a clearly developing tendency in the assessment of his social class and sophistication. No longer is he regarded as a relatively ordinary minstrel. If he actually read and used half of the German, French, and Latin works that have been proposed as direct sources of parts of his poem, he was a cultivated man indeed. The very degree of this cultivation has led most authorities to place him in the one class where such sophistication is most to be expected, and make him a cleric (probably *not* a priest)—not excluding thereby the possibility that he was at the same time a noble. Recently, certain scholars have revived the once popular notion that the same Kürenberg who is identified with the lyric strophe (p. vii) also wrote the *Nibelungenlied*. Here, however, we have reached the no man's land which separates firm ground from spiraling imagination, and it is better to stop.

PART I

✠ FIRST ADVENTURE

1   Wondrous things are told in ancient tales
Of famous men and bold, of great travails,
Of joy and festive life, of woe and tears,
Of warriors met in strife—the wonder shall fill your ears!

2   There grew a royal child in Burgundy—
In all the world none lovelier than she.
Her name was Kriemhild. Great her beauty when,
In womanhood, she cost the lives of many men.

3   Love was fitting tribute where she reigned—
Desired by valiant men, by none disdained.
Her charms exceeded praise; she was refined
And virtuous enough to grace all womankind.

4   Three lofty kings were guardians of her ways:
Gunther and Gernot, warriors high in praise,
And a knight preeminent, young Giselher.
This lady was their sister, and she was the princes' care.

5   Those lords were generous men, and well descended,
Unmatched in strength and valor, in station splendid.
Their country bore the name of Burgundy.
Attila's land would witness their feats of bravery.

6   At Worms on Rhine they dwelt in all their power,
Served by their proud knights—until the hour
Of their death—in high and honored state.
They ended wretchedly, from two women's hate.

7   Their mother's name was Uta, mighty queen;
       Their father, Dankrat—he whose youth had been
       So full of glory, whose courageous name
       Was greatly honored still. From him their heritage came.

8   The three kings were, as I have said before,
       Men of highest valor. What is more,
       They had as subjects knights whom men accounted
       Best in strength and brave, in bitter war undaunted.

9   Hagen of Trony was one of them, another
       Was Ortwin of Metz; also Hagen's brother,
       Able Dankwart; Counts Gere and Eckewart;
       And Folker of Alzei, armored with a stalwart heart.

10   Rumold the Kitchener managed household things
       With Sindold and Hunold—men of the three kings,
       Paying courtly form their full attention.
       Other lords they had, more than I can mention.

11   Dankwart was the Marshal; Royal Steward,
       His nephew Ortwin. Sindold (he was no coward)
       Served as the King's Lord Butler; as Chamberlain,
       Sir Hunold. Masters of courtly taste were all these men.

12   The story of this vast court, their dignity
       And great extent of power, of Chivalry,
       Which all their days they cherished as their goal—
       Truly, no one has the gift to tell it all.

13   Surrounded by this glory, Kriemhild dreamed
       She raised a fair, wild falcon, which it seemed
       Two eagles clawed to death while she looked on.
       No sorrow could be worse than this, that it was gone.

44

14 She told the dream to Uta, who could see
    One meaning only: "In life this bird must be
    A noble lord. Unless God's hand is strong
    In his defense, I fear he'll not be yours for long."

15 "Sweet mother, do not speak of that again;
    I mean to live without the love of men,
    And I will keep the beauty given me,
    Till death, and no man's love shall bring me misery."

16 Her mother said, "Oh make no vow so bold!
    Whatever happiness this world may hold
    Comes from a man's love. If God provide
    A noble lord for you, you'll be a lovely bride."

17 "An end to our debate, my Lady dear!
    In many women's fate this much is clear:
    Pain is the price of pleasure when all is done.
    But I am safe from danger, for I'll have neither one."

18 From love the lady turned her thoughts away,
    And thus she lived for many a happy day,
    Knowing no man by whom her heart was stirred.
    And yet one day, in state, she wed a gallant lord.

19 He was the falcon of her dream, the one
    Foretold by Uta—by her own kin undone,
    On whom she took most awful vengeance then.
    And one man's dying brought the death of many men.

✝ SECOND ADVENTURE
Sigfrid

20   In Netherland lived the son of a royal house,
Child of King Sigmund and Siglind, his spouse.
They dwelt in a mighty city, wide in fame,
Set on the lower Rhine—Xanten was its name.

21   This was Sigfrid, of all bold men the best.
Strong in will, he put whole lands to test,
And many, in strength of limb, he rode to see.
Ah, what courageous knights he found in Burgundy!

22   They tell great things of Sigfrid in his prime,
His days of youth, and how he grew in time
To be a man of high renown and handsome—
How he was loved by many women, fair and winsome.

23   His education there was duly nourished,
While in his heart courtly virtues flourished.
His ever noble bearing people found
A splendid thing by which his father's land was crowned.

24   And soon he was of age to go to court,
Where he found welcome. It would please the heart
Of many maids and ladies if he desired
Soon to return. He knew that he was much admired.

25   They seldom sent him riding unescorted.
His parents dressed him well, and he consorted
With masters of chivalry, who lent their hands
To teach him ways of knighthood, winning of men and
    lands.

26   Now his strength was such that he could look
To bearing arms—he had the stuff it took;
And taste enough with lovely ladies to broach
His suit with them. Loving him was no reproach.

27   The king now had his vassals summoned in,
Announcing a tourney for all his kith and kin.
To other sovereigns' lands they bore the tiding.
He gave to stranger and friend good clothes and steeds for
    riding.

28   Whatever noble youths his heralds met
Who were by age and background fit to get
The promise of accolade, these they invited
To the feast, there to be with Sigfrid knighted.

29   What stories one could tell of the tournament!
Sigmund and Siglind gained, for the wealth they spent,
Increasing honor. They gave with a generous hand,
Bringing a host of strangers riding to their land.

30   Four hundred squires were robed at his accolades,
And out of love for Sigfrid beautiful maids
Busied their hands, working each precious stone
Into the cloth of gold, for in this way alone

31   Could all the clothes be made for lords so proud.
Their host gave out command that for the crowd
Of stalwart men seating be provided,
For the summer-solstice feast at which his son was
    knighted.

32   Many the lord and squire who went to service
At minster. Master there attended novice—

The custom, once accorded him as boy.
This they did in pleasure and thought of future joy.

33   Men sang mass to God. Through the crowd,
A mighty motion surged, as squires vowed—
New made knights, in knighthood's regimen,
With splendor such as the world will hardly see again.

34   They hurried where the saddled horses waited.
Melee and noise continued unabated,
Till Sigmund's palace rang, and the halls around.
Gay and haughty knights raised a mighty sound.

35   And you could hear from knight and novice blows
So numerous the shatter of lances rose
To the sky—and see the splinters whirl and fall
From the eager hands of men, all the way to the hall.

36   The host cried halt, the horses were led away.
Bosses were broken, and many jewels lay,
Precious stones from rims of the bright shield tossed
Upon the grass—and all of this from the crash of the joust.

37   The guests were given seats. Excellent food
In plenty put an end to their weary mood—
And the best of wines, served with a generous hand—
Paying to stranger and friend the honors of the land.

38   They turned their time to pleasure all the day,
While many minstrels gave up sleep to play
And sing for rich reward their songs and lays.
And through them all the lands of Sigmund shone in
    praise.

39   In grant of fief the king now asked his son
To give out lands and towns as he had done.
Richly Sigfrid gave to his friends who took
The sword with him. How sweet it made their journey
    look!

40   The celebration lasted one whole week.
The wealthy Lady Siglind, to bespeak
The love she had for her son, gave of her gold,
Repaying the people's love for him, as they did of old.

41   There wasn't a minstrel poor in all the land.
Horses and clothes ran from their hands like sand,
As if they hadn't another day to live.
I doubt if ever court has had such wealth to give.

42   The tourney now dispersed, with splendid rites.
Soon this wish was heard from powerful knights:
Might not the young prince now be king alone?
But their desire did not accord with Sigfrid's own.

43   With both Sigmund and Siglind hale and sound,
Their son had no ambition to be crowned.
He wished instead to gain the upper hand
Of that which worried him: injustice in the land.

✠ THIRD ADVENTURE

How Sigfrid Came to Worms on the Rhine

44 The prince's heart was rarely sorrow-laden!
Once he heard there lived the fairest maiden
In Burgundy, the model of loveliness—
Later cause of his many joys, and deep distress.

45 Word of her beauty traveled far and wide,
Nor did she make a secret of her pride
From the countless heroes who, as strangers, came
To royal Gunther's land, attracted by her fame.

46 However many came to press their case,
Kriemhild in her heart would never face
The thought of yielding to any lover's will.
The man she later wed—he was a stranger still.

47 Now courtly love took hold on Sigfrid's mind.
Others' wooing was a sigh of wind
Compared to his! Well he knew the way
To court a beauty, and Kriemhild would be his one day.

48 All of Sigfrid's courtiers and his kin
Advised him now that he should try to win
A lady worthy of him, since he was filled
With visions of courtly love. "Then I will have Kriemhild,

49 Princess of Burgundy, for none is fairer,"
Sigfrid said. "In this I make no error:
The greatest emperor, if he would marry,
Could give this princess his love—never would he be sorry."

50   Sigmund heard this tale, told around
      Among his vassals. Thus it was he found
      His son's intent—and with misgiving viewed
      The choice of the brilliant lady for whose hand he sued.

51   Siglind, too, found out, and worry grew
      In her mind, for the sake of her son. Well she knew
      King Gunther and his men. With common voice
      They joined in showing him the folly of his choice.

52   Sigfrid made reply, "I always planned,
      My dear father, to live without the hand
      Of any lady, unless I were disposed
      By heart and love to court. In this my mind is closed—

53   Let people talk as they will." Replied the king:
      "If you will not give in—well, everything
      You wish is fine with me; I'll help you out
      As best I can, but Gunther has proud men about.

54   Hagen alone would be sufficient trouble—
      Such a proud and overbearing noble,
      That we may well regret it, I'm afraid,
      If we should set our minds on courting your fair maid."

55   Sigfrid said, "How is that to hold us back?
      What can't be got from them on a friendly tack
      I'll take with the strength of my hand—valor's course;
      I think I can seize their country, men and all, by force."

56   "These," said the king, "are words I must deplore.
      Let news like that be heard by the Rhenish shore
      And you will never ride to Gunther's land!
      He and Gernot are men I know and understand."

57   "Force will never win the princess' love,"
Spoke Sigmund, "that much I am certain of.
But if you must approach their land in force,
We'll summon whatever friends we have, from every
     source."

58   Sigfrid replied, "I have no wish to see
Warriors off to the Rhine, following me—
Or any kind of expedition sent
To help me conquer my love. That's not what I meant.

59   This hand alone can win her. I shall go
As one of twelve to Gunther's land, and so,
My father, help me in this!" (He gave away
To Sigfrid's men clothes of fur, vair and gray.)

60   His mother Siglind also heard the news.
She mourned for the child she loved and feared to lose
To Gunther's men. In her anxiety
The noble queen commenced to weep most bitterly.

61   Lord Sigfrid saw his mother, in compassion
Went to her, and said in kindly fashion:
"You must not cry for me, my lady dear.
Let any warrior face me, I shall have no fear.

62   Support my trip to Burgundy! Provide
For my knights and me the kind of clothes with pride
And honor worn by men of lofty mood—
For that I pledge to you my trust and gratitude."

63   She spoke, "Since you will not be reconciled,
I'll help you with your trip, my only child,

Making clothes for you and your men, of stuff
The best that knights have worn. You'll take with you
    enough."

64   At this young Sigfrid bowed and said to her,
"Twelve knights will go with me, for I prefer
To take no more. Let clothes for them be planned.
I mean to find Kriemhild and see how matters stand."

65   Night and day lovely women stayed
At work—no rest for them until they made
Sigfrid's clothes. The trip was on his mind,
And he refused to hear advice of any kind.

66   At Sigmund's word, they adorned with lavish hand
The clothes in which he left his father's land.
His vassals readied arms to take along:
Bright byrnies, sturdy helmets, shields broad and strong.

67   The day of their trip to Burgundy drew near.
In hearts of men and women grew the fear
That they might not return, once they were gone,
But they had ordered clothes and weapons loaded on.

68   Their steeds were handsome, their harness red with gold.
How could there live a man so overbold
As to rank himself with Sigfrid's company?
And now for the royal leave to go to Burgundy:

69   They granted it in sadness, queen and king.
He spoke in loving kindness, comforting,
And said, "Never weep, for sake of me.
My life is safe, you need have no anxiety."

70   Knights were sad and many maidens cried.
I think the heart within had prophesied
How vast a death of friends would now ensue.
Oh, they did well to mourn—they had good reason to.

71   The seventh morning, the heroes reached the shore
Of the Rhine at Worms. All the clothes they wore
Were red with gold, their harness skillfully wrought,
Smooth the gait of the steeds that Sigfrid's men had
    brought.

72   The shields they had were new and broad and bright,
Their helmets proud, as now the valiant knight
Lord Sigfrid rode to Gunther's land and castle.
Such splendid gear was never seen on lord or vassal.

73   The tips of their pointed swords hung to the spur,
Sharp were the spears these perfect warriors bore.
Sigfrid's measured two hands broad in the blade,
And what a fearful cut its double edges made!

74   In hand they carried golden colored reins,
The horses' martingales were silken chains.
Thus they came to the land. Everywhere
The crowds of common people stopped to stare.

75   Many of Gunther's men, knights and squires
Proud in bearing, ran (as form requires)
To welcome them—guests to their master's land.
Here they took their steeds and all their shields in hand.

76   About to lead the horses to food and stall,
They heard Lord Sigfrid loud and boldly call:

"Leave our mounts alone—my men's and mine.
We shall soon be leaving. This is my firm design.

77   Speak up, if you know—do not conceal it.
Where do I find the king? Come now, tell it.
Mighty Gunther, I mean, of Burgundy."
Someone told him (well he knew where the king would
    be):

78   "If it's the king you want, he's easily found.
I saw him there in the hall. All around,
His knights were standing. Go where I told you to,
You'll find he has some worthy men in his retinue!"

79   By now the king himself had heard report
How lusty-looking men had come to his court
In splendid clothes and gleaming coats of mail.
But none in Burgundy knew them or knew whence they
    might hail.

80   On this the king was greatly curious, too—
About these elegant knights whose garments' hue
Was shining bright, whose shields were new and wide.
His question went unanswered, the king was not satisfied.

81   Then it was that Ortwin of Metz spoke out
(A powerful man and brave, beyond a doubt):
"Since none of us can say, have someone go
And get my uncle Hagen; show him these men below.

82   He knows our realms and foreign lands as well.
Let him see them—if he knows he'll tell."
The king now sent for Hagen and his men—
A splendid sight they were, as they came to court again.

83   Hagen asked his king's desire. "My hall,"
He answered, "is host to strangers. If you recall
(As none here can) seeing them anywhere,
I want you to tell me, Hagen, the truth of this affair."

84   Hagen walked to the window. "That I'll do."
He turned his gaze to the strangers, whose aspect drew
His pleased attention, in garb and general grace.
But never in Burgundy had he seen a single face.

85   "These riders to the Rhine, wherever be
Their home, are princes or prince's embassy.
Their steeds are handsome, the cut of their clothing grand.
These are men of spirit, whatever be their land."

86   And then he spoke: "It would come as no surprise—
Although I never saw him with my own eyes—
If that were Sigfrid walking so proudly along.
This at least is my opinion, right or wrong.

87   His coming means great news within our land.
The sons of mighty Nibelung died by his hand:
Shilbung and Nibelung, each a valiant prince.
And his amazing strength has worked more marvels since.

88   Once as he rode along, without escort,
By a mountainside—I have it on good report—
He found some stalwart men by the treasure-store
Of the Nibelungs, men he had never seen before.

89   They had brought the cache from the hollow mountainside—
Nibelung's men, preparing to divide

The Nibelung hoard. (This is the strange account.)
When Sigfrid saw them there, his wonder began to mount.

90   He came so close he could see the men and they,
      In turn, had noticed him. One rose to say,
      'Here comes Sigfrid, Netherland's champion.'
      (Among the Nibelung men there would be strange things done!)

91   The two young princes made him welcome there,
      In common council asked that he set the share
      That each of them should get of all this treasure.
      They urged and plead, till he agreed to do their pleasure.

92   A hundred carts, they say, could hardly hold
      The precious stones he saw, and more red gold
      From the land of Nibelung. All this they planned
      Should be divided out for them by Sigfrid's hand.

93   By gift of the sword of Nibelung they bought
      His services, and ill return they got
      In the job he did for them, Sigfrid the fair.
      The task was never done, there was anger in the air.*

C 94 He had to leave the treasure undivided.
      The two kings' men commenced a fight and sided
      Both against him. With Balmung, their father's sword,
      He wrested from them their lands and all the Nibelung hoard.

---

* The sequence of stanzas in MS B gives a confusing picture of the scene. The next stanza is interpolated from C, and one of B's succeeding quatrains omitted.

57

94 Beside them twelve courageous vassals stood,
Giants all—it did them little good!
The angry hand of Sigfrid cut them down,
And seized the seven hundred knights of the Nibelung
  crown.

96 The two great kings as well he struck and slew,
And out of this his trouble with Alberich grew,
Who hoped to avenge his lords that very hour,
Until he learned the true extent of Sigfrid's power.

97 In battle, the fearsome dwarf could not prevail.
Like savage lions they raced the mountain trail,
Where the Magic Cloak fell prize to the dreaded lord,
And with it Sigfrid's title to the treasure-hoard.

98 Those who had dared to fight lay slain and dead.
The rest should haul and carry the gold, he said,
To where the Nibelungs had it previously.
He left it there in mighty Alberich's custody.

99 The dwarf was forced to swear an oath of service,
And willingly has done his every office."
Thus said Hagen. "All this he has done.
Greater power never fell to anyone.

100 And I recall one other thing I knew:
Once there was a dragon Sigfrid slew
And bathed himself in his blood. His skin was turned
To horn no blade will cut, as many men have learned.

101 We'll make the warmth of our welcome that much
  stronger
Lest somehow we incur the young man's anger.

So bold a knight, whose past has thus disclosed
So many marvels done—let's keep him well-disposed!"

102 The mighty king replied, "You may be right.
See how like a battle-eager knight
He stands with all his men. It seems but fair
That we go down the stairs and meet this warrior there."

103 "No loss of face," said Hagen, "if this be done.
He comes from a noble line, a great king's son—
God knows he looks the part. And I dare say
No trivial thing would bring him riding here this way."

104 The king of the land now spoke, "Then let him be
Our welcome guest. Your words have pictured me
A bold and noble man; he shall be rated
High in Burgundy." Gunther went where Sigfrid waited.

105 The host and his men received their guest so well
That not the slightest flaw could Sigfrid tell
In their demeanor. He felt well inclined,
Their way of greeting him had been so very kind.

106 "Tell me," said the king without delay,
"From where, oh noble Sigfrid, you come our way,
Or what you hope to do, here at Worms."
His guest replied, "That I shall, in the plainest terms.

107 I heard reports of you our country over,
The truth of which I wanted to discover:
You have the bravest men, so people claim,
That ever served a king. And that is why I came.

59

108 I also hear that you yourself enjoy
   A name for courage. Never king could toy
   With danger, all the people say, like you.
   I'll not give up until I see if this is true.

109 I also am a knight, crown and throne
   Will soon be mine. I want all men to own
   That I have gained my whole domain by merit.
   I offer pledge for that: by honor and life I swear it!

110 Since you are brave—this is the word I've got—
   I don't much care if anyone likes or not,
   I mean to conquer what you have—your castles,
   All your lands. And all your people shall be my vassals."

111 The king was much amazed at what he heard,
   As were his men, to find that it occurred
   To him to seize their lands. Anger broke
   Upon them all as they listened to him. Gunther spoke:

112 "And do I merit this? To let another
   Take by show of power what my father
   Long in honor cherished—that would be
   A sorry show of how we practice chivalry."

113 Undaunted, Sigfrid answered, "This is my stand,
   From which I will not yield. Unless your land
   Gain its peace by your power, I'll have it all—
   And mine besides, which if you win, to you shall fall.

114 Thus it shall be: my heritage and yours
   Alike at stake. Whichever one secures
   The victory, all is his: people, town,
   And country." Hagen and Gernot tried to talk him down:

115   "We have no intention," Gernot said,
      "Of seizing any place, when men lie dead,
      At heroes' feet, as price of it. Our lands
      Are rich and rightly ours. They rest in proper hands."

116   In angry mood his friends were standing by,
      Among them Ortwin of Metz. "I loathe this try
      At soft appeasement," Ortwin answered back,
      "When Sigfrid threatens you with unprovoked attack.

117   If you and your brothers had no armed defense
      And if he brought with him a force immense
      As any king's, I still am confident
      That I could give him cause to be less arrogant."

118   The hero Sigfrid cried, his anger fanned:
      "Not against me shall you dare lift your hand!
      I am a mighty king, and what are you?
      A vassal! This is more than twelve of you could do."

119   Ortwin called for swords, with a mighty shout.
      He was Hagen's kin, beyond a doubt!
      (The king was vexed by Hagen's lengthy silence.)
      Gernot, the bold and merry, stepped in, forestalling
        violence—

120   Crying out to Ortwin, "Stop the fuss!
      Sigfrid has done nothing so bad to us
      That we cannot secure some peaceful end,
      With honor, and more to our credit, gain him as a friend."

121   Said mighty Hagen, "All of us may rue
      His riding here—the love of strife that drew

This man to the Rhine! He never should have come.
What hostile act of my lords has he ever suffered from?"

122   Mighty Sigfrid answered him this way:
"Does it bother you, Hagen, to hear what I say?
Then I will give you, instead, a chance to see
What power my hands will wield, here in Burgundy!"

123   "I'll see to that myself," Gernot cried,
Forbidding his men to speak a word in pride,
By which he might be angered. It happened too
That Sigfrid began to think of the woman he came to woo.

124   "What cause have we to fight you?" Gernot said.
"Think of all the heroes lying dead—
Small glory to us, and little good to you."
Sigfrid, son of Sigmund, cried, when he was through:

125   "What's Hagen waiting for? Why not rush in—
Ortwin too—and fight, with his friends and kin,
Of whom the land of Burgundy is full?"
They dared not say a word, for this was Gernot's will.

126   "You all are welcome," answered Uta's son,
"You and your companions, every one.
My kin and I will gladly do our best
To serve you." Gunther's wine was poured for every guest.

127   "All we have is yours," the king declared.
"So long as you take it in honor, be it shared
Equally with you, our men and the wealth we own."
(Sigfrid's mood took on a somewhat gentler tone.)

128   They had their garments brought and stored away,
And found for Sigfrid's men a place to stay,
The best they could, to make them feel at home.
Their guest became a welcome sight, in time to come.

129   Men came to pay him homage, many a day,
A thousand times more often than I can say.
His valor earned it, on this believe my word.
In no one's heart who saw him was any rancor stirred.

130   With kings and men at play, whatever test
They turned their hand to, he proved himself the best.
So great his strength that none of them came near,
Whenever they hurled the heavy stone or cast the spear.

131   And if the merry knights made love their sport,
For sake of chivalry, and paid their court
To the ladies, Netherland's lord was welcome there.
Chivalric love had now become his constant care.

132   In all of their pursuits he gladly joined,
The fairest maid envisioned in his mind—
And he in the mind of one he'd never seen,
Who secretly often spoke of him with kind esteem.

133   And when the younger knights and men would fill
The courtyard with their games, from the windowsill
The gracious princess Kriemhild now would gaze—
And wanted no more pleasant way to pass her days.

134   What lasting joy for him, if he had known
That she whom he loved was watching! Her sight alone,
Of this I'm certain, would have been so sweet
That all this world could hold no pleasure more complete.

135   When he stood with heroes at court, as still is done
By men for their pleasure now, Siglind's son
Looked so handsome that he greatly swayed,
For heart's love of him, many a highborn maid.

136   And many times he thought, "How may it be
That ever with these eyes of mine I see
The princess I have loved so long and well,
For she and I are strangers still, sad to tell."

137   Whenever the kings would visit their domain
The knights were called upon to join the train,
And Sigfrid too, for which his lady grieved.
For love of her, what blows of fortune he received!

138   And so he dwelt in the land of Gunther here,
Among the noble lords, for one whole year.
No glimpse in all this time did he ever gain
Of the beauty who was to bring him pleasure, yes, and
    pain.

✠ FOURTH ADVENTURE
How He Fought the Saxons

139   At this time now there came a strange report
Sent by distant heralds to Gunther's court,
Of unknown knights whose anger they'd incurred.
Truly, it made their spirits sad to hear this word.

140   I'll tell you who they were: from Saxony
Lord Liudeger—a powerful prince was he;
And Liudegast, monarch in Denmark reigning.
They brought a splendid host for their campaigning.

141   His foes had sent out men to make their entry,
Coming as heralds, into Gunther's country.
They summoned the strangers to royal audience,
Asking them to tell the purport of these events.

142   "Welcome," cried the king, with a friendly word.
"Who may have sent you here I have not heard.
And this is what I'd have you tell me," he said.
The thought of Gunther's fierceness gave them much to
dread.

143   "Grant us your permission to reveal
The news we bring and we shall not conceal
But name the lords who sent us: Liudeger
And Liudegast together—they come here bent on war.

144   You have roused their wrath. The story goes
That both regard themselves as your bitter foes.

Worms on Rhine is the goal of their campaign,
And many knights are with them—the truth I tell is plain.

145   Within twelve weeks they march. If you have friends
Good enough to help in your defense
Of lands and castles, let that be soon revealed,
For they will shatter here many a helm and shield.

146   Or if you'd rather sue for peace, then send
The message to them and they will not descend
In all their great and hostile force on you,
With havoc and pain and the death of knights that must
     ensue."

147   Answered the king, "Wait for a moment or so,
That I may think it over and let you know.
If I have loyal friends, I must not turn
This serious news from them but tell them my concern."

148   Mighty Gunther felt in full the smart
Of the secret pain he bore within his heart.
He summoned Hagen and many another vassal,
And sent men out to find Lord Gernot at the castle.

149   They came, the greatest lords of high position.
"Powerful forces plan an expedition
Against our land. Take this to heart," he cried.
To which Lord Gernot, champion gay and bold, replied:

150   "Well then, our swords must see to that," he said.
"Only the doomed will die, let them lie dead.
For this I can't forget my own good name.
Welcome these foes of ours, let us be glad they came."

151 "That seems to me unwise," Lord Hagen cried.
"Liudegast is a man of violent pride,
And Liudeger. We cannot recruit so fast,
In so few days. Why not tell Sigfrid what has passed?"

152 They had the heralds lodged within the town.
Foes or not, the king would have them shown
The best of care (and this was right to do),
Till he could learn what friends of his would see him
 through.

153 Still the king was saddened by his care.
A certain lord, who could not be aware
Of what had happened, saw him deep in worry
And bade King Gunther tell him what might be the story.

154 Sigfrid spoke, "It greatly surprises me
How you have put an end to the gaiety
Which up to now was your accustomed way
Of treating us." Handsome Gunther turned to say:

155 "Not to everyone can I impart
The secret fear that occupies my heart.
True friends alone can share our deep concerns."
Noble Sigfrid's face grew pale and flushed by turns.

156 He said to the king, "There's nothing I've denied you.
I'll help to see that future ills avoid you.
If you are looking for friends, let me be one.
That I can promise, with honor, till my days are done."

157 "God reward you, Sir, your words are pleasant!
Your valor may never help me, and though it doesn't,
I still am glad to hear of your loyalty.
If I should live you'll be repaid, and suitably.

158   I'll tell you why I stand thus deep in worry.
Heralds of my foes bring me this story,
Saying they have planned a great invasion—
More than knights have dared on any past occasion."

159   Sigfrid answered, "Set your mind at rest.
Never worry, do as I suggest.
Let me secure your interest and your honor.
And ask that they too help who serve beneath your banner.

160   Though your mighty foes had thanes to assist them
As many as thirty thousand, I'd resist them
With only a thousand men. Count on me."
Said the king, "For that I promise constant fealty."

161   "Give me a thousand of your men on loan,
Since I have brought with me of all my own
Barely a dozen, and I'll defend your land.
You shall have loyal service always from Sigfrid's hand.

162   Hagen shall give us help, Ortwin too,
Dankwart and Sindold, lords of your retinue.
Another who shall ride: Folker the Brave,
As standard-bearer—there's no one I should rather have.

163   Send the heralds home to their masters' land.
They'll see us first—make sure they understand.
This is the way to protect our towns and castles."
Gunther the king sent word to summon kin and vassals.

164   Back to Gunther's court went Liudeger's men,
Happy to be going home again.
He offered them rich gifts and guaranteed
Safe conduct through his lands. Proudly they agreed.

165   "Now," said Gunther, "tell my powerful foes
They'd best stay home, as far as this war goes.
But if they mean to encroach on my domains,
Unless my friends desert me, they'll suffer for their pains."

166   They handed Liudegast's men expensive things
Which Gunther could give in number like few kings.
To this the heralds did not dare say no.
They left rejoicing as soon as they had leave to go.

167   When the messengers arrived at the Danish court
And gave King Liudegast their full report
Of how they left the Rhine, he was irritated,
Through and through, at the tale of arrogance they related.

168   They told him Burgundy had brave men to spare,
And they had seen a knight among them there,
A hero of Netherland, Sigfrid he was called.
When Liudegast heard this, his heart was greatly galled.

169   And when the Danes found out, they called their kin
And friends in haste, bringing more troops in,
Until Sir Liudegast had managed to gain
Twenty thousand men to join in his campaign.

170   The King of Saxony also armed for war,
Until they counted forty thousand or more
Ready to ride with them to Burgundy.
At home King Gunther too recruited a company

171   Of kinsmen and his brothers' men to lead
Into combat now that war was decreed—

Together with Hagen's troops—the only path
Now open to them and one on which brave men faced
   death.

172   They hurried preparations. Leaving there,
      Folker took the standard (his to bear).
      As soon as they had quitted Worms and planned
      To cross the river Rhine, Hagen took command.

173   With them Sindold and Hunold rode away,
      Well equipped to merit Gunther's pay;
      Dankwart, Hagen's brother; Ortwin too,
      An honor and credit to this warlike retinue.

174   Said Sigfrid, "Stay at home, your Majesty,
      Since all your knights will come along with me.
      Remain with the ladies, proudly, nothing loath!
      I surely can guard for you honor and property both.

175   Those who thought to hurl their full attack
      At Worms on Rhine—I'll see that they stay back,
      Close to home. We'll strike their country yet,
      So hard that we shall turn their pride to sad regret."

176   From the Rhine they rode through Hessia with their lords
      Toward Saxony. There was fighting afterwards!
      They burned and pillaged, laying the country waste,
      Till both the kings knew well the bitter fear they faced.

177   They reached the border, there the squires withdrew.
      Mighty Sigfrid asked, "Our retinue
      Of service troops—who'll stay and be their chief?"
      (No one ever rode to the Saxons' greater grief.)

178   They said, "En route let Dankwart guard the pages—
        A stalwart man, bold when the battle rages—
        Liudeger's men will hurt us all the less.
        Ortwin and he can watch the rear with all success."

179   "I shall take the van," Lord Sigfrid chose,
        "Riding on the lookout for our foes
        Till I discover where their men may be."
        They armed fair Siglind's son and did it speedily.

180   He gave command of the knights in their main body
        To Hagen and to Gernot, brave and sturdy.
        Alone to Saxony he rode away.
        Many helmet straps he cut in two that day!

181   Soon he saw a mighty host deployed
        Across the field, outweighing his, but void
        Of true distinction—forty thousand or more.
        This was a happy sight, causing his pride to soar.

182   There too a knight had taken up his post,
        Well armed for war, to watch for the enemy host.
        Sigfrid saw this man, and he saw him.
        They followed one another, their gazes fierce and grim.

183   I'll tell you now by whom the watch was manned.
        A shining shield of gold was in his hand;
        King Liudegast it was, guarding his force.
        The noble stranger, stately and proud, spurred on his
        horse.

184   Liudegast also had his foeman spied.
        Each one put the spurs to his horse's side

And, aim on shield, lowered his mighty lance—
For all the king's great power, a threatening circumstance!

185   Their lances crashed. The horses bore them past,
One prince crossing before the other so fast
They seemed like wind. Reining, these gallant lords
Wheeled and savagely took up the fight with swords.

186   Sigfrid struck so hard the whole field crashed
With the echoing blow and fiery red sparks flashed
From the helmet stroke like flames that fan
From some great conflagration. Each had found his man.

187   And fierce the strength that Liudegast revealed
In the blows he hit him. Heavy on each man's shield
Lay the other's valor. Thirty came on the run
To cover the king—before they reached him Sigfrid won,

188   Wounding the king three times, striking through
To pierce his excellent mail. The sword blade drew,
Where the edges cut, blood from the wounds it made—
By which the royal Liudegast was much dismayed.

189   He begged for his life, pledging his domains,
And said he was Liudegast. All his thanes
Came running up, for they had seen full well
What both were doing at their post, and what befell.

190   About to lead him off, he faced attack
By thirty of Liudegast's men. He fought them back,
Guarding his mighty hostage with savage blows.
The gallant knight would cause more losses for his foes!

191   All thirty he was strong enough to slay,
Except for one, who promptly rode away
And gave the rest report of what occurred.
The red on his helmet vouched to them for the truth of
his word.

192   Told the king was a prisoner, every Dane
Was struck with wrath at the news and filled with pain.
They told his brother, who began to storm
In a great and towering rage, for this was grievous harm.

193   And so he led away King Liudegast then—
Sigfrid in all his power—to Gunther's men.
He gave him over to Hagen, in his safekeeping.
Hearing it was the king, they felt no need for weeping.

194   They bade the Burgundians fasten their pennants on.
"Forward!" Sigfrid cried. "More's to be done
Before the day is through. If I keep my life,
We'll leave in care and sorrow many a Saxon wife.

195   Warriors of the Rhine, listen to me.
I'll guide you to Liudegast's army. Then you'll see
Helmets hewn to bits by heroes here.
Before we head back home, they'll learn the taste of fear."

196   Gernot and his men leaped to their horses.
A mighty minstrel rode at the head of their forces,
Noble Folker, taking in hand their banner.
Their troops were ready for war, armed in the finest
manner.

197   They had a thousand men—only those
And Sigfrid's twelve. Clouds of dust soon rose

Along the roads. They rode across the fields,
And you could see before them the glitter of splendid
    shields.

198   Now there came the army of Saxony,
With sharpened swords—so it was told to me—
Swords that could really cut, in the warriors' hands,
To push the strangers back and defend their towns and
    lands.

199   The king's commanders moved the army ahead.
Sigfrid also came with the knights he led
In company with him from Netherland.
That day's fighting left many a bloodstained hand.

200   In battle Sindold and Hunold and Gernot slew
More than one before he even knew
The measure of their valiant bravery—
A cause of grief for women of noble ancestry.

201   Folker and Hagen and Ortwin in the fight
Put out with flowing blood the flashing light
Of numerous helmets—heroes in battle heat!
And Dankwart too performed many a marvelous feat.

202   Men of Denmark also tried their mettle.
The sound was loud of shields in the crash of battle,
And of sharp swords, swinging constantly.
Damage enough they caused, bold fighters of Saxony!

203   When Burgundy's men rushed into battle there,
They plied their swords, and many wounds lay bare.
Over the saddles streams of blood ran down.
Thus did valiant warriors seek to gain renown.

204   The sound of sharpened blade in hero's hand
    Resounded loud when the men of Netherland
    Followed their lord, to join the mighty throng.
    Models of knighthood, they and Sigfrid rode along.

205   Where Sigfrid went no Rhenish knight would go,
    But one could see a bloody river flow
    Through rows of shining helmets—the work of his hand—
    Till he found Liudeger at the head of his warrior band.

206   Through his foes for the third time he rode,
    To the end and back, when out Lord Hagen strode,
    To help him sate his spirit in the fray.
    Many warriors had to die at their hands that day.

207   When Liudeger saw Lord Sigfrid riding by,
    And saw that in his hand he held on high
    Balmung the mighty sword and that he killed
    So many men, with savage anger his heart was filled.

208   Now with a mighty surge and noise of swords
    The armies approached each other, both the lords
    The more intent to find which one was stronger.
    The others now withdrew. The air was full of anger.

209   By now they had informed the Saxon chief
    Of his brother's capture, a cause of pain and grief.
    Not knowing yet that it was Siglind's son,
    They blamed Lord Gernot. He found out soon by whom
      it was done!

210   Such was the power Liudeger revealed
    That at his blows Lord Sigfrid's charger reeled

Beneath his saddle. Gaining control of his horse,
Sigfrid renewed the fight with savage and cruel force.

211   Hagen and Gernot helped him, Dankwart too,
And Folker the minstrel—many men they slew.
Sindold and Hunold and Ortwin there in the heat
Of warfare struck them down in numbers dead at their
        feet.

212   Fighting they kept each other close in view,
These splendid princes. Over helmets flew
Spears from heroes' hands to strike their way
Through shining shields on which the color of blood now
        lay.

213   In storm of battle many a fighting man
Dismounted from his horse. Two heroes ran
At one another, Sigfrid and Liudeger.
Lances and sharpened spears went flying through the air.

214   Sigfrid cut the straps that held his shield.
He thought that he would make the Saxons yield,
Brave though they were, with their many casualties.
Dankwart cut through shining rings of mail with ease.

215   Then Liudeger saw a shield with crown all painted
In front of Sigfrid's hand. Well acquainted
Now with its owner—a valiant man, he knew—
The king called out aloud to all his retinue:

216   "Men of mine, stop now, the fight is done.
The man that I see here is Sigmund's son,
Sigfrid the strong—I know that it is he.
The cursed devil himself has sent him to Saxony."

217   In the midst of battle he had them lower the standard,
And sued for peace—in which he was not hindered,
But had to go as hostage to Gunther's land—
Tribute forced from him by the power of Sigfrid's hand.

218   In common council they set an end to war.
Punctured helms and the massive shields they bore
Were now put down—and not a one was free
Of marks the color of blood, from the hands of Burgundy.

219   They took as hostage (having given no quarter)
Whomever they chose. By Gernot and Hagen's order
The wounded were put on stretchers. They carried off
Five hundred captives to the Rhine—all brave enough.

220   The Danes rode home deprived of victory,
Nor had the Saxons fought so gloriously
That one could praise them for it—much to the pain
Of proper heroes. Friends and kinsmen mourned the slain.

221   They packed their arms and armor home again
By horse to the Rhine. Sigfrid and his men
Had proved their merit—his was a noble deed.
This the men of Gunther would readily concede.

222   The king sent Gernot back to Worms to tell
His friends and kin at home, and say how well
He'd fared himself, and all his retinue:
Brave men were they, honor was their guide and due.

223   The pages came running, and passed the message on.
Faces were bright with joy, all sorrow gone,
At such auspicious word as now was passed.
Noble women's questions soon came thick and fast:

224   How, they asked, had the great king's warriors done?
To Kriemhild went a messenger alone—
A secret others could not be witness of,
For one among those warriors was her heart's true love.

225   When she saw the herald coming to her place
The lovely lady spoke with kindly grace:
"My gold is yours if you have good news to repeat.
I'll always owe you thanks if you do it without deceit.

226   How did my brother Gernot leave the field—
And my other kin? Did we lose many killed?
And who gained most distinction, tell me this."
Quickly the herald replied, "No one showed cowardice.

227   But in real combat no one rode so well,
My noble queen (since I have this to tell),
As did our highborn guest from Netherland.
Amazing was the work of valiant Sigfrid's hand!

228   However well our heroes fought the fight—
Dankwart or Hagen or any other knight
Of our great king—however they fought for glory,
What Sigfrid did alone was quite another story.

229   In battle they accounted for many slain.
And yet I doubt if anyone could explain
The wonders Sigfrid did when he rode in.
He fashioned women's grief from what he did to their kin.

230   Many sweethearts fell and never rose.
So loud upon their helmets were his blows
That they brought forth from wounds the flowing blood.
He excels in every point—a gallant man and good.

231   Much as Ortwin of Metz accomplished there
      (For if his sword could reach them it was rare
      To find them whole—and mostly they were dead!)
      Still your brother Gernot gave them more to dread—

232   The worst that could befall in battle-hue.
      One must give these excellent men their due:
      Such the work of our proud Burgundian nation
      That not a hint of shame could touch their reputation!

233   Men of the Rhineland emptied saddles bare
      Before their hands, as swords flashed in the air
      And the field resounded. So hard they rode and fought
      That what their foes had started it were better they had
        not.

234   Men of Trony inflicted bitter losses
      When the armies met (and both supporting forces).
      Brave Hagen himself accounted for many killed—
      Feats with which reports to Burgundy are filled.

235   Sindold, Hunold, Gernot's warriors there,
      And Rumold, fought so well that Liudeger
      Had something to be forever sorry for:
      His message to your kinsmen here, declaring war.

236   The noblest fight that anywhere has been
      Or, first and last, ever men have seen—
      This was the willing work of Sigfrid's hand.
      And he brings mighty hostages to Gunther's land,

237   Conquered in valor by this handsome knight—
      For Liudegast the king a bitter plight,

And for his Saxon brother Liudeger.
Now hear, most noble, gracious queen, the news I bear.

238   Sigfrid captured them both! Never before
Have so many come as hostages of war
To Burgundy as by his work at present
Approach the Rhine." For her, no news could be more
    pleasant.

239   "We bring five hundred men or more, my lady,
All unhurt. Of the badly wounded eighty
Who come on blood-red stretchers to our land,
Most of them struck down by valiant Sigfrid's hand.

240   Those who sent to the Rhine their arrogant call
To battle now must be in Gunther's thrall,
And carried back to this land, a joy to their foes."
The tidings made her bright skin blossom like a rose,

241   Her lovely face all red with blushing to hear
That out of combat in good health and cheer
Gallant Sigfrid had come, her fine young knight.
She also rejoiced for her kinsmen—which was only right.

242   Fair Kriemhild said, "You've brought good news to me,
And you shall have rich clothes as herald's fee
And ten marks of gold I'll have them get."
(How nice when good news puts a lady in your debt!)

243   They gave him his reward, his gold and clothes.
To the windows many lovely maidens rose,
To watch the road below—there to see
Riding in all their pride the knights of Burgundy.

244 Sound of limb or wounded, on they came,
To hear their kinsmen's welcome—joy without shame.
The king rode out to them with a cheerful face.
His trouble and pain had ended and joy was in their place.

245 He greeted his foreign knights like his own force—
For a mighty king no other fitting course
Than generous thanks for those who came to his aid,
For the victory they had won and the merit they displayed.

246 Gunther asked for news of kin and friend:
Who in this campaign had met his end.
Their losses were only sixty. An end of sorrow
Had to come for these, as still with the death of a hero.

247 Uninjured men brought back their shields, all shattered,
To Gunther's land, and helmets badly battered.
Before the royal hall the troops dismounted,
And there the cheerful noise of welcoming resounded.

248 They took the knights to town and found them quarters—
Good treatment for his guests, by the king's orders,
And for the wounded shelter, care, and rest.
In the treatment of his foes his merit was manifest.

249 "I offer you welcome," he said to Liudegast.
"Much that through your doing I have lost
Will now be repaid if my good luck holds through.
For all my friends' support may God give them their due."

250 "You give them thanks," said Liudeger. "Well you may!
More noble hostages never fell to the sway
Of any king. For honorable custody
We'll pay you well—and mercy to your enemy."

251   "On your parole I'll let you both go free
      Provided that my foes stay here with me,
      And not without permission leave my land;
      On this I want some pledge." And Liudeger gave his
        hand.

252   They found them all a comfortable place to rest
      And good beds for the wounded. Meanwhile they pressed
      On those who were well excellent wine and mead,
      Until they were a joyous gathering indeed.

253   They stored away their shields, all hacked in battle,
      And ordered hidden many a bloody saddle—
      No lack of these!—that women might not weep.
      Good knights arrived from that campaign in need of sleep.

254   What full and generous service the king bestowed
      On all his guests! His country overflowed
      With friends and strangers. He ordered the finest care
      For the badly wounded. All their pride was vanished in
        air.

255   Physicians there were given rewards untold:
      Silver without a scale, and shining gold,
      To heal the heroes after battle stress.
      The king gave proof to all his guests of his largess.

256   Those who had a journey home in mind
      They begged, as one does friends, to stay behind.
      The king took counsel now on how to pay
      The men who had done his will in such a glorious way.

257   And Gernot said, "We ought to let them ride.
      In six weeks' time—so have them notified—

They shall return again for a festival.
Many who now lie wounded will then be healed and
well."

258 Then Sigfrid too requested leave to go.
When Gunther heard that he'd decided so,
He asked that he remain, most courteously.
(Except for his sister's sake, this would never be.)

259 Too high in wealth and power to take reward,
He well deserved the king's most fond regard—
Shared by all his kin who had been witness
To what occurred in battle through his strength and
fitness.

260 For his fair lady's sake he thought to stay,
On chance of seeing her—which he would one day.
(He met the maiden, as he had hoped and planned;
And afterward rode happily to Sigmund's land.)

261 The king arranged full tests of chivalry,
Which youthful knights pursued most willingly.
Meanwhile he ordered seats upon the strand
For those who were to come to Worms in Burgundy land.

262 At this same time, when all the guests were due,
The news had come to lovely Kriemhild too
That for his friends the king had planned a fete,
And lovely women now were busy early and late,

263 Preparing the clothes and headdress they would wear.
Great Uta also heard the tidings there
Of the warriors soon to come—men proud and bold.
Lavish clothes were taken from the garment fold.

264   For sake of her children Uta ordered made
Clothes in which they all would be arrayed—
Ladies, maids, and knights of Burgundy—
And fashioned for the strangers elegant livery.

✠ FIFTH ADVENTURE
How Sigfrid First Saw Kriemhild

265   To the Rhine they rode, guests on their eager way
To the tourney—you could see them every day.
Out of love for the king they gathered there.
Many were given steeds, and splendid things to wear.

266   Seats were all set up in preparation
For the high and the mighty who came to the cele-
bration—
No less than thirty-two princes, they say. Meanwhile,
Fair ladies planned ahead—a rivalry of style.

267   Young Giselher had no lack of things to do,
He and Gernot (with each his retinue),
Greeting all the guests, strangers and friends—
The sort of generous welcome chivalry extends.

268   Saddles the red of gold, shields ornate,
And clothes of splendor they brought with them to the
fete,
These guests who came to the land along the Rhine.
Many among the injured soon were looking fine!

269   And those who lay in bed and those who bore
The pain of wounds forgot how close was the door
Of bitter death. People soon had ceased
To pity the injured and ill—for joy at the coming feast.

270   They thought of times they'd have as guest or host.
Delight was boundless, joy was uppermost

In all their hearts, overflowing on every hand.
Great was the happiness that came on Gunther's land.

271   The morning of Pentecost, from every door
They poured, in elegant dress, five thousand or more—
Stalwart warriors bound for the festive scene.
Each vied to show the other what sport and pleasure mean.

272   The host was not a fool. He long had known
How fond of his sister Netherland's lord had grown,
Though he had never seen the fair princess,
Whose beauty, they said, excelled all other loveliness.

273   His vassal Ortwin spoke to the king. He cried,
"If you would earn in full the honor and pride
That go with this feast, let the beautiful girls appear,
Who to our greater glory live in Burgundy here.

274   What is a man's delight, to still his care,
If not a pretty girl or a lady fair?
So let your sister come before your guests."
For heroes' hearts he spoke. "Agreed as he suggests!"

275   Thus the king replied, "So be it done."
The news they heard delighted everyone.
To Uta, and her comely daughter too,
Went word to come to court, with maids of her retinue.

276   They chose from wardrobes clothes of the finest kind,
All the noble garments they could find;
Bracelets, too, with silk-and-golden chains,
And all the maidens dressed and primped with endless
    pains.

277 Every novice knight was out to make
     A fine impression for the ladies' sake—
     He wouldn't take a kingdom for his chances.
     Women he'd never met he watched with eager glances.

278 As escort for his sister Gunther sent
     A hundred men or more. On service bound they went,
     Kin of his and hers, sword in hand.
     They were the vassal lords in liege of Burgundian land.

279 Uta also came, Her Majesty.
     In many lovely ladies' company,
     All richly dressed—perhaps a hundred or more.
     Charming maidens followed, her daughter walked before.

280 From ladies' chambers people saw them go.
     Among the heroes moved a surge and flow,
     A pressing forward in the hope, meanwhile,
     If luck was kind to them, they'd see their princess smile.

281 She came in loveliness, as does the dawn
     From somber clouds. His many cares were gone,
     Who bore her in his heart (as long he'd done).
     She stood before him now, his fair and radiant one.

282 Bright from her garments shone the precious stones,
     And sweet the cast of her flesh, its rose-red tones.
     No man who lived, however prone to error,
     Could say that in all this world he had seen a woman
       fairer.

283 As the clear moon stands alone in starry skies,
     Its image bright on clouds, in similar wise

She stood before these comely women then,
To lift with pleasure the hearts of many handsome men.

284   Chamberlains, resplendent, walked in advance,
But dashing knights would not give up their chance
Of pushing out in front where they might gain
A glimpse of the charming princess—Sigfrid's pleasure
    and pain.

285   He thought to himself, "What ever made it seem
That I could hope to love you? A childish dream!
But if I should give you up, I'd rather be dead."
Reflecting thus, he swiftly paled and then blushed red.

286   The handsome son of Sigmund, standing there,
Was like a portrait done with artful care
By a master, on a parchment page,
The fairest knight, they say, of this or any age.

287   The lords in escort bade a path be made
For the ladies. Falling back, the knights obeyed,
Their eager hearts the cause of much delight.
What lovely women they saw! How gracious, how polite!

288   Lord Gernot spoke, "He who kindly made
Offer of service now should be repaid,
Dear brother, in equal fashion, before the eyes
Of all these knights. This I'm not ashamed to advise.

289   Have Sigfrid come before my sister in state
That she may greet him—our profit will be great.
Let her who has never greeted knight extend
Her welcome to him, and we have won our handsome
    friend."

290   Kin of the royal host went out to bring
The news to Sigfrid. "As honor from the king,"
They said, "you shall come to court and there receive
Your welcome from his sister, by the royal leave."

291   His heart was lifted up, his soul was stirred
With pleasure free of pain, as now he heard
That he should see the princess, Uta's child,
She welcomed him—with tact and sweetness reconciled.

292   The proud knight stood before her. Color broke
Like flame upon his face. The maiden spoke,
"Sir Sigfrid, here be welcome, noble knight!"
Her greeting left his spirits high; his heart was bright.

293   Attentively he bowed; she clasped his hand.
How charmingly the young lord took his stand
Beside the lovely lady. Tenderly
They glanced at one another—they meant no one to see.

294   Whether lovingly, in heart's devotion,
White hand was pressed, I have no notion,
But I cannot believe it otherwise:
She never tried to hide her love from Sigfrid's eyes.

295   These were the days of May, the time of summer.
His heart would never hold a feeling warmer
Than the joy he felt as now he walked
With her he hoped to win, their two hands interlocked.

296   And many a warrior thought, "That I could stand—
His sort of luck—to wander hand in hand
With her the way he does, as I have seen—
Or sleep with her." (No knight has better served a queen.)

297   Whatever land the guests might call their own,
      Their eyes were fixed on this one pair alone.
      They gave her leave to kiss the handsome knight,
      And all this world had never brought him such delight.

298   The King of Denmark cried on seeing this:
      "Men have paid with life and limb for that kiss,
      As well I know, for Sigfrid's hand is clever.
      God keep him out of my domains henceforth forever."

299   And now on every side they cleared the road
      For her to the church. Respectfully they strode,
      The knights who walked as escort on the way.
      But here her gallant lord was forced to turn away.

300   She went to the minster then, in company
      Of many women, adorned in such degree
      That many high-flown hopes were left forlorn.
      To many a knight she seemed for his eyes' own pleasure
         born.

301   Sigfrid could hardly wait till mass was through.
      He owed eternal thanks that she was true
      In her affection for him—she whose image
      Filled his heart—to whom in turn he rendered homage.

302   When, like him, she left the minster door,
      They summoned the valiant lord to come before
      The lovely princess again. She spoke her thanks
      For the splendid way he fought at the head of her
         brothers' ranks.

303   "Sir Sigfrid, God reward you. You have earned
      The loyal trust of your men, as I have learned

From their ungrudging words." With this he cast
A tender glance at her, and so replied at last:

304   "I mean to serve them always, nor even sleep
At evening, Lady Kriemhild, unless I keep
My deeds to their desire, and never waver
All my life. This I do in hope of your favor."

305   The space of twelve whole days, from start to end,
They saw the gracious maid with her warrior friend,
Whenever before the eyes of all her kin
She went to court—all for the love she held him in.

306   And all this time the joys and robust sounds,
The great delight of jousting filled the grounds
And palace of Gunther. Valiant men were there,
But Ortwin and Hagen performed feats beyond compare.

307   What any one would do, they were ready for.
In generous measure, too, these men of war.
They made themselves well-known on every hand,
Among the many guests—to the glory of Gunther's land.

308   Wounded men were seen to rise and start
Off to the games, eager to take their part,
To feel the shock on their shields and shoot the spear.
No lack of those to help them—a mighty throng was here.

309   On the festive day, the host decreed
His guests be royally fed, for he had freed
His name of all reproach that strikes a king.
A friend among his guests he walked, in welcoming.

310   He spoke, "O noble knights, before you leave,
       Accept the gifts I offer. I would grieve
       If you should turn them down, for I am true
       In this my purpose: to share my worldly goods with you."

311   The men of Denmark answered, "Sir, once more
       Before we journey home, we all implore
       A lasting peace, our need for which is plain:
       Your men have cost us many friends—our battle-slain."

312   The Saxon chief and Liudegast were healed
       From all the wounds they suffered in the field,
       But not a few were dead, and left behind.
       Now Gunther went to Sigfrid and bade him speak his
           mind:

313   He asked, "Advise me what you think is best.
       Our foes would leave tomorrow. They request
       A guarantee of lasting peace from me.
       Sigfrid, what do you think the wisest course would be?

314   I'll tell you now the terms they swear to keep.
       They'll give me all the gold that they can heap
       On five hundred horses, if I accede
       To letting them go in peace." "A most unworthy deed,"

315   His stalwart guest replied. "Let them rather
       Go from here at once, with no more bother,
       And take the two kings' pledge that never again
       Will hostile warriors dare encroach on your domain."

316   "I'll do as you advise." So the foe was told,
       After their talk: "No one wants your gold."

And now at home families longed once more
To see their men, and they who fought were tired of war.

317   Shields were brought and in them gold was laid.
He gave in plenty to his friends, unweighed.
Five hundred marks or so—to many, more.
(Gunther had the counsel of Gernot on this score.)

318   As they desired, so now they took their leave.
They went to Lady Kriemhild to receive
Her word of parting, or to Uta the queen.
Finer granting of leave the world has never seen.

319   Lodgings were empty as they rode away
But many noble men were still to stay:
King and kin, of perfect breeding all,
Who daily came to Kriemhild to pay her formal call.

320   Sigfrid, too, was ready to depart—
Renouncing the hopeful wishes of his heart.
But now the king found out how matters lay,
And youthful Giselher persuaded him to stay:

321   "Where are you riding, Sigfrid, proud as ever?
Stay with our warriors here—do me this favor.
Stay with Gunther the king and his retinue.
There are beautiful women here, as we'll gladly prove
    to you."

322   Then Sigfrid said, "Leave our mounts behind!
I was about to ride—I've changed my mind.
Take back our shields, though we were homeward bound,
Giselher, with his loyal heart, has won me around."

323   So he remained by friends' affection there.
Not in all the world, not anywhere,
Would life be sweeter. And here the reason lay:
That he could see the lovely princess every day.

324   In pleasure he passed the time with them, detained
By her great beauty there, and never pained
But by his love, through which he was sadly tried—
And for which later, wretchedly, the brave man died.

✠ SIXTH ADVENTURE

How Gunther Went to Iceland in Quest of Brunhild

325   Along the Rhine was heard a new report
      Of lovely maidens, filling Gunther's heart
      With hope of wooing one to be his bride,
      And lifting up his knightly mind with joy and pride.

326   They said there was a queen beyond the sea.
      Her like was never known, of such degree
      Her beauty was, her strength without a peer.
      She challenged every suitor to contest with the spear.

327   In two more tests she threw the heavy stone
      And made a great leap after. Not one alone
      He had to win, but all, and if instead
      The suitor failed a single trial he lost his head.

328   (Precisely this had many times occurred.)
      Such is the news our handsome knight had heard.
      He turned his thoughts to winning her as bride,
      And all for this, in time, many a warrior died.

329   The lord of the Rhineland spoke, "Down to the sea
      To Brunhild I will go, whatever the cost may be,
      And for her love I will risk my very life.
      Rather dead than never to have her as my wife."

330   "I advise against it," Sigfrid warned,
      "This queen is a thing of terror. Many have mourned

The price they paid to sue for her love and hand.
So you might well give up this journey you have planned."

331   "I'll tell you what to do," Lord Hagen spoke.
"Ask that Sigfrid share with you the yoke
Of this great burden. I think you'll find it pays,
Since he seems to know so much of Brunhild's ways."

332   Then Gunther spoke, "My Lord, will you then aid
My wooing of her? If so, and if the maid
I love becomes my lover, I will stake
My honor and my life for noble Sigfrid's sake."

333   In answer Sigfrid, Sigmund's son, replied,
"Give me your sister then, to be my bride,
And I will do it. The princess, gracious and noble—
She is the sole reward I want for all my trouble."

334   "I give you my word and hand," Gunther swore,
"If beautiful Brunhild comes to the Rhenish shore,
Then I will give my sister to be your wife,
And you may live with her for the whole of your happy
        life."

335   On that the noble warriors took their oath.
Far more trouble lay ahead for both
Before they brought the lady back to the Rhine—
Men of highest valor, plagued by fate's design.

336   Sigfrid had to take the Magic Cloak,
The same that he had gained when once he broke
The power of Alberich the dwarf in fearful battle.
(They all prepared for the journey, men of proven mettle.)

337   When Sigfrid had the magic mantle on
     His power was great enough! The cape alone
     Brought the strength of twelve to his renewing.
     And thus he set his subtle skill to the great queen's
       wooing.

338   This cloak was also made in such a fashion
     That any man, secure from mortal vision
     Could in it do whatever things he chose.
     And thus he won Brunhild—and a multitude of woes!

339   "Now tell me, Sigfrid, sir, before we start,
     Should we take knights to Brunhild's land, as part
     Of our good name and fame on this trip to sea?
     Thirty thousand we can have and readily."

340   "Whatever troops we take," was his reply,
     "So fearsome is the queen, that they would die
     At the mercy of her pride. But I submit,
     Brave lord, there is a better way of doing it.

341   Go down the Rhine like knights adventure bound—
     I'll name you the only lords that need be found,
     Four in all, to go with us to sea,
     And we shall win the queen, whatever else may be.

342   I shall be one, the second one is you.
     Let Hagen be the third. And Dankwart, too—
     That valiant man shall be the fourth to go.
     In war with us a thousand men won't stand a show."

343   "Another thing I'd like to have you say
     Before we leave (I'd gladly be on our way!):

What sort of clothing we should take to wear
Before Brunhild. Tell me what is proper there."

344   "The best of clothes that can be found they wear
Always in Brunhild's land. Let us take care,
Therefore, to let her see us richly dressed,
That when they tell of us we need not be distressed."

345   Said the noble knight, "Then I shall go and see
If I can get my mother to agree
To set her maids at work on such array
That we may go before this queen in a fitting way."

346   Said Hagen of Trony (his words bespoke refinement):
"Why do you give your mother this assignment?
Let your sister know what you intend.
Your trip will profit from the help that she can lend."

347   Word was sent to his sister they would call—
Sigfrid and he—to see her. But first of all
The lovely maiden dressed in perfect taste,
Not displeased at the gallant visitors she faced.

348   Suitably adorned was all her court.
The two princes came. At this report,
She rose from her chair, in perfect form and breeding,
And went to give her noble guest and brother greeting.

349   She spoke, "I welcome my brother and his friend,
And I am curious, what does this portend,
Your visit here at court? So let me hear,
My great and gentle lords, how both of you may fare."

350 Gunther spoke, "My lady, you shall know.
  We face with pride and courage the risk of woe.
  Far in foreign lands on chivalry
  We ride and must be dressed for the journey splendidly."

351 The princess said, "Sit down, my brother dear.
  Who are these women—I do so want to hear—
  Whose love you seek in other monarchs' lands?"
  With this the lady took the lucky heroes' hands.

352 She walked with them back to her former seat,
  On a couch with splendid pillows, all complete
  With pictures, rich in gold, a lovely thing.
  They found good entertainment, here in the women's
   wing.

353 Friendly glances and sweet meeting of eyes
  Between the couple then—and no surprise!
  Her image was in his heart, much as his life
  Was she to him, this lovely woman, soon his wife.

354 The mighty king then spoke, "Without your aid,
  Sister dear, our trip could not be made.
  We go to Brunhild's land, in search of pleasure;
  Before these ladies we need clothes of richest measure."

355 "Believe me, dearest brother," she replied,
  "My fullest help shall never be denied,
  If in any way it may avail you,
  And I should be displeased if any one should fail you.

356 Do not ask, hesitant or fearing,
  Command of me, in high and noble bearing!

99

Whatever you wish of me, I shall do,"
This the charming princess added, "and gladly, too."

357   "Dear sister, we must have fine clothes to wear.
Let preparations be in your gracious care.
Your maids must do their work with never a slip
In fit and good appearance. Our hearts are set on this trip."

358   The princess replied, "Remember just one thing.
I have the silk; your men, however, must bring
Jewels to us in their shields. That's all we need
To make the clothes you want." Gunther and Sigfrid
      agreed.

359   "And who are the friends," she asked, "who go with you,
For whom such splendid courtly dress is due?"
Gunther answered, "I am one of four.
Two vassals, Dankwart and Hagen, go with us—no more.

360   And take good note, my lady, of what I say.
The four of us must have, for every day
Of four, three changes of clothes, in perfect taste,
Lest when we leave Brunhild's land we go disgraced."

361   The lords now said good-bye. To the separate hall
Where the women lived, the queen sent out a call
For thirty maids in waiting, every one
Renowned for special skill whenever such work was done.

362   Silks from Arabia, white as the winter snows,
And green from Zazamanc, as the clover grows—
Into such fabric they worked the precious stone,
For lovely clothes, cut by the fair princess alone.

363   A picture strange to see: on the undersides
       A marvellous lining made of otter hides.
       This they covered with silk (it is worn that way).
       Now listen to the wonder of their bright array.

364   Silks from the lands of Morocco and Libya, the best
       That ever any king or queen possessed,
       In lavish stock: thus Kriemhild, for her part,
       Made known to all the sweet affection of her heart.

365   With the lofty purpose of their trip now sure,
       Ermine trim alone seemed much too poor,
       Hence the woolen cover, black as coal—
       Fitting still for heroes in their festive role.

366   On a ground of Arabian gold the brilliant light
       Of jewels played. The cost was nothing slight
       In women's work—and seven weeks all spent,
       But now it was done and with it, too, their armament.

367   And while the women toiled, a sturdy ship
       Was swiftly in the building, to speed their trip
       Upon the Rhine, and take them down to the sea.
       What weariness for women of noble pedigree!

368   But now they could tell the knights that what they willed
       In the way of elegant clothes was all fulfilled,
       Ready for them to wear. They did not choose
       To tarry by the Rhine, once they had heard this news.

369   To friends went out a message, to inquire
       If they would come and view their new attire—
       And say if they thought the fit too short or long.

The ladies earned their thanks, their friends found
  nothing wrong.

370   And everyone who saw must needs agree
No better clothes in this world did he ever see.
So they could wear them there at court with pride—
The best that knights have ever owned, no one denied.

371   Great was the gratitude that they expressed.
But now in courtly style they made request
That the ladies grant them leave, these merry peers,
And eyes that once were bright were moist and sad with
  tears.

372   Kriemhild said, "You still could stay, dear brother
(I'd think it wise), and seek the hand of another.
Your life would not be wagered in the try.
You'll surely find as noble a wife—and nearer by."

373   I think their hearts foretold what the future kept.
No matter what was said, the women wept,
Until the gold upon their breasts was flecked
And tarnished by the tears that fell from their eyes
  unchecked.

374   The princess said, "Sir Sigfrid, I commend
My brother to your care. Your favor attend
His ways in Brunhild's land, lest ill ensue."
Which, on Kriemhild's hand, he boldly swore to do.

375   "So long as I shall live," the warrior said,
"From your heart, my lady, banish dread!
I shall bring him back, as surely as I have vowed,
In safety to the Rhine." The lovely maiden bowed.

376 Down to the beach they carried their shields of gold,
And took along their clothes. Their men they told
To bring the horses, for they were ready to ride.
Great was the weeping then, as lovely women cried.

377 Beautiful damsels stood at the windows watching.
The sails of the ship were moved by a strong breeze
  catching.
The proud companions now put out from land
And royal Gunther spoke, "Who shall take command?"

378 "I will," Sigfrid said, "since I can guide
Your way across the sea. Be satisfied,
My friends, I know the way by water there."
And so they left from Burgundy, without a care.

379 Sigfrid took a pole, with it began
To shove away from the shore, a sturdy man;
And Gunther the bold himself took up an oar.
Off from the land they went, these valiant men of war.

380 They had good food with them, and excellent wine,
The best that they could find along the Rhine.
Their horses were quartered well, in a decent stall,
The ship rode an even keel, they had no trouble at all.

381 The powerful stays of their sails were stretched out tight.
They had covered twenty leagues before the night,
Down with a favorable wind, down to the sea.
(From all of their haughty labor, grief and misery!)

382 Twelve mornings after that, so goes the tale,
The wind had borne them far, until their sail

Was in sight of Isenstein, in Brunhild's realm
(Familiar only to the hero at the helm).

383   When royal Gunther saw so many towers,
And the size of the place, he cried, "Good friend of ours,
Tell us, if you know, whose might they be,
All these many towers, the splendid land we see?"

384   Sigfrid replied, "I know, for the truth is plain.
This is Brunhild's people, her domain,
And the fortress Isenstein, as you've heard me say.
There are lovely women there—you'll see this very day!

385   And here is some advice I have for you:
All of you say the same and carry it through.
(This I think is best.) If we are seen
By her today, take care how we approach the queen.

386   Before her court and the lovely lady's throne,
No two reports, my sirs, but this alone:
That Gunther is my lord, and I am one
Among his many vassals, and what he wills is done."

387   He bade them swear to this, and they complied.
And not a one that failed, for all their pride.
They spoke as he desired, when Gunther was bid
Before the lovely Brunhild, and it was well they did!

388   "Not so much for love of you I take
This step, as for your lovely sister's sake,
Who is like my soul to me, my very life.
For this I gladly serve: that she should be my wife."

✠ SEVENTH ADVENTURE
How Gunther Won Brunhild

389   Meanwhile their ship had come so close to land
      The king could see the fairest maidens stand
      Far above in the windows of the city—
      But none he recognized, which seemed to him a pity.

390   He turned to question Sigfrid, his companion:
      "Who might these maidens be, in your opinion,
      Looking down at us on the ocean tide?
      Whoever their lord may be, there's spirit there and pride."

391   Noble Sigfrid answered, "Cast a glance,
      In secret, among these girls. Given the chance,
      Now tell me, which would you choose to be your bride?"
      "All right, I shall," bold and eager, Gunther cried.

392   "I see one now, by the window over there,
      Dressed in a snow-white dress, of such a rare
      And lovely form—my eyes would never err,
      If they had the chance to choose, and I would marry her."

393   "The light of your eyes served you well in the choice,
      For that is noble Brunhild, the lovely prize
      Toward which your heart and mind and will, unceasing,
      Urge you." Her every gesture seemed to Gunther pleasing.

394   The queen soon ordered her maids to stand away
      From the window ledge: it was not right to stay

Where strangers could stare at them. And they obeyed her.
But we shall also hear of them what they did later.

395   With the strangers in mind, they put their finery on,
Like lovely women always, and were gone
To the narrow windows where, looking through,
They had seen the heroes stand—all this for a better view.

396   But they were only four who came to the land.
Sigfrid led Gunther's horse out on the sand—
Maidens watched from the window as he did it,
Which seemed to Gunther all to his greater fame and
       credit.

397   He led him by the bridle, the graceful steed,
Big and strong and handsome, of perfect breed.
Royal Gunther rose to the saddle then.
This was Sigfrid's service, soon forgotten again.

398   He went to the ship and brought his horse to land.
No common thing was this, that he should stand
Beside the stirrups of another knight,
And from the windows highborn ladies watched the sight.

399   In perfect harmony the princely pair:
White as the snow the clothes they brought to wear
And of their steeds the same; their shields well made,
From which, as they held them high, the bright reflection
       played;

400   Their saddles studded with jewels; fine and small
The gauge of their martingales. To Brunhild's hall
They came in splendor. Bells of bright red gold

Hung on their saddles. They rode to this land as suits the bold,

401 With newly whetted spears and well made swords
Broad and sharp, held by the handsome lords
So that the point reached down to the very spur.
This fair Brunhild watched, nothing escaping her.

402 With them came Sir Dankwart, and Hagen came,
Their noble vassals, wearing garments the same,
Richly made, in color black as the raven.
Their shields were things of beauty—massive, broad, and proven!

403 From India came the splendid jewels fastened
Upon their clothes, which with their moving glistened.
Unguarded they left their craft by the waterside,
And turning toward the castle now, began to ride.

404 Eighty-six towers they saw in all,
Three palaces, and a nobly fashioned hall
Of marble green as the grass, and it was here
That with her lords and ladies dwelt Brunhild the fair.

405 The city was open wide, the gates unlocked,
Toward them quickly Brunhild's vassals walked,
Eager to welcome guests in their mistress' land.
They took their horses in charge, the shield from each one's hand.

406 A chamberlain said, "Now give your weapons over,
And your suits of mail." Said Hagen, "That's one favor
We will not do you. We'll keep them close at hand."
Sigfrid answered: "Let me explain how matters stand.

407   That is their custom at court. They let no guest
Carry weapons here. So it is best
To let them take our arms and lay them aside."
Much against his will, Gunther's man complied.

408   Wine was poured for them; the guests were made
To feel at home. At court a bold parade
Of warriors dressed to suit their princely station,
Still the strangers got their share of admiration.

409   The news had been conveyed to Brunhild, the queen,
That unknown men in elegant clothes were seen
Arriving at court, borne by the ocean tide.
Now the lovely maiden asked of this; she cried:

410   "These men, these strangers, tell me who they are,
Coming all unknown and from afar,
To stand so proudly here within my walls—
And to whose honor and credit this heroes' voyage falls."

411   One of her retinue spoke, "This much I can say:
None have I ever seen until this day—
Except that one among them I can tell
Looks like Sigfrid. Truly I counsel you: welcome him well.

412   The second is a man of such good breeding
That he would be a king—only needing
Wide lands to rule. Perhaps he really is—
To stand among those men with dignity like his!

413   The third among these men appears so gruff,
And yet in form, my Queen, handsome enough;
Look at those flashing eyes and the angry stare.
I'll wager anything there's a fierce temper there.

414   The youngest of the group is most refined—
His bearing and his breeding seem the kind
We cherish in maidens, such his gentle charm.
Things would go hard with us if he ever came to harm.

415   For all his handsome form and gentle tone,
Many a winsome wife would weep alone
If he ever turned to rage. He seems indeed
A bold and dauntless man, a knight of the noble breed."

416   The queen cried out: "My dress, my battle-gear!
If mighty Sigfrid has made this journey here
With thought of winning my love, he'll pay with his life.
I'm not so afraid of him that I mean to be his wife."

417   Soon the fair Brunhild, in fitting dress,
Came with her beautiful maids, surely no less
Than a hundred in all, fair and handsomely clad.
Here they could see the strangers—at which their hearts
    were glad.

418   As escort for the ladies, Iceland's lords,
Vassals of Brunhild, came, bearing their swords—
Five hundred, and maybe more. Alarmed by that,
The doughty guests arose from the couches where they sat.

419   And now would you like to hear the words that passed,
When Brunhild saw the prince of the Rhine at last?
"Welcome to Iceland, Sigfrid," said the queen,
"And will you tell me, please, what does this voyage
    mean?"

420   "Your gracious favor, Lady, has reversed
The order of your greeting. He is first

Who stands before me here, this noble lord,
My liege—I must decline the honor you accord.

421   Born to the Rhenish throne—what more to say?
And all for the love of you we are here today.
He means to marry you, at any cost.
Reflect on this! My lord will not yield, and you are lost!

422   Gunther is his name, a glorious king.
In all the world he wishes this one thing:
To gain your love. This trip I did not choose,
But that was his command and I could not refuse."

423   "If you are a vassal, and he the one who bears
The crown, the challenge is his. In case he dares
To take it up and wins, I'll be his wife.
But if I vanquish him, all of you lose your life!"

424   Hagen spoke, "Lady, let us see
These mighty contests. Awesome they must be
Before you hear surrender from Gunther, my king.
For you are the sort of beauty he thinks of marrying."

425   "He shall throw the stone, and jump, and shoot the spear.
Before you answer rashly, let this be clear;
Life and honor both you stand to lose,"
The beautiful woman said. "Think before you choose."

426   Sigfrid said to the king, as he stepped up near,
"Say what you feel like saying. Have no fear
Because of the queen or the hurt you might incur.
I know some tricks to keep you safe enough from her."

427   Said royal Gunther, "Gracious lady, decree
As suits your pleasure. If more—so let it be!

For I shall brave it all for your sweet sake.
I must have you in marriage—for this my life is at stake."

428   Now that Brunhild knew the king's intent,
She told them to hasten the start of the games and sent
To get good armor for the battlefield:
Mail of red gold, and a hard-bossed shield.

429   Here was the silken tunic that she wore
In many battles. No weapon ever tore
Its lovely Libyan wool, carefully made
With light designs in shining woven work and braid.

430   During this time, arrogant taunt and threat
Were the strangers' lot. Dankwart was much upset,
And Hagen worried over Gunther's fate.
They thought: "The good we get from this trip will not be
   great."

431   Meanwhile crafty Sigfrid walked away,
Unnoticed, back to where their vessel lay,
And took the Mantle from its hiding place,
And quickly slipped it on, so none could see his face.

432   Returned, he found a crowd of knights, who came
To hear the queen decree her lofty game.
He wisely came upon them unaware.
Not a soul could see him, of all the people there.

433   The place for the game was set, the ring was drawn,
Ready for the host of lookers-on—
More than seven hundred referees,
For they would say who won; in armor all of these.

434   Brunhild now had come, weapons in hand,
As if she meant to conquer some monarch's land—

In silks with golden brooches fastened in,
Beneath which gleamed the shining whiteness of her skin.

435   Then came her retinue of knights, to hold
The mighty breadth of shield, of pure red gold
With heavy straps as hard as steel and bright,
Under the guard of which the lovely maid would fight.

436   The enarmes upon her shield were a noble braid,
With precious stones, green as the grass, inlaid,
Their many gleams competing with the gold.
The man who won her love must certainly be bold.

437   People say that, at the boss, her shield
Was three hands thick, and this the maid could wield!
A splendid mass of gold and steel so great,
Four of her chamberlains could hardly bear its weight.

438   When mighty Hagen watched them bring the shield,
His mood of bitterness was unconcealed:
"What now, King Gunther? A nice farewell to life!
This woman you hope to marry is surely the devil's wife!"

439   But listen, too, how ample her attire!
A tunic of silk from Azagouc, with the fire
Of many precious stones, whose color shone
From the rich and noble cloth and the queen who had
    it on.

440   .They also brought the maiden a mighty spear,
Enormous in size, yet part of the battle gear
She always used. The stock was heavily made,
The point was sharp and true, a fearsome cutting blade.

441   I tell you, amazing tales have made the rounds
About how heavy it was. A hundred pounds
Of metal alone, they say, went into the spear;
It was all three men could lift. Great was Gunther's fear.

442   He thought to himself, "Is our whole plan amiss?
How could the devil in hell get out of this?
If I were back alive in Burgundy,
She'd wait a long, long while for any love from me!"

443   Now Hagen's brother spoke, the brave Dankwart:
"I rue this trip from the bottom of my heart.
They call us knights—is this the way we die,
Here, at the hands of women, under this foreign sky?

444   I'm sorry that I ever came to this land!
But if my brother had his weapons in hand,
And I the use of mine, they'd soon dispense,
All these men of Brunhild's, with some of their insolence.

445   They'd learn to watch their step, take that from me!
This beautiful woman here—before I'd see
My master die, her own life-breath would cease,
Though I had sworn a thousand oaths to keep the peace!"

446   "They'd never stop our getting out of here,"
His brother Hagen said, "if we had the gear
We need when the fighting breaks, and swords at our side.
We'd teach this mighty woman a humbling of her pride!"

447   The noble lady heard what Hagen said.
With a smile about her lips, she turned her head,
And looking back she spoke, "If he feels so brave,
Give them back the armor, the sharp swords they gave."

448   When at the lady's behest they got their swords,
Dankwart flushed with joy. "And now, my lords,
We'll take the game as it comes. Since we are armed,"
The valiant warrior cried, "Gunther cannot be harmed."

449   But Brunhild's strength was clearly an awesome thing.
They brought a heavy stone up to the ring,
A mammoth piece of rock, huge and round.
It took a dozen men to lift it off the ground.

450   She used to throw it after she threw the spear.
The men of Burgundy were filled with fear.
"Great God," said Hagen, "he's chosen his lover well!
She ought to be the cursed devil's bride in hell."

451   Back from her white and gleaming wrist she rolled
Her sleeves, and took her shield in hand to hold,
And lifted up her spear. The games were on.
At the thought of Brunhild's wrath, their confidence was
    gone.

452   If Sigfrid had not come to Gunther's aid,
The king would have lost his life to the mighty maid.
Now secretly he went and touched his hand.
Sigfrid's stratagem left Gunther all unmanned.

453   "What touched me?" Gunther thought. He looked
    around—
And all about him no one to be found!
"It is I, Sigfrid, your loyal friend.
As for the queen, let all your fears be at an end.

454   Hand over now your shield for me to hold
And make a careful note of what you're told.

You go through the motions, the work is mine."
Gunther knew his man; this was a welcome sign.

455 "Keep my trick a secret. Tell no one of it.
The queen shall not increase her fame nor profit
At your expense—which is what she wants to do.
Look how that woman stands undaunted in front of you!"

456 The maiden made her throw, a mighty one,
Against the great new shield that Siglind's son
Held in his hands. As if a wind had chanced
To sweep across the steel, the sparks of fire danced.

457 Clear through the shield the mighty blade-point came,
And over the rings of mail there flashed a flame.
Both of the heroes staggered under the blow—
But for the Magic Cape it would have laid them low.

458 Blood burst from Sigfrid's mouth, but he was swift
In leaping back to the ring, there to lift
The spear she had hurled with force enough to cleave
His shield, and send it back at her with a mighty heave.

459 "I do not want to kill the girl," he thought.
He turned the blade of the spear around and shot,
Shaft first, and straight at her tunic he aimed the throw.
Her coat of mail rang loud with the powerful force of the
 blow.

460 Out of the rings of mail the fire swirled
Like sparks in the wind. The son of Sigmund hurled
A mighty spear; her power gone, she fell
Beneath the blow. Never would Gunther have done so
 well.

461   How quickly the fair Brunhild sprang to her feet!
"My compliments, Gunther! The noble lord I greet
Who made that throw." (For so she thought him to be.
But she was tricked at her game by a mightier man than
     he.)

462   Straight to her place she went, with an angry frown;
High in the air the maiden raised the stone.
She gave it a mighty heave—and how it flew!
Her armor clanging, she jumped after the stone she threw.

463   The stone had traveled twenty yards or so,
And still the jump she made surpassed her throw.
Now the hero Sigfrid walked to the stone.
Gunther hefted it, but Sigfrid threw it alone.

464   Sigfrid was tall and powerfully built. He threw,
And the stone went farther. His jump was farther, too.
His vast skill and cunning made him so strong
That he could make the leap and carry Gunther along.

465   The jump was over, the stone was on the ground,
And none in sight but Gunther, all around.
Beautiful Brunhild flashed an angry red:
Except for Sigfrid's feat, Gunther would be dead.

466   Now that she saw him standing safe and sound
At the end of the ring, she shouted, "Gather 'round,
Kin of mine, men of my retinue,
You shall be in liege to Gunther, all of you."

467   And all the warriors laid their weapons down,
And knelt in obeisance to the Burgundian crown
Of Gunther the mighty, thinking the while, of course,
That he had won the contest by his own sheer force.

468   He greeted her graciously, like a perfect knight.
       She placed her hand in his, granting the right
       Of command to him and giving him full domain—
       Much to the joy of Hagen, his great and valiant thane.

469   She asked the noble king to come with her
       Into the palace, this time to confer
       Upon the warriors services multiplied
       (Which Dankwart and Hagen had to accept and be
         satisfied).

470   Sigfrid was not the least ingenious of men.
       He took his mantle back to store it again,
       And then returned where all the women sat,
       And asked the king a question (a wise precaution, that):

471   "What do you wait for, sir? Why do we need
       Delay these many games the queen decreed?
       Let's see what kind they are!"—all this a show
       He cunningly put on, as if he didn't know.

472   The queen inquired, "How could it possibly be,
       Sigfrid, my lord, that you should fail to see
       The victory which the hand of Gunther gained?"
       Hagen of Burgundy it was who thus explained:

473   "True, my lady, by some unhappy slip
       Our good companion here was down at the ship
       When the lord of all the Rhineland conquered you,"
       Gunther's man went on, "and so he never knew."

474   "I'm glad to hear that news," Sigfrid cried.
       "So now at last someone has leveled your pride;
       A mortal man has proved he could best you. Fine!
       And now, my noble lady, follow us back to the Rhine!"

475 The fair maid answered, "Not yet! Before I go,
All my kin and all my men must know.
I cannot lightly leave my native land;
First I must have my friends and family close at hand."

476 So out on every path her heralds flew
Till all her troops, her kith and kin all knew
That they were summoned to court without delay.
For them she ordered splendid clothing given away.

477 And every day they came, from dawn to late,
Down to Brunhild's castle, like streams in spate.
"Hello," said Hagen of Trony, "what have we here?
This waiting for Brunhild's men is apt to cost us dear.

478 What if they now descend on us in force—
(We don't know what she has in mind, of course.
What if she's mad enough to plot our death?)
Then an evil day for us was the day she first drew breath!"

479 Stalwart Sigfrid said, "Leave this to me,
The thing you fear will never come to be,
For I shall bring you help, to Iceland here,
Knights you have never seen, men who have no peer.

480 Now I shall go and do not ask me where.
Meanwhile your honor stands in God's good care.
I'll not be long. You'll have a thousand men,
The finest fighters I know, when I come back again."

481 "Just so you aren't too long!" replied the king.
"We're duly grateful for the help you bring."
"I shall be back in hardly more than a day,
Tell Brunhild that it was you who sent me away."

✝ EIGHTH ADVENTURE
How Sigfrid Went to Get the Nibelung Warriors

482   **S**igfrid walked to a gate by the waterside,
Wearing his magic cape. There he spied
A boat and, boarding secretly, was gone.
As though a swift breeze blew, he pushed the vessel on.

483   No one saw the pilot. The boat moved off
By Sigfrid's strength alone—great enough
To make it seem there blew some special wind.
But no, this was the work of the son of fair Siglind.

484   In what remained of day and one brief night
He reached the land he sought, so great his might—
A trip of a hundred miles and even more.
These were the Nibelungs, here was his treasure-store.

485   All alone he landed on an isle,
Gaily moored and tied his boat meanwhile,
And walked ahead to a castle on a hill,
And sought for lodging there, like tired travelers still.

486   He came before the gate. They had it locked,
A guard of their good name, and so he knocked,
Unknown, upon the door. The one he tried
He found was guarded well. A giant stood inside,

487   The guardian of the castle. Always near,
In readiness, he kept his battle gear.

"Who's beating on the door like that?" he cried.
Sigfrid changed his voice and waited there outside.

488   "A wandering knight," he said, "adventure-bound.
And any man who'd rather lie around
And take his ease today—I'll stir him up!
Open the gate!" It vexed the guard that he would not stop.

489   That giant now had put his armor on,
His helmet on his head, and swiftly drawn
His heavy shield. He opened wide the gate,
Rushing out at Sigfrid, fierce and full of hate.

490   How dare he come and wake so many men?
And from his hand the blows descended then,
Like rain. The splendid stranger parried back.
The giant warder used an iron mace to hack

491   His shield-rim off. Thus was the hero harried.
The chance of dying even had him worried,
Since his giant gateman fought so hard,
And yet, as master, he was proud of such a guard!

492   They struggled so, the castle echoed 'round
And in the Nibelungs' hall they heard the sound.
Sigfrid won, and tied him foot and hand.
The news of it soon spread through all the Nibelung land.

493   Far across the hill the fearful clash
Had roused up Alberich the dwarf, wild and rash.
He put his armor on, ran and found
The noble stranger there, the giant warder bound.

494   The dwarf was fierce, and anything but frail.
He had his helmet on, his coat of mail,

And in his hand, all made of gold, a knout.
In search of Lord Sigfrid he boldly sallied out.

495   This knout had seven iron-knotted bands.
The shield before courageous Sigfrid's hands
He struck so violently it smashed apart.
Fear for his very life laid hold on the stranger's heart.

496   Sigfrid threw aside his broken shield
And sheathed his long blade, which he would not wield
To kill his chamberlain; and thus restrained,
Preserved his perfect breeding, as worthy knights are
      trained.

497   He ran at Alberich with those hands men feared,
And grabbed the grey-haired fellow by his beard,
And brought him up so short that Alberich screamed—
A hero's bringing-up, and painful, so it seemed!

498   Alberich cried aloud, "Let me live!
If my oath of bondage were free to give
To any but the master I swore to cherish"—
Craftily he spoke—"I'd be yours before I'd perish."

499   Sigfrid bound the dwarf, like the giant before.
The knight's great power left him hurt and sore.
The dwarf inquired, "What's your name, pray tell?"
He said, "My name is Sigfrid. I thought you knew me
      well."

500   The dwarf replied, "That is good news to hear!
Your warrior's handiwork has made it clear
That you have every right to rule this land.
Only let me live—I'll do what you command."

501   Sigfrid answered, "Quickly go and call
A thousand Nibelung knights, the best of all,
And have these men report to me today."
What he wished them for, no one heard him say.

502   The giant and the dwarf he let go free.
Alberich ran where he knew the knights would be,
Anxiously woke the Nibelung retinue:
He cried, "Get up, you men, Sigfrid summons you!"

503   They leaped from bed, a thousand of the best,
Eagerly prepared, and quickly dressed,
And hurried where they found Lord Sigfrid waiting.
Then, in words and actions, came a handsome greeting.

504   Candles were lit and spiced wine was poured.
For such a swift response he gave reward
Of thanks to all. "You and I shall go,"
He said, "across the sea." And who would answer no?

505   Thirty hundred knights had come in all
Of whom a thousand men received the call.
To these—the best—they carried sword and helm,
For he was about to lead them back to Brunhild's realm.

506   "At court, my lords—this much I'll tell you here—
Have on your finest clothes when you appear.
Many charming girls must see us there,
And so provide yourselves with splendid things to wear."

507   By early morning, men were journey-bound.
Bold companions these, that Sigfrid found.
They took the finest clothes, and steeds to ride.
They came to Brunhild's land in full chivalric pride.

508   Winsome maidens lined the parapet.
"Does anyone recognize these travelers yet?"
The queen inquired. "They ride the waterflow,
And the sails they fly are rich, whiter than any snow."

509   Replied the king of the Rhine, "Those are my men!
En route, I left them near; I sent again
To bid them come, my queen, and here they are."
All eyes were turned upon the strangers from afar.

510   There was Sigfrid standing at the bow
In splendid dress, with many men, and now
The queen inquired: "Say what course to choose:
To greet these guests, my lord, or silently refuse?"

511   "Go out to meet them on the palace ground,
That they may know what welcome they have found,"
The king replied. She did as Gunther told;
She greeted all the rest, to Sigfrid she was cold.

512   They found them rooms and put their things aside.
So many strangers came—there seemed a tide
Of pushing crowds, wherever they might be.
But now the knights would leave for home and Burgundy.

513   "All thanks to any man who might divide
My store of gold and silver," Brunhild cried,
"Among my guests and his—so much is there."
Answered Dankwart, thane of royal Giselher:

514   "Let me have your keys in custody,
And I'll divide it well, depend on me!
Oh noble queen, let me take any blame."
(He clearly proved that he deserved his generous name.)

515   When Hagen's brother took in charge the key
He gave with a hero's hand, so fast and free
That he who wanted half a pound was given
All a poor man needs to think himself in heaven!

516   Times untold, he offered a hundred pounds—
Or more; and many left the palace grounds
In better clothes than they had ever possessed.
This the queen found out, and she was much distressed.

517   She cried, "My lord, this goes a bit too far.
The way your steward gives, what clothes there are
Will all be gone, my gold—he will have spent it!
My thanks to any person who can now prevent it.

518   He must assume I've sent for Death to come,
Such gifts he gives. I'd thought of keeping some,
And spending what my father left to me."
(No queen's steward could match his generosity!)

519   Hagen of Trony said, "You should be told
That Gunther has so much in clothes and gold
To give away that we can well afford
To take no single garment out of Brunhild's hoard."

520   Said she, "But let me fill, for my own sake,
Twenty trunks with gold and silk to take
And give away as gifts, from my own hand,
When all of us have reached our goal in Gunther's land."

521   They filled the trunks with jewels—and not a flaw!
Gunther and Hagen laughed at what they saw:
Chamberlains of hers must needs be there,
For she refused to trust the thane of Giselher!

522   The queen now thought to whom to leave her lands:
      "This should be confirmed by our two hands,
      Before we go." "Bid the man appear
      Who seems most fit," he said. "We'll make him regent
         here."

523   She saw her uncle standing close beside,
      High in rank among her kin. She cried,
      "I here commend to you my towns and land
      Until the whole be ruled by royal Gunther's hand."

524   Two thousand men she chose as company
      From all her court, to sail to Burgundy,
      Besides the thousand knights from Nibelung land.
      Prepared for the journey now, they rode along the strand.

525   Eighty-six matrons she took from here,
      Perhaps a hundred maids, in person fair,
      They wished to hurry now—no more delay.
      The ones they left behind, how full of tears were they!

526   In perfect courtly grace she left her land.
      She kissed her friends who waited close at hand.
      They took their formal leave and left the shore—
      Her father's land to which the queen would come no
         more.

527   En route they played at every kind of game,
      And every pastime known. There also came,
      To speed their sail, a fair and steady breeze.
      They left the lady's land in joy and pleasant ease.

528   She'd not embrace her lord upon the way—
      Pleasure saved until another day:
      At Worms, the castle, and the festive night—
      Where soon they all would be, in joy and much delight.

✠ NINTH ADVENTURE
How Sigfrid Was Sent to Worms

529   When they had been nine days upon the way
       Lord Hagen spoke, "Hear what I have to say!
       We've sent no one to Worms to tell our story;
       Heralds by now should be in Burgundian territory."

530   Gunther answered, "What you say is true;
       No better man for such a trip than you,
       My friend, so ride ahead to Burgundy!
       Finer herald of our journey could never be."

531   "I'm no good as messenger," Hagen cried.
       "I'll watch the stores and be at the ladies' side,
       Guard their lovely things, and stay at sea
       Until we bring them home to the land of Burgundy.

532   Ask Lord Sigfrid to carry back the news,
       He's more than man enough. Should he refuse
       To make the journey, then politely frame
       Your same request again, in your dear sister's name!"

533   They sent to find him and he came. "And now,"
       Said Gunther, "we are nearing home, somehow
       Word must be dispatched to kin of mine,
       My sister and the queen, that we approach the Rhine.

534   This I ask of you. If you will do
       My bidding, I'll always be obliged to you."
       Sigfrid, stalwart lord, would not agree
       Till urgently the king began to press his plea:

535 "I beg you make this ride for me," he prayed
 "And for my sister's sake, the lovely maid,
 That she may join with me in fair reward."
 When Sigfrid heard these words, he spoke, in full accord:

536 "Anything you ask, I'll undertake,
 And do it gladly, too, for her sweet sake.
 Why should I refuse the very one
 My heart holds dear? Ask in her name and it is done."

537 "Then to Uta the queen, my mother, say
 That on this trip of ours our hearts are gay.
 Let my brothers know how we have fared.
 Seek out our friends as well, and let the news be shared.

538 Let my lovely sister hear from you.
 Pledge her my regard and Brunhild's too.
 Tell all the court, the vassals in my hire,
 To what a perfect end I brought my heart's desire.

539 Tell my cousin Ortwin he shall see
 To having places set at Worms for me.
 And look up all my other friends and say
 Brunhild and I intend to hold a gala day!

540 Tell my sister also, when she hears
 My company of guests and comrades nears,
 That she shall take good care to greet my lover;
 I'll not forget my gratitude for Kriemhild's favor."

541 At once the hero sought, from Brunhild's hands,
 The formal leave that etiquette commands,
 And from her court as well. He rode to the Rhine—
 Never in all the world a herald half so fine!

542   With twenty-four good knights he came to Worms—
      Without the king. Reported in these terms,
      The news alarmed the court with grief and dread;
      They feared their royal lord was left afar and dead.

543   His men dismounted now, their spirits high,
      How soon the fine young Giselher came by!
      His brother Gernot, too—how quick to shout,
      Seeing Sigfrid there, the king nowhere about:

544   "Welcome, Sigfrid! Tell me everything!
      Tell me where you left my brother, the king.
      Have we been robbed by Brunhild's mighty arm?
      If so, her lofty love has brought us fearful harm."

545   "Discard your fears! To you and every friend
      The lord I journeyed with bade me extend
      His loyal word of greeting. I left him well.
      He sent me here as herald, and gave me news to tell.

546   Arrange it any way, but this you must do:
      Let me see the queen—your sister, too,
      For they must hear this embassy of mine
      From Brunhild and the king (both of whom are fine)."

547   "Well," said Giselher, "go pay your call;
      The favor you do my sister is far from small.
      Gunther's trip has caused her much disquiet.
      She'll gladly give you welcome, I swear she'll not deny it!"

548   Sigfrid said, "However I may serve her,
      It shall be done in willing faith and fervor.
      Now who will tell the ladies I am here?"
      They sent the word by Giselher, that handsome peer.

549 And this bold knight announced, when he had seen
His sister and his mother, Uta the queen:
"The prince of Netherland has reached the Rhine,
Despatched to visit us, by Gunther's own design.

550 Of his condition now he brings report,
So let this lord appear before your court,
For he will tell of Iceland." Still the minds
Of noble ladies weighed with fears of many kinds.

551 They ran to get their clothes and quickly dressed
And bade the lord appear, with which request,
In joy to see them both, he soon complied.
Noble Kriemhild spoke, in greeting sweetly cried:

552 "Accept our welcome, Sigfrid, master sword!
Where is my brother Gunther, king and lord?
I fear, by Brunhild's mighty power torn
From us and dead! Alas that I was ever born!"

553 "Messenger's reward, I ask no less!"
He said, "You have no cause for such distress,
My ladies, hear! I left him safe and well.
This is the very news they sent me here to tell.

554 He and his love, in warm and kindred meeting,
Send you, noble lady, cordial greeting.
Have an end of tears. They'll soon be here!"
Not in a long, long time had she heard such words of
cheer.

555 She wiped her lovely eyes, after her tears,
With a fold of her snow-white hem. She filled his ears

With thanks for the news that he as herald brought;
Her sorrow and her woe were all reduced to naught.

556   She bade him sit, which he was glad to do.
Charmingly she said, "I'd give to you
My gold as herald's pay, but this would be rude
To one so mighty. You'll always have my gratitude."

557   "If I alone were lord of thirty lands
I still should welcome presents from your hands,"
Said he, and the princess spoke: "So be it then,"
And after herald's pay she sent her chamberlain.

558   Two dozen armlets set with jewels she gave
As his reward. His thought was not to save
But give them all away, with none to spare,
To members of her court, in her apartment there.

559   Her mother, in kindly greeting, wished him well.
The knight replied, "There's more I have to tell:
On coming home, one thing that he would ask—
And he will love you much, if you will do this task:

560   Receive them well—for thus he spoke his mind—
These splendid guests of his. Be so kind,
And ride to meet him on the beach by Worms.
This the king required in fair chivalric terms."

561   "I shall," the lady said, "with joy comply.
No favor I can do will I deny;
It shall be done in friendly faith and trust."
And for the pleasure that she felt the lady blushed.

562   What prince's messenger has better fared?
       She would have kissed him, too, if she had dared.
       He took his leave from the ladies, gallant and bold.
       Men of Burgundy went to do as Sigfrid told.

563   Sindold, Hunold, Rumold—all these three
       Had very little time for leisure free.
       They built the stands at Worms, along the strand;
       Among the royal staff was not an idle hand.

564   Ortwin, too, and Gere would not miss
       The chance to tell their kin and friends of this—
       Inform them of the coming celebration.
       Lovely ladies planned for dress and decoration.

565   For honored guests the palace, walls and all,
       Was richly hung and trimmed, and Gunther's hall
       Redone for the many strangers coming here.
       The grand event began upon a note of cheer.

566   They rode the many paths across the land,
       Kin of three great kings, at high command
       To wait attendance on the crowd that neared.
       Out of wardrobes then resplendent garb appeared.

567   Word was passed: men approach, on horse—
       Brunhild's train! Excitement ran its course
       Through all the gathered mass of Burgundy.
       On either hand, what a host of knights, what gallantry!

568   "The maids who join with me in welcoming,"
       Said lovely Kriemhild now, "I ask to bring
       The finest clothes of all from the garment chests,
       That we may gain esteem and praise from all our guests."

569   And now the knights arrived, and men were told
To bring the saddles worked with splendid gold
For ladies at Worms to ride to the river Rhine.
Nowhere has anyone seen harness quite so fine.

570   How bright a flash of gold from the horses shone!
From gleaming reins with jewels fixed thereon,
And golden stepping stools on carpets laid,
Which serving men had brought for each vivacious maid.

571   The noble ladies' mounts, as I said before,
Were ready in the yard, and each one wore
About its chest a silken martingale
As good as you will find in mine or any tale.

572   In formal headgear all the matrons came,
Eighty-six of them, in Kriemhild's name,
Ladies comely in their gleaming dress,
And beautifully appareled winsome maids, no less

573   Than fifty-four, from all of Burgundy,
The country's highest aristocracy,
Blond of hair beneath their shining bands.
Such was the eager crowning of the king's commands.

574   They wore for their guests the richest silks on earth—
So well arrayed as to reflect the worth
Of their great beauty. The man who would disdain
A single one of them could hardly pass for sane.

575   Sable wraps and furs of ermine graced
Many arms and hands, in charming taste,
And over the satin, golden rings extended.
No one could tell you all the effort they expended.

576 Rich and long the artful girdles placed
By many hands on many a lovely waist;
Made of Arabian silk the farandine
On their noble coats—and joy in noble maidens' mien!

577 Pretty girls were sweet in lacing framed
Across their breasts, and each would be ashamed
If her clothes outshone the brightness of her skin.
No finer retinue for any king or kin!

578 Now the lovely ladies all were dressed.
Their escorts soon arrived, the very best
Of haughty knights, a company large and good;
Shields they carried there, and spears of ashen wood.

✠ TENTH ADVENTURE
How Brunhild Was Received at Worms

579   Across the Rhine, as far as the eye could reach,
The train of the king and his friends approached the beach.
Here too were soldiers leading by the reins
Many maidens riding. Their welcome spared no pains.

580   When those from Iceland and the Nibelung host,
Sigfrid's men, had reached the waiting boats,
They sped across (never an idle oar!)
For there were Gunther's people, lining the other shore.

581   Hear now my words of Uta the glorious queen,
How when she left the town her maids were seen
To follow her on horse as she appointed.
(And thus would many ladies and knights become acquainted.)

582   Duke Gere held the reins of Kriemhild's steed,
But just to the gate, where Sigfrid came to lead
The lovely princess on, so to afford
The service of chivalry, and sweet was his reward.

583   Ortwin rode along at Uta's side—
Maidens and men in pairs, a social ride.
Never were lovely women, safe to say,
Seen in such multitudes on so gala a welcoming day!

584 And lovely Kriemhild watched the great behourds
Staged along the road by worthy lords,
All the way to the ships—their joy and duty.
They lifted from their steeds women of fairest beauty.

585 The king and his worthy guests were now across.
In crowded joust the crash of boss on boss
Echoed loud, and shield on shield-rim battered—
The ladies were looking on—and sturdy lances shattered.

586 The graceful maidens stood by the landing quay,
As Gunther and his guests debarked. And see!
Brunhild came herself, on Gunther's arm.
Costumes shone and jewels gleamed in rival charm.

587 Kriemhild came, as perfect ladies do,
To welcome Brunhild and her retinue.
Bright hands lifted ladies' veils
For the sweet exchange of kisses etiquette entails.

588 Kriemhild spoke, gently bred, polite:
"I bid you welcome here, in my own right,
And for my mother, too, and all the dear,
Devoted friends we have." Brunhild bowed to hear.

589 Often now the regal pair embraced.
Never such kind regard and perfect taste
As Uta and Kriemhild showed the bride-to-be.
And on her sweet mouth they kissed her repeatedly.

590 When Brunhild's maids were all upon the beach,
In courtly fashion they were taken each
By a handsome knight in hand. With pleasing grace,
Before their lady Brunhild the maidens took their place.

591   A long time passed before their words could tell
The joy of welcome there, and kisses fell
On rose-red lips. Together still they stood,
Two princesses. To heroes' hearts the sight was good.

592   Men who once had heard that in all their days
No lovelier sight would ever meet their gaze
Than these two women, found that judgment fair.
(Nor did they see a trace of make-up anywhere.)

593   Connoisseurs of woman's charm and grace
Lauded Gunther's wife for her lovely face.
Yet men who looked with more experienced eyes
Vowed that Kriemhild, more than she, deserved the prize.

594   Ladies and maids drew near—and what a sight
Of lovely figures gaily decked and bright!
Silken canopies and tents galore
Graced the town of Worms and filled the fields before.

595   Great was the crush among the royal kin.
They bade Brunhild and Kriemhild now turn in
And all the ladies, where the shade was fair.
Knights of Burgundy had come to lead them there.

596   Now they had all come up, the guests on horse,
And lances shot through shields with all the force
Of mighty jousting, and clouds rose from the field,
As if the earth were aflame. Valor stood revealed.

597   These deeds of theirs were all the ladies' concern.
I picture Sigfrid riding many a turn
Before their tents, up and back again,
With his handsome Nibelung troop (he had a thousand
   men).

598   Then Hagen of Trony came, at the king's request,
In courtesy to call an end to the test,
And stop the joust lest too much dust should fly
And cover the pretty girls. The guests were glad to comply.

599   Gernot spoke, "Let the horses rest,
Until the cool of evening. Then we'd best
Pay our ladies court before the hall.
When Gunther decides to ride, be ready one and all!"

600   Over the whole field the tilt was spent.
Now, for entertainment, warriors went
To the tall tents, and the pleasant life inside,
And so they passed the time, until the word to ride.

601   The hour was near to evening, and setting sun;
The day was growing cool, delay was done:
The time had come for man and maid to rise.
Lovely women shared the fond caress of eyes.

602   Valiant heroes rode their clothes to tatters,
After the country's custom in such matters,
Until the king dismounted by the hall.
They served the ladies well, men of spirit all.

603   Here at the palace they parted, queen from queen.
Uta and her daughter left the scene,
Went to a grand apartment, with both their trains—
Everywhere such noise as comes when pleasure reigns.

604   Seats at table were set, to be occupied
By king and royal guests. There at his side
Lovely Brunhild stood, wearing her crown
Within the king's own land, befitting her renown.

605   A very host of chairs, tables broad
    And set with many foods! It would be odd
    To find this meal were lacking any thing
    To suit the lofty guests who gathered 'round the king.

606   Water was brought, in basins made of gold,
    By the royal chamberlains. If anyone told
    Of service more refined, seen or heard
    At any prince's feast, I'd not believe his word.

607   Before the lord of the Rhine had dipped his hand
    In the finger bowl, Sigfrid made demand,
    As well he might, recalling the promise made
    Before in distant Iceland he sought the lovely maid.

608   He spoke, "Remember now what on your hand
    You swore to me: when Brunhild came to this land,
    You'd give me your sister. What's become of the oath?
    Your journey cost me much in labor and trouble both!"

609   Said Gunther, "Justly you recall my vow.
    In this my hand shall not turn perjurer now,
    And I shall help you out as best I may."
    They called the princess in to audience straightway.

610   With lovely girls of her train she neared the hall.
    Giselher sprang to the foot of the stair, to call:
    "Send these maidens back. None shall appear,
    Except my sister alone, before his Highness here."

611   And so they brought the princess where she found
    The king with knights from royal lands around.
    In the vastness of the hall they bade her stand.
    Lady Brunhild came to the table, close at hand.

612   Gunther spoke; these are the words she heard:
      "Sister, by your goodness redeem my word!
      I promised you in marriage. Will you fulfill,
      By granting him your hand, the tenor of my will?"

613   "Dearest brother," the noble maid replied,
      "You need not plead with me. As you decide,
      So I would do—and thus is your promise kept.
      The man you choose for me I willingly accept."

614   Eyes he loved were on him, his color warmed.
      As Sigfrid vowed his service, a circle formed,
      Which now they bade them walk together toward.
      They asked her then if she would have this handsome lord.

615   Maidenly breeding made her seem embarrassed,
      But such was fate and Sigfrid's star, she cherished
      No desire at all to turn him down.
      He swore to be her husband, the heir to Netherland's
      crown.

616   When each to the other they had pledged their troth,
      He took her in his arms—and was not loath
      To hold in sweet embrace the lovely princess.
      He kissed the fair young queen, with many knights as
      witness.

617   Lords in waiting parted. Opposite,
      In the place of honor, Sigfrid went to sit
      With Kriemhild and receive great homage rendered.
      (Along with Sigfrid all the Nibelung knights had entered.)

618   The king was seated. Brunhild, too, was there—
      This was her greatest sorrow, to see this pair

Sitting together. Her eyes began to well,
Over her bright cheeks the hot tears fell.

619 "What troubles you, my dear," said the king at last,
"That eyes so bright should be thus overcast?
You've better cause for joy; my lands and castles
Stand in liege to you, and many handsome vassals."

620 "I've cause enough for tears," the lady cried,
"I'm sick at heart for your sister! Here at the side
Of your own vassal she sits; I must weep
At seeing her degraded thus and sunk so deep."

621 "Take this all in silence," said the king.
"Another time I'll tell you everything—
Why I gave my sister as Sigfrid's wife.
Well may she live with him, happy all her life!"

622 "I pity her, so nobly bred and fair!
I'd run away, if only I knew where,
And never sleep with you, unless you say
Why it is that Kriemhild was given him this way."

623 "I'll tell you the truth of it," came his reply.
"He has castles and lands as well as I.
Of this be sure: that he is a mighty king;
I gladly grant him the princess, for his love and marrying."

624 In spite of his words, her mood was far from bright.
Now from the tables rose many a knight.
The castle rang with din of melees and tests,
Until the host was irked with all his many guests.

625   He thought he'd like it better, to lie at her side.
         The hope within his heart would not subside
         Of all the pleasant favors she would render.
         He looked at lovely Brunhild—his glance was long and
            tender.

626   The guests should cease their jousting now, they said—
         Time for the king and queen to go to bed.
         Kriemhild and Brunhild met, there in the palace
         Before the stairs—neither yet with trace of malice.

627   Their courtiers followed. Mindful of what was right,
         Chamberlains lit the way with candlelight.
         The two kings' men now took their separate course.
         All eyes watched as Sigfrid's knights withdrew in force.

628   The two lords came to where their sleep would be,
         And each one thought of lover's victory
         Over lovely women, by which their state
         Of mind grew gentler—and Sigfrid's pleasure then was
            great.

629   By Kriemhild's side he found his resting place.
         The offices of love, with noble grace,
         He tendered her. As much as his life was she,
         And more to him than could a thousand others be.

630   I'll say no more of what he did with her,
         But listen now and hear what things occur
         Between the king and Brunhild! Gunther might,
         With someone else, have spent a far more restful night.

631   His retinue had left, and soon the door
         Was closed and locked. The sweet embrace in store

He pictured to himself. The time was wrong.
She was not yet his wife, and still his wait was long.

632   She walked to the bed in a gown of linen-white.
"Here and now I have," so thought the knight,
"All that in all my days I ever desired!"
Great must be the joy such beauty as hers inspired.

633   The king reached out and put the light away.
He turned and walked to where his lady lay,
Himself lay down beside her, in pure delight.
He took his love into his arms and clasped her tight.

634   He would have pressed caress upon caress,
Had his noble spouse allowed. To his distress,
She turned instead in anger, so irate,
That where he looked for a friend, he found a foeman's
    hate.

635   "You must stop it now, my Lord," cried she,
"What you are hoping for, cannot be.
I mean to stay a virgin—of that be sure—
Until I know the truth." Then Gunther turned on her.

636   He struggled for her love, and disarrayed
The gown she wore. Then the marvelous maid
Reached for the girdle of braid she wore at her waist—
And treated him so that he was hurt and left disgraced.

637   She tied him, hand and foot, nor was that all;
She found a nail and hung him on the wall!
He spoiled her sleep, and she withheld her love—
A cruel show of strength he nearly perished of.

638 He who would be master now must plead:
"Untie me, noble queen! If I am freed,
All my hopes of winning you are through,
Never, never again will I lie so close to you."

639 She cared not how he felt, her sleep was soft.
All the night till dawn he hung aloft,
Till into the room the light of morning shone.
If ever strength was his, now it was surely gone.

640 "Now tell me, royal Gunther, would you mind
If chamberlains of yours should come and find
Their master strung up here, by a woman's hand?"
"They'd think it ill of you," replied the lord of the land;

641 "And little credit to me!" the warrior said.
"So out of your goodness, let me back in bed.
Since my attentions cause such bitterness,
I swear my hands shall never so much as touch your dress."

642 She loosed and let him down. He made his way
To the bed again, where his fair lady lay,
And stayed so far from her, her lovely clothing
Was safe from his touch. (She would have greeted that
with loathing!)

643 The servants came to bring their change of clothes,
The numerous things held ready when they rose.
Perhaps all those around were light and gay—
The king was filled with gloom, though he wore his
crown that day.

644 After the country's custom—rightly so—
Gunther and Brunhild did not forgo

The early trip to church, where mass was held.
Sigfrid also came, the multitude was swelled.

645   Clothes and crown were ready, before their eyes,
All that royal privilege implies.
Then came the rites of anointment! The crowd around
Beheld the happy sight of four sovereigns crowned.

646   A good six hundred youths (an honor paid
The two great kings) received the accolade.
Joy in Burgundy beyond compare!
The shock of shafts in hands of lancers filled the air.

647   In the windows sat the pretty girls and gazed,
As the light from countless shields before them blazed.
The king had left his men and stood apart.
Whatever others did, he stood with a gloomy heart.

648   Sigfrid's mood and his were not the same.
The warrior knew what the trouble was; he came
To where the monarch stood and asked outright:
"Tell me truthfully, how did you fare last night?"

649   His host replied, "With shame and injury!
I've brought the very devil home with me.
I had in mind to love her, that was all.
And she tied me up and hung me on a nail in the wall!

650   There I hung, in danger, till dawn of day
When she untied me—how quietly she lay!
I tell you this for help and sympathy,
And as a friend." "This truly troubles me,"

651   Sturdy Sigfrid said. "If you agree,
I promise—and tonight I'll guarantee—
She'll lie so close to you that never again
Will she withhold her love." The words were balm to his
    pain.

652   Sigfrid went on, "Things will be all right.
I gather we fared differently last night.
Your sister now means more to me than life,
Before this night is out, Brunhild shall be your wife!"

653   He said, "I'll come to your room this very day,
Wearing my Magic Cloak, by a secret way,
That not a soul shall see my stratagem.
Your chamberlains must go home, be sure to get rid of
    them.

654   I'll blow the candles out in the page's hand.
That shall be the sign; you'll understand
That I am there to help. I'll tame your wife
For you to love tonight, or else I'll lose my life!"

655   "Providing you don't make love," the king replied,
"To my wife—otherwise I'm satisfied.
So do whatever you please. If it should be
The death of her, I'd let it pass, so fearsome is she."

656   "You have my word that I won't touch your queen.
Of all the women I have ever seen
Your sister is the only one for me."
Gunther put his faith in Sigfrid's guarantee.

657   They took their pleasure now in strenuous joys,
Until they called a halt to joust and noise,

For soon the ladies were about to ride
Back to the hall, and chamberlains ordered folk aside.

658 The courtyard soon was cleared of horse and men.
Each of the queens was led by a bishop then,
In the king's presence to the dining tables.
And they were followed to their seats by handsome nobles.

659 The king's fond hope and happy humor grew.
He thought of what his friend had pledged to do.
This day seemed like a month! His lady's love—
That was the only thing that he was thinking of.

660 He could hardly wait until the meal was through.
But then the time was come—the queens withdrew
To privacy, each to her own apartment
With valiant knights attending, men of bold deportment.

661 Sigfrid sat by his wife, as lovers sit,
In perfect joy, with hate no part of it.
She stroked his hands with her own white hand.
But suddenly he was gone—she could not understand.

662 As she was caressing him he disappeared.
She turned to his men and said, "How very weird!
I wonder now, where could the king have gone?
Who took his hand from mine?" But she did not go on.

663 He made his way meanwhile until he found
Chamberlains with lights, all standing 'round.
In the pages' very hands he blew them out.
Thus did Gunther know his friend was close about.

664   He knew why he was there. Gunther bade
The maids and ladies leave, and when they had,
The vaunted king himself then locked the door,
And quickly threw the heavy double bolts before.

665   He hid the light behind the canopy,
And now began the struggle that had to be:
Fair maid and mighty lord. Whatever pleasure
Gunther felt was matched by pain in equal measure.

666   Sigfrid now lay down, close to the queen.
"Stop it, Gunther," she cried, "unless you mean
To get yourself in trouble once again."
Before the night was out she hurt this prince of men!

667   He hid his voice and uttered not a word.
Though he could not see, still Gunther heard
No sound of wantonness from them at all.
Indeed, the comfort such a bed could give was small.

668   He acted just as if it were Gunther there,
And put his arms around the lady fair.
Then all at once she threw him out of bed.
He crashed against a stool, hitting it with his head.

669   Up he jumped again with all his might,
To make one more attempt, and when he tried
He paid with hurt and pain for this violence.
I doubt if woman ever put up such defense!

670   When he would not give in, she sprang from bed.
"I will not have you touch a single thread
Of my white gown. For your rudeness you will be
A sorry man," she cried. "I'll show you—wait and see!"

147

671   She closed her arms around the marvelous knight,
       And meant to pack him off, thus fastened tight,
       As she had before, in peace to have her sleep.
       He disarrayed her clothes, and her revenge ran deep.

672   What good his mighty strength of muscle and bone?
       She proved to him the measure of her own,
       She dragged him off (he had no choice at all)
       And rudely squeezed him between a cupboard and the
          wall.

673   "Good Lord," he thought, "am I to lose my life
       At a maiden's hands? If so, how many a wife
       Will turn in scorn and pride against her lord,
       Who otherwise would not do it of her own accord?"

674   What his Highness heard did not assuage
       His worry! Sigfrid turned in shame and rage,
       Fighting back again with main force,
       Wildly, trying her strength. His was a risky course.

675   It seemed an age to the king, before he won.
       She crushed his hands, making the blood run
       Gushing from his nails. His joy was scant!
       Shortly though he made the glorious queen recant

676   What once she vowed—her rude and harsh intention.
       (The king had heard, though neither word nor mention
       Came from Sigfrid.) He pinned her on the bed—
       She screamed aloud! For now his strength hurt her in-
          stead.

677   She reached down at her side and found the sash,
       To tie him up. He gave her such a lash

With his hand, her body cracked in every bone.
With that the fight was done, and she was Gunther's own.

678 She cried, "Oh, noble sovereign, let me live!
Whatever I have done to you, I'll give
Full payment back, your love shall not be spurned,
For you can master a woman, as oh so well I've learned."

679 She lay upon the bed, and Sigfrid rose
As if he intended taking off his clothes.
But first he slipped from her hand a golden ring—
All the while the queen did not perceive a thing.

680 He took her girdle, a sash of silk and gold.
(I cannot say if being overbold
Made him do this. He gave it to his bride—
To his later grief.) Now Gunther lay at Brunhild's side.

681 Rightfully he lay there, making love.
Much she had to be forgetful of:
Both wrath and modesty. She paled at the touch
Of his embrace. Ah, love had ebbed her strength so much!

682 No stronger than any woman then was she.
He caressed her lovely body tenderly,
Nor could she now by fighting back demur.
This is what the love of Gunther did to her.

683 With what sweet charm at Gunther's side she lay,
In tender love, until the break of day!
Meanwhile Sigfrid left to seek his bride—
A lover's welcoming, at a lovely lady's side.

684 He brushed aside the question she had thought
   To ask of him, and hid what he had brought,
   Until she took the crown in his own land.
   But what he was destined to give he gave with open hand.

685 The king next morning felt more cheerful far
   Than he had felt before. The only bar
   To perfect joy in all his land was gone,
   And all his noble guests were nobly waited on.

686 The celebration lasted fourteen days,
   And all the while no end of the noise men raise
   In following after every sort of pleasure—
   A heavy burden, too, on royal Gunther's treasure!

687 To further the king's repute his friends were told
   To give to the poets there shining gold
   And silver, clothes to wear, steeds to ride.
   If they came in hope of gifts, they left there satisfied.

688 The lord of Netherland, his thousand men—
   Why, all the clothes they brought were gone again,
   Given away, till nothing was left to give—
   Horses and saddles, too. They knew how to live!

689 Before their great largess had ceased its flow,
   It seemed an age to those who wished to go.
   Never guests received more elegant care.
   So Gunther willed, and that was the end of the festival
    there.

✚ ELEVENTH ADVENTURE
How Sigfrid Went Home with His Wife

690   When all the foreign guests had gone their way,
Sigmund's son addressed his friends to say:
"It's time that we made ready to return."
This was the sort of news his wife was pleased to learn.

691   She asked her husband then, "When shall we go?
Not in haste—I should not like it so.
My brothers first must share with me our lands."
(He was not pleased to find her making these demands.)

692   The princes came to him and spoke, all three:
"Know this, my lord: our services shall be
In fealty yours, as long as we shall live."
He bowed to them in thanks for the love they pledged to
      give.

693   "We shall divide with you," said Giselher,
"The castles and lands we own, and you will share
With Kriemhild then, as full and rightful gain,
In all the far-flung lands that make up our domain."

694   The son of Sigmund said, as he saw and heard
How much the princes meant their every word,
"God save you all your heritage intact,
And all your subjects, too! If Kriemhild ever lacked

695   For anything, it's not this proffered share.
Her wealth at home, where the crown is hers to wear,

Shall pass (if I live to see it), all power known
To mortals. In all things else, your wishes are my own."

696   Said she, "My dower perhaps you cannot use—
Burgundian knights are harder to refuse!
A king would gladly take them to his land.
And I should like my share from my dear brothers' hand."

697   "Take your pick," said Gernot, when she was through.
"You'll find no lack of men who'll ride with you
Of our three thousand thanes we'll give a third
To be your men-at-arms." Kriemhild now sent word

698   To Hagen and Ortwin, asking if they would agree,
With all their men, to bear her fealty.
Anger filled the answer Hagen hurled:
"The king has no right to give us to anyone in this world!

699   Let others of our courtiers follow you.
Well you know what men of Trony do:
Our job it is to stay with the kings at court;
We followed them here. We cannot cut our duty short."

700   There they left it. Kriemhild, going through
With her plans to leave, gathered her retinue:
Thirty-two young maids, five hundred men.
Count Eckewart went with them, following Sigfrid then.

701   Now they asked their leave—as form requires—
All the dames and maids, knights and squires.
They kissed farewell, for time had come to part.
They left the land of Gunther, gay and happy at heart.

702   Their kinsmen rode along, to guide them right.
       Instructions were that they might spend the night
       In the king's domain, wherever they cared to stay.
       Heralds to royal Sigmund started on their way,

703   Bearing word to him and Siglind, too:
       Their son and lovely Kriemhild soon were due,
       Uta's child, from Worms across the Rhine.
       No other news in all the world could be so fine!

704   "Thank God," said Sigmund, "I shall be around
       When lovely Kriemhild walks our land, and crowned,
       Shall add her glory to my dominions' fame.
       My son, the noble Sigfrid, shall rule in his own name."

705   Siglind gave a weight of gold away,
       Silver, and red velvet—herald's pay—
       For what she heard had brought her happiness.
       Eagerly her maids gave thought to proper dress.

706   They asked who else was coming to their land,
       And had the seats erected and the stand,
       From which his friends would see the prince appear,
       New crowned. Sigmund's men rode out to bring him here.

707   I never heard of such reception yet
       As these great knights in Sigmund's country met.
       The lovely Siglind rode to meet Kriemhild,
       Escorted by charming ladies and lords. The journey
          filled—

708   Before they met the strangers—one whole day.
       They suffered great impatience on the way,
       Friend and stranger alike, until they found

The mighty castle Xanten, where they would soon be
   crowned.

709   Siglind and Sigmund, laughing in joy and pleasure,
Gave Kriemhild many kisses—in equal measure
To Sigfrid too. Gone was all their pain.
They granted heartfelt welcome to them and all their
   train.

710   They asked that the guests be brought to Sigmund's hall.
Now they came to lift the maidens all
Down from their steeds. And many men were there,
Serving the lovely ladies with every zealous care.

711   Great as was the tourney by the Rhine,
Here they gave the heroes clothes so fine
They never had the like in all their days—
What wonders I could tell you about their wealthy ways!

712   They lived in splendor, with all they wished and more.
Such golden-colored skirts her ladies wore,
With pearls and jewels woven through and through.
On such a scale the queen maintained her retinue.

713   Among his friends assembled, Sigmund came
And spoke, "To the kin of Sigfrid I proclaim:
Before these lords my crown shall be his to wear."
This news the men of Netherland rejoiced to hear.

714   He commended him his crown, his courts and land.
All who came to justice at his hand
He truly judged, and so maintained the law,
The name of Sigfrid soon was held in general awe.

715   In splendor passed ten years of Sigfrid's life,
Of law beneath his crown, and then his wife,
The lovely Kriemhild, bore to him a son—
Kin or friend, a source of joy for everyone.

716   Soon the christening and then his name:
After his uncle, Gunther—no cause for shame
Should he take after him, how good and right!
They brought him up with zealous care, as well they
    might.

717   In these same days Dame Siglind passed away.
Uta's daughter now held rightful sway,
Mighty mistress in all the land was she.
Death had taken the queen. They mourned her grievously.

718   And far by the Rhine, as soon all people knew,
A son was born to mighty Gunther, too,
By lovely Brunhild, queen of Burgundy—
For love of Sigfrid christened, and so his name should be.

719   They watched and cared for him with zealous joy.
Gunther picked out tutors for the boy
Who brought him up to be a stalwart lord.
What awful toll of friends he paid as fate's reward!

720   Many tales were told, on many days,
How cheerful warriors lived a life of praise
In Sigmund's country always. They said the same
Of royal Gunther's courtiers, men of peerless fame.

721   Nibelung's land and Shilbung's thanes and all
The wealth of both now stood at Sigfrid's call.

(The power of his greatest kin was nothing near it—
Even prouder pleasure to his valiant spirit!)

722 To him belonged the greatest treasure hoard
That, but for its former owners, any lord
Had ever won, the prize he had fought to gain
By the mountainside, at cost of many warriors slain.

723 The honors men desire he possessed.
But lacking these, he still must be confessed
One of the best who ever sat a horse.
People had good cause to fear his potent force!

✝ TWELFTH ADVENTURE

How Gunther Invited Sigfrid to the Festivities

724   Gunther's wife kept thinking all the while:
       "How can Kriemhild live in such high style?
       Her lord is after all our vassal, and yet—
       Much time has passed and little service do we get."

725   This she held in silence in her heart,
       Embittered that they kept themselves apart,
       That Sigfrid's people rendered service due
       So rarely. How this came about she wished she knew.

726   She tried her way with the king, hoping to find
       Some chance to see Kriemhild. Set in her mind,
       She plotted what she wished, in confidence.
       But what she said, in Gunther's view, made little sense.

727   He answered her, "How can we bring them here?
       The impossibility of that is clear.
       I dare not ask them, the distance is so huge."
       Brunhild countered this with a cunning subterfuge:

728   "However great the power in a vassal's hands,
       He cannot fail to do as his king commands."
       Gunther smiled at her words. When Sigfrid came,
       One could scarcely say he did it in duty's name.

729   She spoke, "My dearest lord, do this for me:
       Help me to arrange that I may see

157

Lord Sigfrid in this land, and your sister, too.
There is no dearer favor I could ask of you.

730   In mind and manners your sister is so well-bred.
How sweet it is whenever my thoughts are led
To the time I spent with her, when we were wedded.
Surely Sigfrid's love for her is to his credit!"

731   She urged so long he said at last, "No guest,
I swear, was ever so welcome, and your request
Falls on willing ears. Heralds of mine
Shall go to both of them, bidding them come to the
    Rhine."

732   The queen replied, "Will you please then say
When you mean to send them—or by what day
Our dear friends are to come here? Those who go
On such a mission I should also like to know."

733   "Gladly," said the prince. "I plan to call
On thirty men to ride." He summoned all,
Telling in Sigfrid's land what news to recite.
Brunhild gave them splendid clothes, for their delight.

734   "My lords," the king declared, "repeat for me,
Omitting nothing, all my embassy
To sturdy Sigfrid and my sister, thus:
They have in all this world no better friends than us.

735   And ask them both to visit us by the Rhine,
Which I and my queen will greet with every sign
Of gratitude. By solstice time he'll see,
As shall his vassals, many who laud his courtesy.

158

736   Give King Sigmund my regards, and tell
How I and my kin as always wish him well,
And tell my sister not to fail this journey
To see her friends. She'll never find more fitting tourney."

737   Brunhild, Uta, and ladies on every hand
Sent their greetings on to Sigfrid's land,
To charming ladies, to men of war, stout-hearted.
With royal friends' assent, the messengers departed.

738   They rode as on campaign, with steeds and dress
For all of them. They left the land, to press
Their journey forward, ever the same direction,
With royal safeguard for his messengers' protection.

739   In three weeks' time at last they made their entry
Into the March of Norway and the country
Where Nibelung Castle was and the knight they sought.
The long trip had tired the steeds the heralds brought.

740   Sigfrid and Lady Kriemhild both were told
Of men-at-arms arriving, whose clothes recalled
The way Burgundian men by custom dressed.
They quickly rose from the couch where they had been at rest.

741   They sent to the window a maid, who soon had spied
In the courtyard valiant Gere, and at his side
All his companions who were ordered there.
What pleasant news to still her homesick heart's despair!

742   She cried to the king, "See them there below,
Walking the yard with Gere, to and fro.

My brother Gunther sent to us these men,
Down the Rhine." Said he, "May they be welcome then!"

743   Out ran all the courtiers, offering each
As best he could in turn a kindly speech
Of welcome to the heralds, whose coming here
Filled the heart of old King Sigmund with good cheer.

744   Lodging was found for Gere and his men,
Their horses cared for. In went the heralds then,
Where at Kriemhild's side Lord Sigfrid sat.
(They had been invited, hence they ventured that.)

745   The host and his wife arose immediately,
With kindly welcome to Gere of Burgundy
And Gunther's vassals who came with him there.
They asked the mighty Gere to come and take his chair.

746   "Grant us our mission first before we sit,
Way-weary guests. Let us stand a bit,
For we must tell you all the news we bear
From Gunther and Lady Brunhild—proudly and well
    they fare!

747   Also the word we have from Uta, your mother.
Young Giselher and Gernot, too, his brother,
Have sent us here, and your excellent family.
They send you pledge of service from lands of Burgundy."

748   "God bless them," Sigfrid said. "With joy I accord
Good faith and wealth to them, the due reward
Of friends—as does their sister. But now go on
And tell if our friends at home are somehow put upon.

749 Has someone since we parted offered ill
  To my lady's kin? Let me know! I will,
  In faith and always, help them bear the blow,
  Until their foes shall weep at the loyalty I show."

750 Margrave Gere cried, "Truest merit
  Abides with them; proud and high their spirit!
  To the Rhine they bid you, for certain festivities,
  They truly want to see you—set your mind at ease.

751 They also ask that my lady come with you
  As soon as the present wintertime is through
  And hope to see you by next solstice day."
  "Hardly," powerful Sigfrid said, "I see no way."

752 Cried Burgundian Gere, in reply:
  "Your mother Uta begs you: don't deny
  Gernot and Giselher! Every day
  I hear them all complain that you're so far away.

753 My Lady Brunhild and all her company
  Rejoice to think of this: for should it be
  That they may see you, in joy their hearts would rise."
  (And all of this found favor in lovely Kriemhild's eyes.)

754 The host asked Gere to sit—he was her kin—
  And ordered wine for his guests. They rushed it in.
  Sigmund also came, having seen
  Burgundian heralds, and spoke to them with a friendly
   mien:

755 "Welcome, men of Gunther! Ever since
  Kriemhild was married to my son the prince,

We surely should have seen you more often now,
Here in our land, if you mean the friendship you avow."

756   They said whenever he wished they'd gladly come.
Their great fatigue they felt delivered from
By all this pleasure. They had the heralds sit
And brought them food, in plenty—Sigfrid ordered it.

757   Nine full days, perforce, the knights remained,
And then at last the gallant men complained
At not returning back to their dominions.
King Sigfrid called his friends, seeking their opinions:

758   "Do you advise my going to the Rhine?
I am asked by Gunther, kin of mine,
And by his family, for a festive day.
I'd go there gladly but his land is far away.

759   They ask that Kriemhild come with me as well.
How is *she* to get there, friends, pray tell?
Had I to fight for them through thirty lands,
Of course they'd have the trip as service from Sigfrid's
    hands."

760   "If this," they said, "is how your mind now lies—
To make the journey—here's what we advise:
Take a thousand knights and ride to the Rhine.
Thus in Burgundy shall your fame and glory shine."

761   Cried Lord Sigmund, "If you mean to go
To these festivities, why not let me know?
I'll ride with you, if you think it worth your pains,
And thus increase your party by a hundred thanes."

762   "My dear father, if you would join our ride
      I should be delighted," Sigfrid cried.
      "We'll leave the land when twelve full days have passed."
      Now they gave apparel and steeds to all who asked.

763   And since the highborn king had set his heart
      Upon this trip, they had the heralds depart
      For home again, back to the Rhine to tell
      His lady's kin: to join their fete would please him well.

764   The story goes that Kriemhild's and Sigfrid's gift
      To the heralds leaving was more than they could lift
      On their steeds to carry home—so rich was he.
      They urged their pack-train off, driving them merrily.

765   Sigfrid and Sigmund gave whatever it took
      To clothe their men. Count Eckewart had them look
      For women's dress, the best they had on hand
      Or could find anywhere in all of Sigfrid's land.

766   Saddles and shields were ready. Gifts they gave
      To every knight and lady about to leave,
      Whatever heart desired, in nothing short.
      He took as guests to his friends a large and splendid court.

767   The heralds made their way home, eagerly.
      Gere the warrior came to Burgundy,
      Where he was welcomed, and they dismounted all
      From charger and steed, in front of good King Gunther's
        hall.

768   The wise and the simple ran, as is the way,
      To ask for news. The good knight stopped to say:

"Wait till I tell the king and you will hear!"
He went with his companions, finding Gunther near.

769 For joy the king jumped up from where he was seated.
Their swift return the lovely Brunhild greeted
With thanks. Gunther called the heralds over:
"How is Sigfrid, who has done us such great favor?"

770 Valiant Gere spoke, "His face was glowing,
As was your sister's. Never such bestowing
Of love, and true regard, has any friend
Had from mortal man as he and his father send."

771 The queen addressed the margrave, "Tell me though,
Is Kriemhild coming? Has she kept some show
Of that refinement which so graced her pure
And lovely form?" Said Gere, "She will come, be sure!"

772 Uta quickly called the messengers
And one could tell from every word of hers
How eager she was: How did her daughter fare?
He told her how they found her, that soon she would be
    there.

773 What Sigfrid gave they did not try to hide
From the three kings' men, but opened wide
The clothes and gold they had for all to see.
Great was their praise for all this generosity.

774 But Hagen said, "It's nothing for him to give.
With all he owns, if he had forever to live
He could not spend it—the Nibelung treasury!
Ah, if only that should come to Burgundy!"

775   All the court looked forward to the day
      When they would come. Men in the three kings' pay
      Found they had no leisure early or late
      Setting up the stands to hold a crowd so great.

776   No idleness for Hunold, surely none
      For Sindold either, with all these things to be done—
      Serving and pouring, setting up benches of wood.
      Ortwin helped, and Gunther gave his gratitude.

777   Kitchener Rumold managed his underlings
      With skill: a multitude of cooking things—
      Kettles, and pots, and pans—there on hand
      To fix the food for those who headed toward their land.

✠ THIRTEENTH ADVENTURE
How They Came to the Festival

778   Let us leave their busy ways and turn
To Lady Kriemhild and her maids, to learn
How they made their way from Nibelung land to the
    Rhine.
Never did horses bear garments half so fine.

779   Saddle-boxes set for the journey, they started
For where they hoped to find it happy-hearted,
Sigfrid, his friends, and the queen. The time was brief
For all of them before it turned to bitter grief!

780   They left Lord Sigfrid's little child, the son
Of Kriemhild, home—what else could they have done?
Out of this courtly journey came great pain:
The child would never see father or mother again.

781   Sigmund rode along. Had he been aware
Of what in after time would happen there,
He would have had no part of the tournament.
On what man's kin was such affliction ever sent?

782   They ordered heralds ahead to give report.
Uta's many friends and Gunther's court
Rode out to meet them in a gay procession—
Guests for whom he spent much time in preparation.

783   He went where Brunhild sat. "When first you came,
How did my sister greet you? You owe the same
In welcome to Sigfrid's wife." "Well and good,"
She said, "I'll do it gladly. I love her as I should."

784   The great king said, "They come tomorrow forenoon.
      If you would welcome them, be at it soon.
      We mustn't wait in the castle till they are due.
      Never have I had guests I so looked forward to."

785   She told her maids and matrons to be quick
      And look for good apparel, the very pick
      Of all things fit to wear before their guests.
      Need I tell you this: that there were no protests?

786   And Gunther's men ran out to offer aid
      And homage while his summons were relayed
      To all his knights. The queen rode out in splendor—
      As vast a welcoming of guests as they could tender.

787   Beloved friends and joyously received!
      This was a day exceeding (so they believed)
      Kriemhild's welcome of Brunhild in Burgundy.
      Meeting them was to meet the pride of chivalry.

788   Sigfrid now had brought his men to ride;
      Back and forth they went, from side to side
      Across the field—so vast his retinue.
      Who could avoid the confusion and all the dust that blew?

789   The king, seeing Sigfrid and Sigmund there,
      Was moved by his affection to declare:
      "My best of welcome to you—to all my friends.
      What pleasure to our spirit your courtly journey lends!"

790   "God bless you," answered Sigmund, a man whose joy
      Lay in honor. "Ever since my boy,
      Sigfrid, became your friend my thoughts have turned
      On meeting you." Said Gunther, "Much pleasure have I
        earned!"

791   Sigfrid they received, in fitting state
        With greatest homage. No one bore him hate.
        Gernot and Giselher, perfect in breeding,
        Joined their welcome. Have any guests had kinder greet-
            ing?

792   And so the two kings' wives approached, and saddles
        Stood empty there as men of many battles
        Lifted ladies down upon the grass.
        Many served and gladly, the time was quick to pass.

793   The charming ladies-in-waiting then drew near
        One to the other, and knights were filled with cheer
        To see on either hand a greeting paid
        With such perfection, as warrior stood by lovely maid.

794   These splendid folk, they took each other's hands
        With all the bowing etiquette demands
        And fairest ladies' kisses, charmingly!
        (A joy for Gunther's men—and Sigfrid's men—to see.)

795   They waited there no more, but rode to town.
        The host gave orders that his guests be shown
        How very welcome they were in Burgundy.
        They charged with lances couched for all the ladies to see.

796   Hagen and Ortwin and all—they left no doubt
        What mighty men they were. And who can flout
        Whatever challenge such a knight suggests?
        They rendered worthy service to all their welcome guests.

797   One heard their shields, echoing thrust and blow,
        Before the castle gate. They tarried so,

Guest and host, a while before they entered.
The day sped by, with all their thoughts on pastime centered.

798   They rode before the palace, full of pleasure,
Artful robes, cut to perfect measure,
Hung beneath the saddles of the fair
And handsome ladies all. Gunther's men were there.

799   They ordered that the guests be shown their lodging.
Meanwhile people noticed Brunhild watching
Lady Kriemhild—her beauty was untold,
Bright against the shining of the very gold.

800   All about the town of Worms one heard
The noise of people. Gunther issued word
To have his Marshal, Dankwart, take in charge
Their retinue and find them a goodly place to lodge.

801   Food was served them, out of doors and in;
Better treatment of guests had never been.
Whatever thing they wanted—that was done
(So rich the king) without refusing anyone.

802   They served them as friends, with not a trace of malice.
His Highness sat at table in the palace
With his guests. He showed Sigfrid the chair
He had before. Handsome knights were with him there.

803   About his circle sat twelve hundred men.
It seemed to Queen Brunhild that never again
In any vassal could such power be vested.
(As yet, she liked him enough to leave him unmolested.)

804 That evening, where the king sat, rich clothes
   Were wet with wine, as many bearers rose
   To make their rounds from table on to table—
   The fullest service done as fast as they were able.

805 They found, as is the way at celebrations,
   For maids and ladies fine accommodations—
   Helped by their host, whatever their country be.
   And courteous people served them well and liberally.

806 At end of night, when day appeared, there glowed
   From traveling cases precious jewels sewed
   In lovely dresses, touched by woman's hand,
   As splendid clothes were chosen and fair attire planned.

807 Day had not quite dawned when knights and men
   Came to the hall and noise grew loud again,
   Before the king's own morning mass was through.
   Young lords jousted, for the royal praise they drew.

808 The mighty crash of trombones swelled around,
   And drums and flutes gave out so great a sound
   That with it echoed all the wide extent
   Of Worms. Lords were mounted, proud and confident.

809 Then in this land began a lofty game
   Of numerous able knights. How many came,
   Armed with shields in hand, men of parts
   And handsome, whose pride and spirit came from youth-
    ful hearts!

810 Splendid ladies sat in each window niche,
   And many lovely maids, their figures rich

With ornament, watching valiant heroes' sport,
When now the king himself rode out, with kin and court.

811   Thus they passed their time—it seemed not long—
Until from out of church they heard the song
Of many bells. Now ladies left on horse,
And noble queens escorted by valiant men in force.

812   On the grass before the minster they dismounted,
All the guests, whom Brunhild still accounted
Friends of hers. They entered church in state,
Crowned as queens—their love soon torn by bitter hate.

813   When they had heard the mass, they all went back,
And later then to table—still no lack
Of joy and honors, pleasure holding sway
Unbroken at the feast until the eleventh day.

✝ FOURTEENTH ADVENTURE
How the Two Queens Hurled Insults at Each Other

814   One vesper time the castle yard was loud
With tumult rising from the eager crowd
Of knights intent on the pleasures of chivalry.
Many men and women hurried up to see.

815   There together sat the mighty pair,
Their queenly thoughts on two whose names were fair,
And Kriemhild spoke, "My husband's hand
Should rightly rule the width and breadth of all this land."

816   The lady Brunhild cried, "How could this be?
If no one were alive but you and he,
No doubt our kingdom might be his domain.
As long as Gunther lives, that hope is all in vain."

817   Kriemhild answered, "See how well he stands,
How proud, before the warriors he commands,
Like the shining moon before a starry sky.
For this my heart has every right to swell with joy!"

818   "However fair and charming your lord may be,
However brave and strong, you must agree
Your noble brother Gunther still is best.
In company of kings, be sure, he leads the rest."

819   Kriemhild again: "My lord is proud and strong.
Surely praising him I do no wrong.

His glories are manifold. Never fear
That I deceive you, Brunhild: he is Gunther's peer."

820   "My dear, you must not take my words amiss.
Not without good right do I say this:
When first we met, I heard them both declare
(When the king imposed his will on mine, and there,

821   In knightly contest, won my love) he came
As Gunther's vassal. Sigfrid said the same;
I take it he's my thane, since he agreed."
Said Kriemhild, "If that were so, I'd be ill-served indeed!

822   What trick do you suspect my brothers of,
That they should let me be a vassal's love?
I ask you, Brunhild, as one of my family,
Stop this talk, in kindliness, for sake of me."

823   "I cannot drop the matter," replied the queen.
"Should I give up these many men, you mean,
Who stand, as Sigfrid does, in our vassalage?"
The lovely Kriemhild answered her, in terrible rage:

824   "Don't think he'll ever serve you! He never can,
In any way, for he is a greater man
Than my good brother Gunther could ever be.
And now you'd best take back the words you said to me!

825   Another thing—it's strange, if he's your thrall
And both of us are at your beck and call,
That he has never bothered to set aside
A penny's tribute! I really should be spared your pride!"

173

826   "You raise yourself too high," cried the queen.
       "Very well, then, let it now be seen
       If you are honored equally with me."
       The wrath of both these queens was a fearful thing to see.

827   Lady Kriemhild said, "Then come what must,
       Since you called my lord your bondsman! Let us trust
       The two kings' own retainers to decide:
       Dare I go to chapel before a monarch's bride?

828   You'll see this day that I am noble and free,
       That my lord is better than yours could ever be.
       And I do not intend to be cried down;
       This night you'll see your bondmaid go before the crown

829   And court of Burgundy, with knights to wait her.
       I intend to be acknowledged greater
       Than any queen this land has ever known."
       And so between them seeds of bitter hate were sown.

830   Said Brunhild, "If you deny your vassalage,
       Don't come to church with me—the privilege
       Of my attendants! You and your maids must leave me."
       To which Kriemhild replied, "That I will, believe me!"

831   "Now dress, my ladies," she said, "dress for church;
       My honor's not for anyone here to besmirch.
       If you have elegant clothes, don't be accused
       Of hiding them. We'll make her rue the words she used."

832   They hardly needed urging, but chose their best,
       Ladies and maids alike, richly dressed.
       With all her suite now, Sigfrid's consort neared:
       The lovely Kriemhild, in lavish garb, appeared

833   With the maids she brought to the Rhine, all forty-three.
Gleaming silks they wore from Araby.
These lovely maidens came to the minster then;
Before the building waited all of Sigfrid's men.

834   The people wondered why it was they saw
The queens in separate companies withdraw
And not together walking as before—
This sight, for many men, held grief and woe in store.

835   Before the minster Gunther's lady stood.
Many warriors thought to themselves how good
Their fortune was to see such beauty there.
Then came Lady Kriemhild, her suite beyond compare.

836   The best that ever royal maidens wore
Compared to this was nothing. Such a store
Of wealth was hers, no thirty queens could add
All their goods together to match what Kriemhild had.

837   With all the will in the world, no man could say
He ever saw such clothes as these today
In which her winsome maidens now were seen.
In this she had no purpose but to hurt the queen.

838   They met at the minster steps. For the hate she bore,
The queen of the land bade Kriemhild walk no more.
She spoke, her words were sharper than a knife:
"Never shall bondmaid go before the king's own wife."

839   Then Lady Kriemhild cried, to anger stung:
"You'd be better off to hold your tongue!
You've sold your beauty cheap and shamed your life.
How can a vassal's mistress pass for a king's own wife?"

840   "Whom are you calling mistress?" the queen outburst.
"You!" said Kriemhild. "The one who loved you first
Was Sigfrid, my own dear lord and good.
Indeed it was not my brother who took your maidenhood.

841   And what a base deception! Where were your brains?
Why did you let him love you—one of your thanes?
All of your complaint is built on air!"
Answered Brunhild, "I'll tell Gunther this, I swear!"

842   "And what is that to me? By your own pride
You stand betrayed. With your own words you tried
To make me out your servant. Honestly,
I hate it all. You'll have no silent friend in me."

843   Then Brunhild wept. And Kriemhild paused no more.
Ahead of the queen, she entered the minster door
With all her train. The mighty hate began
For which, from shining eyes, so many sad tears ran.

844   However God was praised, whatever the song,
The time that passed to Brunhild seemed too long,
For will and body both were dark with gloom—
The price of which in time was noble heroes' doom.

845   She wept with her maids and waited at the door.
She thought, "I must hear from her, if there is more
To the noisy libel of her bitter tongue.
If Sigfrid boasted this, I swear I'll have him hung."

846   Now with her warriors, Kriemhild came outside.
"Stand where you are!" Lady Brunhild cried.
"You say that I'm a harlot. Prove what you say!
You know what pain you've caused me—to talk of me
    that way."

847 Said Kriemhild, "You'd do better to let me go!
This gold upon my hand is the proof I show;
My lover brought me it when he lay with you first."
Of all of Brunhild's days this was far the worst.

848 "This precious ring—someone made bold to steal it,"
She said, "and long maliciously conceal it.
Now I see too well who was the thief!"
The rage and fury of both these women passed belief.

849 Said Kriemhild, "I will not play your stealing game
And you would hold your tongue if your good name
Meant much to you. Who says I lie, be cursed!
The proof is the belt I wear: my Sigfrid had you first."

850 From Nineveh the silk that made the sash
She wore about her. On it played the flash
Of splendid gems. When Brunhild saw, she wept.
Not from Gunther nor Burgundy could this be kept.

851 "Ask the prince of the Rhine to come," she cried.
"He shall hear how I am vilified
By his own sister—giving me the name
Of Sigfrid's mistress." He and his retainers came.

852 He saw his own dear lady weeping greatly.
"Tell me now," he questioned her most sweetly,
"Who it is that has hurt you so, my dear."
She said to the king, "I stand bereft of joy and cheer.

853 Your sister has tried her best to slur and taint
My good repute. I bring you my complaint:
She says her husband Sigfrid slept with me."
King Gunther spoke, "If so, she acts most evilly."

854   "And here she wears my belt, which I had lost,
    My red gold ring. I rue the bitter cost
    That I was born. Defend me, Sire, and set
    An end to this disgrace, or I shall not forget!"

855   King Gunther spoke, "Let him come forward now.
    If he has made this boast, he must so avow
    Or else he must deny what here you say."
    They sent for Kriemhild's lord to come without delay.

856   Sigfrid saw their tears, their patience tried,
    And had no notion why. He quickly cried,
    "Why do these women weep, I'd like to know,
    And by what cause I get the royal summons so."

857   King Gunther answered, "I am deeply pained.
    My lady Brunhild here has just complained
    You boast you conquered her and first became
    Her paramour. Or so at least your wife would claim."

858   Sigfrid answered, "Would she? If this is true,
    She will be very sorry before I'm through.
    I'll swear there's nothing to be offended at.
    Your men shall hear my oath: I never told her that."

859   "Let us see," announced the king of the Rhine;
    "If you will swear this oath you offer, fine!
    I'll judge you free of every evil thing."
    They bade the proud Burgundians join to form the ring.

860   Sigfrid swore the oath with upraised hand.
    Said mighty Gunther, "I fully understand
    Your innocence, and I declare you quit
    Of all my sister's charge: you've done no part of it."

861   Said Sigfrid, "If my wife has got some gain
Or comfort out of causing Brunhild pain,
Believe me, I am moved to deep regret."
At this the dashing courtiers turned, and their glances met.

862   "Women should be trained in a proper way,"
Said Sigfrid, "to curb the haughty things they say.
Warn your wife, and I will do the same.
Their immoderate conduct fills my heart with shame."

863   Many women's tongues were now at rest,
But Gunther's men beheld their queen depressed
And full of gloom, and pity at what they'd seen
Stirred their hearts. Hagen came and spoke to the queen.

864   He asked what the trouble was. In tears she told
What just had happened. He swiftly vowed to hold
A pledge that Kriemhild's husband should be punished—
Else from his life all joy should be forever banished.

865   Ortwin and Gernot joined the plotting twain,
As they discussed how Sigfrid might be slain.
And Giselher, the highborn Uta's son,
Came and heard their talk; he spoke as the loyal one:

866   "Noble warriors, why should you do this?
Does he deserve such hate, to prejudice
His very life? The things that women find
To get upset about are a vain and petty kind."

867   "Shall we raise cuckoos then?" Lord Hagen cried.
"That would give us little cause for pride.
He has boasted of my lady, my king's wife.
For that I swear to die unless he pays with his life."

868   The king spoke up: "What did he ever give
But good and glory? Let him live.
What use if I become his enemy?
He was always loyal and served us willingly."

869   "Indeed," said Ortwin, warrior knight of Metz,
"From all his mighty strength small good he gets!
I'll see that he's hurt—if you permit, my lord."
So most wrongfully the men gainsaid their word.

870   None but Hagen pressed this counseling.
He, at every moment, urged the king
That with his death the lands that Sigfrid had
Would surely fall to his crown. The king grew troubled
    and sad.

871   But there they left it. Again the jousting sounds,
As lances broke on shields, from the minster grounds,
As Sigfrid's wife went forth, to the castle hall—
With many of Gunther's men in no good mood at all.

872   The king declared, "Forgo this mortal fury.
He was born for our good, our greater glory.
He is, besides, a man of strength so grim—
If he should find this out, who'd dare face up to him?"

873   "He won't," said Hagen. "You shall keep it quiet.
I have in mind a secret plot and by it
He'll pay in sorrow for my lady's weeping.
Hagen has no further bond with him worth keeping."

874   King Gunther said, "How could that ever be?"
"I'll tell you how," said Hagen. "We shall see
That heralds come to our land declaring war,
In public, men whom no one here has seen before.

875   Then you, before your guests, bid every one
Take up our arms and march. When that is done,
He'll surely pledge his help—and lose his life!
I'll get the facts we need—straight from his own wife."

876   The king fell in with Hagen's evil plan.
Without a soul suspecting, they began
To shape their perfidy, these men of pride.
From two women's wrangling many heroes died!

✠ FIFTEENTH ADVENTURE
How Sigfrid Was Betrayed

877 The fourth day dawned; thirty-two men were sighted
Riding to court. News was soon recited
To mighty Gunther, of truce revoked, and war—
A lie that held for women bitter woe in store.

878 The men were granted audience and told
How they were men of Liudeger the Bold.
The monarch bested once by Sigfrid's hand
And brought by him as hostage to royal Gunther's land.

879 He welcomed them and bade them take a seat.
"Let us stand," said one, "till we repeat
The message we have brought. This you must know:
That many a mother's son, my lord, is sworn your foe.

880 Our king and Liudegast call off the truce,
Who suffered at your hands such grave abuse.
They mean to ride in force against your land."
When Gunther heard the news it seemed his wrath was
    fanned.

881 They sent to their lodgings now the traitorous crew.
What could Sigfrid—what could any man do
To guard against this plotting? They would in time
Themselves be forced in pain to suffer for their crime.

882 The king took whispered counsel with his kin.
Hagen would not let his lord give in.

Though many would have willingly forgot,
Trony refused to hear of giving up the plot.

883   Sigfrid passed them once as they conspired
In whispered tones. The valiant lord inquired:
"Why are king's and courtier's faces so long?
If any one has harmed you, I'll help avenge the wrong."

884   "If I am pained, I have good cause to be,"
Said Gunther. "The Danish kings have challenged me.
They will, in open war, invade my land."
The stalwart warrior cried, "That let Sigfrid's hand

885   Prevent for you—as royal honors bid.
I'll deal with them as once before I did.
Their castles and their lands I'll level flat
Before I rest my hand. My life is pledge for that.

886   You and all your men can stay right here.
I and mine shall ride, and thus make clear
How willingly I serve. Bitter woes,
Be sure of that, shall come through me to all your foes!"

887   "This is good news to me!" And Gunther made
As if he honestly were glad of aid.
The faithless man, all in deceit, bowed low.
And Sigfrid cried, "You need have little worry now."

888   They mobilized the men of their company—
All this for Sigfrid and his men to see.
He ordered his Lowland troops in readiness.
The knights of Sigfrid sought their gear and battle dress

889   "Father Sigmund, stay. There is no need
For you to go," he said. "With God's good speed

The shortest time will see us back again.
You'll have a pleasant stay, here with the king and his
    men."

890   They fixed the banners on, as if to go.
Many of Gunther's vassals did not know
The true account of all these steps they took.
A crowd was there with Sigfrid, gathered around to look.

891   Helmet and corselet tied upon their horse,
Stalwart knights prepared to set their course
Away from home. And now Lord Hagen went
To Kriemhild, ready to leave, asking her assent.

892   "How lucky for me," she said, "that I should win
The sort of man who dares, for friends and kin,
To be defender, as Sigfrid does for mine!
In the pride and joy of this," she cried, "my heart shall
    shine.

893   Lord of Trony, loyal friend, reflect!
I never bore you hate, but full respect.
Grant me reward of this in my husband's name!
If I insulted Brunhild, he should not bear the blame.

894   Whatever I did I've since regretted roundly,
And he himself it was who thrashed me soundly
For saying what so weighs upon her mind.
My lord exacted penance, and that of the strictest kind."

895   "The two of you will shortly reconcile
Your differences, oh Queen. But say meanwhile
How by helping him I might serve you—
None I'd rather help, and nothing I'd rather do!"

896   "I should never fear," replied Kriemhild,
      "In any battle-storm his being killed,
      Had he not this rash and headstrong will,
      For then my gallant lord could never suffer ill."

897   Said Hagen, "Lady, if you have cause to feel
      That he is vulnerable, do not conceal
      By what devices this may be averted.
      Afoot or riding then I'll be on guard, alerted."

898   "You are kin to me, and I to you.
      I commend to you my lord, and this I do
      In faith that you may guard the one I love."
      She told him things that better were not spoken of.

899   She said, "My lord is bold, and strong as well.
      By the mountain when he fought and the dragon fell—
      He bathed himself in its blood, and never since,
      In any battle waged, could weapons wound my prince.

900   Still, whenever he fights, I have my fears,
      Where warriors hurl so many heavy spears,
      That I shall lose my dearest husband there.
      Alas, he causes me such great and frequent care.

901   I tell you now, upon your charity—
      And may you ever keep your faith with me!—
      Where my beloved husband may be hit
      And hurt. In trust to you, my friend, I utter it.

902   When in the dragon's wounds, and in the well
      Of steaming blood he bathed himself, there fell
      Between his shoulder blades a linden leaf.
      There he can be hurt. This is my cause for grief."

903   Hagen of Trony said, "If you will sew
A little mark on his coat, then I shall know,
When we are fighting, where to shield my friend."
She thought to save his life—she caused his bitter end!

904   "With finest silk I'll sew upon his cloak
A secret cross, and there," the lady spoke,
"Protect my husband when the battle flows
Around him violently, and he must face his foes."

905   "Dear lady," Hagen answered, "I will do it!"
And so she thought her lord would profit through it,
But thus it was instead he stood betrayed.
Hagen took his leave, his happiness was made.

906   The spirits of the court were gaily keyed.
I doubt if ever knight will do such deed
Of treachery as by his will occurred,
When Kriemhild put her trust in Hagen's faith and word.

907   In all good cheer, at dawn the following day,
His thousand men and Sigfrid rode away,
Avenging, as he thought, his friends' distress.
Hagen rode so close that he could scan his dress.

908   When he had seen the cross, he sent two men,
In secret, to tell a different tale again:
How peace should be restored to Gunther's land,
And how they came to him at Liudeger's command.

909   Sigfrid now rode back, in sad dismay;
His friends were not avenged in any way.
They hardly talked him into turning 'round.
He rode to see the king. What words of thanks he found!

910 "Sigfrid, noble friend, may God reward
Your willingness to do what I implored.
I'll always give you thanks, as I should do.
More than all my friends, I place my trust in you.

911 Since this campaign has ceased to be our care,
Let us hunt the Vosges for boar and bear,
As I have often done." This was a plan
That Hagen first proposed, the false and faithless man.

912 "Send to all my guests and let them know:
We'll make an early start. Prepare to go,
All those who wish to hunt. And those who stay
To pay the ladies court will please me well that way."

913 With perfect sense of form, Sigfrid cried:
"Whenever you call the hunt, I shall ride.
Lend me a beater then, and if you could,
Some hunting dog, and I shall ride with you to the wood."

914 "Do you want only one?" the king replied.
"If you wish I'll lend you four, well-versed and tried
In woods and forest paths, the tracks of game.
They'll get you safely back to the camp from which you
came."

915 The dashing warrior rode to see his wife.
Hagen took his plot on the hero's life
Straightway to the king—through and through
A deed of faithlessness, and more than man should do.

✠ SIXTEENTH ADVENTURE
How Sigfrid Was Slain

916   Gunther and Hagen, bold, but with the face
Of false deceit, proposed a forest chase:
To hunt with sharpened spears the wild swine,
The bison and the bear—is there any sport so fine?

917   They took with them supplies of every kind.
Sigfrid rode, in grace and noble mind.
Beside a cooling spring he lost his life—
This was the work of Brunhild, royal Gunther's wife.

918   To Kriemhild's side the stalwart knight had gone.
His hunting gear and theirs was loaded on,
Ready to cross the Rhine. Never before
In all her days, had Kriemhild cause to suffer more.

919   He kissed his love upon her lips and cried,
"God grant I see you safe again, my bride,
And may your eyes see me. Now you must find
Diversion with your kin, I cannot stay behind."

920   She thought of the words she spoke in Hagen's ear
(And dared not now repeat). In pain and fear
The princess grieved that she was ever born—
Kriemhild wept, her tears unnumbered, all forlorn.

921   "Give up this hunt!" she cried. "Last night I dreamed
A painful thing. Two wild boars, it seemed,
Pursued my lord across a field. In sleep,
The flowers all turned red. I have my right to weep;

188

922   I fear from many hands an evil plot—
What if someone here should think he'd got
Ill use from us and turned this thought to hate?
Dear lord, I say, turn back, before it is too late."

923   "I'll soon return, my dear, I swear I will.
I know no persons here who wish me ill,
For all your kin are well disposed to me,
And I have always acted so that this should be."

924   "Oh no, my lord, I fear it can't go well.
Alas, I dreamed last night two mountains fell
On top of you, and I never saw you again.
If you should leave me now, my heart will be heavy with
    pain."

925   He held his perfect wife in arms' embrace,
With lover's kiss caressed her lovely face.
He took his leave and soon he went away.
Alas, she never saw him safe beyond that day.

926   They rode to a certain heavy wood, in quest
Of hunt and sport, and many of the best
Were they who followed Gunther's party there.
The only ones who stayed were Gernot and Giselher.

927   The horses went ahead, across the Rhine,
Full laden with the hunters' bread and wine,
Their fish and meat, and other good supplies
To suit a wealthy king in full and fitting wise.

928   At the forest edge they had their camp site placed.
By this device the haughty hunters faced
Where game would run, there on a spacious isle.
They told the king that Sigfrid had ridden up meanwhile.

929 The hunters' stations now were occupied
At every major point. Lord Sigfrid cried,
That stalwart man, "And who shall show the way
To the woods and the waiting game, you lords in bold
array?"

930 Hagen said, "Before the hunting starts,
Why not split our group in several parts?
Thus my lords and I may recognize
Which hunter masters best our forest enterprise.

931 All the men and hounds we shall divide.
And each one choose the way he wants to ride.
Whoever hunts the best, his be the praise!"
The hunters did not wait, but went their separate ways.

932 "One dog is all I need—more's a waste,"
Lord Sigfrid said, "a hound that's had his taste,
To help him hold the scent through all this wood."
Thus said Kriemhild's lord: "This hunting will be good."

933 His ancient huntsman chose a goodly hound
Who soon had led them to a spot of ground
Where game in plenty ran. They bagged at will
Whatever rose from cover—experts do it still.

934 All the hound could flush fell to the hand
Of valiant Sigfrid, prince of Netherland—
So fast his horse that nothing got away.
His was the greatest praise for work in the hunt that day.

935 In all respects a skilled and sturdy man!
He made the kill with which the hunt began:

A mighty boar that fell at a single blow.
Shortly then he saw a monstrous lion go.

936 He strung and shot as the dog flushed his prey.
The sharp and pointed arrow sped its way.
The lion sprang three times—then it fell.
His fellow huntsmen praised him, saying he hunted well.

937 He added elk and bison to his bag,
Aurochs—four of them—and a giant stag;
His horse was fast, it never fell behind,
And they could not escape—no hope for hart or hind.

938 The hunting dog now found a giant boar.
It fled, the master hunter on the spoor
Without a moment's pause, and sticking tight.
The angry pig turned back and rushed the gallant knight.

939 What other hunter could have drawn his sword
To slay as easily as Kriemhild's lord?
After the kill they brought the hound-dog in.
Now the Burgundians learned how good his luck had
  been.

940 His fellow sportsmen said, "If you don't mind,
You might, my lord, just leave a few behind.
You've emptied hill and forest all this while.
Please let something live!" At this he had to smile.

941 There still was noise and clamor all around
Of hunters, and hunting dogs, so great a sound
That hill and forest answered. (The men released
A full two dozen packs, to hunt the forest beast.

942   And many animals would not survive.)
The other hunters thought they might contrive
To win the prize—an honor not for earning
With hardy Sigfrid there, where hunting fires were
    burning.

943   The chase was over now—and yet not quite.
Returning hunters brought to the camping site
Hides of many beasts, a host of game.
And ah, what wonderful things for the royal kitchen came!

944   The king was ready now to take repast,
And ordered the hunt informed. A single blast
Upon a horn sufficed to signify:
The noble prince had come to the camping site nearby.

945   A hunter of Sigfrid's cried: "My lord, I hear
By the sound of horns they want us all to appear
At camp again. I'll send an answer back."
(They blew for the other hunters, by way of keeping
    track.)

946   "We'd better leave the woods," Sir Sigfrid cried.
They hurried on, his horse at an even ride.
Their noise aroused a savage beast who broke
And ran—an angry bear. The hero, turning, spoke:

947   "I think we'll have some sport for our comrades there.
Let go the hunting dog, I see a bear.
He'll come to camp with us—as good as done!
He cannot save himself, unless he can really run."

948   The hunting-hound was loosed, the bear took flight.
Off to ride him down went Kriemhild's knight.

He came where trees lay felled and blocked the path.
The mighty beast now felt secure from the hunter's wrath.

949   The haughty warrior leapt at once from his steed
       And ran on foot. The bear, forgetting heed
       And caution, failed to run and soon was caught
       And swiftly tied—and not a scratch had Sigfrid got!

950   The captured beast could neither claw nor bite.
       He tied him to the saddle, the fearless knight,
       And mounting, rode to camp. The feat was done
       In a hero's pride of heart and all for the sake of fun.

951   He came to camp arrayed in his splendid gear:
       Broad-bladed and massive, his mighty spear,
       Down to his very spurs a handsome sword,
       And a horn of reddish gold in the hand of the gallant lord.

952   Of finer hunting garb I never heard.
       He wore a black silk cape; his cap was furred
       With sable skins and very richly made.
       He had a quiver, too, adorned with costly braid,

953   And covered with panther hide—by purpose so
       Because its smell was sweet. He had a bow
       No man except himself could bend an inch,
       If he were asked to draw, without an archer's winch.

954   His suit was made throughout of otter's skin
       With patches sewn from head to hem therein.
       The gleaming pelts had golden buckles on;
       At the hunter's right and left the clasps of red gold shone.

955   He carried Balmung, too, his handsome sword,
So broad and sharp as never to fail its lord
In helmet strokes, its edges true and tried.
This was a huntsman great in confidence and pride.

956   And since I have the full account to tell:
The choicest arrows filled his quiver well,
Spliced with gold, the blades were a good hand wide.
Whatever felt their cut, so stricken, swiftly died.

957   He rode with spirit, the way of hunting men.
Gunther's thanes could see him coming then.
They hurried out to hold his tourney-mare.
There at his saddle, tied, was a big and vicious bear!

958   Jumping down, he loosed the ropes that bound
The bear by foot and maw. The dogs around,
As many as saw the beast, gave tongue and bayed.
The bear was all for the woods; the men—a bit afraid!

959   Into the kitchens he went, confused by the noise.
Ho, but that place was not for the kitchen-boys!
Kettles were tumbled, hardly a fire was whole.
And oh, what foods were strewn among the ash and coal!

960   Men were leaping up on every hand.
The bear was angry now. At the king's command
The dogs that still were leashed they cut away.
With a better end that would have been a merry day.

961   No waiting now, but up with spear and bow
And after the bear, to see where he would go.
They dared not shoot with all the dogs around.
They raised a fearful racket and made the hills resound.

194

962   The bear, pursued by dogs, began to flee.
Kriemhild's lord kept up—and none but he.
He ran him down, with his sword he struck him dead;
Later they brought him back to camp and the fire-stead.

963   All that saw it praised a mighty deed.
They bade the noble hunters come and eat.
The whole assemblage sat on a pleasant sward.
What marvelous foods were set before each noble lord!

964   The stewards took their time in bringing wine.
Otherwise no service quite so fine
Was ever seen. These men would have no reason
To fear a word of censure, but for their stain of treason.

965   Sigfrid said, "It gives me some surprise
When they send us from the kitchen such supplies
Of excellent food, and no one brings the wine.
If they serve their huntsmen thus, the next time I'll
    decline.

966   I think I merit better service," he cried.
Falsely spoke the king, from the tableside:
"We'll make up later what you missed at first.
This is Hagen's fault—he'd let us die of thirst."

967   Said Hagen of Trony, "Listen, my lord, to me.
I thought the hunt today was meant to be
In Spessart and that is where I sent the wine.
We missed our drinks today; I'll not forget next time."

968   "Confound them," answered Sigfrid then, declaring:
"They should have brought me seven sumpters bearing
Spiced wine and mead. And failing that,
Was there no place closer to the Rhine we could have sat?"

969   Said Hagen of Trony, "Noble knights, my king,
Not far from here I know a cooling spring.
Do not be angry now—why not go there?"
(Counsel fraught, for many, with sorrow and grievous
    care).

970   The pang of thirst was all that Sigfrid feared.
He ordered the table that much sooner cleared,
That he might go to the hills and find the spring.
There they worked their plot—a black and faithless thing.

971   They placed on carts the game Sigfrid had killed
To have it carried home, and all who beheld
Granted Sigfrid honor in high degree.
(Hagen broke faith with him—and he broke it wretchedly).

972   As they were about to go to the linden tree
Lord Hagen said, "They're always telling me
How nothing is fast enough to keep the pace
With Sigfrid running. I wish he'd show us how he can
    race!"

973   Cried the Prince of the Low Lands, Sigmund's son:
"Find out for yourself, my friend! If you want to run
A race to the spring, all right. Whoever's faster
To the finish we shall all acknowledge master."

974   "Very well," said Hagen then, "let's try."
Stalwart Sigfrid made a bold reply:
"I'll first lie down in the grass before your feet."
Royal Gunther smiled, the words he heard were sweet.

975   Sigfrid had more to say: "I'll tell you what.
I'll carry every bit of clothes I've got,

My spear and shield, and all my hunting gear."
He put his quiver next to his sword and laced it there.

976 Gunther and Hagen removed their clothes and stood
In their white underwear. It did no good.
Across the clover like two wild panthers burst
The pair of running men, but Sigfrid got there first.

977 (In all, from many men, he won renown!)
He loosed his sword, and put his quiver down
And leaned on a linden branch his giant spear.
The splendid stranger stood by the waters flowing clear.

978 With perfect sense of form in everything,
He laid his shield on the ground beside the spring
And would not drink, however great his thirst
(Evil thanks he got!) till Gunther drank there first.

979 The spring was pure and good and cool.
Gunther bent his head above the pool
And after drinking rose and stepped away.
Ah, if Sigfrid could have done the same that day!

980 He paid the price for the courteous thing he did.
His sword and bow Lord Hagen took and hid
And hurried back where the spear had lain before.
He looked for a certain mark on the cape that Sigfrid wore.

981 As Sigfrid leaned to drink, he took his aim
And hurled it through the cross. The heart-blood came
Welling from the wound, richly to spill
On Hagen's clothes. No knight has ever done so ill.

982 He left the spear embedded by Sigfrid's heart.
  Never in all this world did Hagen start
  And run so fast from any man before.
  When good Lord Sigfrid knew the vicious wound he bore,

983 He leapt from the spring like a man out of his mind.
  Up from his heart and towering out behind
  Rose the shaft of the spear. His bow and sword
  He sought in vain, or Hagen would have his due reward.

984 The wounded man could find no blade to wield,
  And nothing left to fight with but his shield.
  He snatched it up and after Hagen he ran—
  Even thus he still caught up with Gunther's man.

985 Mortally wounded as he was, he hit
  So hard with his shield that from the edge of it
  The precious jewels spun, and the shield was shattered.
  For that most splendid knight revenge was all that
   mattered.

986 Hagen stumbled and fell at Sigfrid's blows—
  So violent all the island echoes rose!
  Had Sigfrid sword in hand, he would have killed him.
  What rage in the wounded man, as hurt and anger filled
   him!

987 The color of Sigfrid's skin had turned all pale.
  He could not stand. His strength was doomed to fail;
  He bore the mark of death in all his pallor.
  Many lovely women later mourned his valor.

988 So Kriemhild's husband fell where flowers grew.
  They saw the blood that left his wound burst through,

And then from bitter hurt he cursed them all,
Whose faithless plotting first designed his cruel fall.

989   Cried Sigfrid dying, "Cowards, knave on knave!
      Is murder your reward for the help I gave?
      I kept my faith with you, and so I pay!
      A shame upon your race, what you have done today.

990   Every child that's born to you will bear
      The stain of this forever. Far too unfair
      Is this revenge you take for your hate of me!
      You should be banned in shame from decent company."

991   The other knights ran up where he lay slain.
      It was, for many there, a day of pain,
      For he was mourned by all that ever served
      A loyal cause—no more than a gallant man deserved.

992   Another mourned: the king of Burgundy.
      The dying man looked up; "What need has he
      To weep for hurt who caused it? Scorn of men
      Is all it earns," said he. "Why not forget it then?"

993   Cried Hagen, "I don't know what you're mourning for.
      Our fears are at an end. How many more
      Will dare to stand against us? A fortunate hour,
      I say, when I destroyed his pride and all his power!"

994   Cried Sigfrid, "Boasting is an easy art.
      If I had seen the murder in your heart,
      I should have taken care to guard my life.
      I worry not so much for me as for my wife.

995 And God have pity that my son was born,
   Whom men in later days will heap with scorn
   For having kin who bear the murderer's taint.
   If only I had strength!—I have a just complaint."

996 Said the dying man, in anguish: "Noble king,
   If you intend to do a loyal thing
   In all this world for any man, then take
   My wife in your protection, for grace and mercy's sake.

997 And let it profit her that she's your sister,
   As you are a well-born prince, in faith assist her.
   My father and men have a long time to wait.
   Never did woman's pleasure end in pain so great."

998 The flowers all around were wet with blood.
   He fought with death but not for long—what good?
   Death has always owned the sharper sword.
   He had no longer strength to speak, that gallant lord.

999 Soon, when the warriors saw the knight was dead,
   They placed him on a shield all golden red,
   And then debated how they might proceed
   Best to conceal the fact that Hagen did this deed.

1000 And many spoke: "We have seen evil done.
   Hide it then, and all shall speak as one
   That Kriemhild's husband rode a forest lane
   To hunt alone, was met by bandits there, and slain."

1001 "I'll take him back," said Hagen. "Have no doubt:
   It's all the same to me if she finds out.
   She caused my lady Brunhild misery—
   Now let her weep as much as she wants, for all of me!"

✠ SEVENTEENTH ADVENTURE
How Kriemhild Wept Over Her Husband and How He Was Buried

1002   They waited for night and crossed the Rhine in force.
Truly, heroes never hunted worse:
The game they slew—a cause for women's tears.
Many warriors paid the price in later years!

1003   Of overweening pride you hear me sing,
And awful vengeance. Hagen had them bring
The murdered lord of the Nibelungs, had him laid
Before the women's hall where Lady Kriemhild stayed—

1004   In secret, by the door where she would pass
And find him as she left for matin mass,
Before the day had dawned. (And rare indeed
The call to such a mass that Kriemhild failed to heed.)

1005   By custom now they rang the minster bell.
The lovely lady roused her maids to tell
What light to bring, what special clothes to wear.
Then came a chamberlain and found Lord Sigfrid there.

1006   He saw him red with blood, his clothing wet,
But who it was he had not fathomed yet.
He took the light in hand to the women's room—
To bring his lady Kriemhild a tale of death and doom.

1007   As she and her maids were about to make their way
To church and mass, the chamberlain shouted, "Stay!

Before your chamber lies a warrior slain."
And Kriemhild now began to weep in boundless pain.

1008   Before she knew it was her husband there
She thought of Hagen's query, his pledge of care
To save his life. Her hurt now passed all measure.
Upon his dying she forswore all joy and pleasure.

1009   Without a word she fell to the floor and lay,
In all her beauty, shorn of joy, the prey
Of endless pain. At last she raised her head
And shrieked till all the chamber echoed. Servants said:

1010   "What if this should be some stranger, though?"
Blood welled from her lips in her heart's woe:
"It is Sigfrid, my own dear lord, I know it.
Hagen did this deed and Brunhild made him do it."

1011   There where he lay she asked that she be led.
In her white hands she lifted his handsome head.
She knew at once, for all the blood and red,
The hero of Nibelung land lay wretched there and dead.

1012   The gracious queen cried out in misery,
"O Lord, my sorrow! Look, your shield is free
Of any mark of swords. They murdered you!
I'd have the death of him who did it, if I knew."

1013   All her attendants mourned with her and cried,
Sad at heart because their lord had died,
Their noble master whom they now had lost—
Brunhild's rage avenged by Hagen, at bitter cost!

1014   The wretched woman spoke, "I ask you, go,
And wake up Sigfrid's men. Tell my woe

To Sigmund too, and ask if he will shed
His tears with mine and help me mourn my husband
    dead."

1015   A herald went where the Nibelung warriors slept,
Sigfrid's men. His painful tidings swept
Their spirits bare of joy. Until they heard
The sound of weeping, they could not believe his word.

1016   And soon the herald came where lay the king.
Sleep for Sigmund was a foreign thing.
I think his heart had told him what befell:
Never again to see his son alive and well.

1017   "My lord, wake up! I come as Kriemhild's thane
Sent to tell the hurt she bears, whose pain
Beyond all other pain strikes to her heart.
Help her mourn this hurt, of which you bear your part."

1018   Sigmund rose. "What hurt is this?" he cried,
"You say the queen has suffered?" The man replied,
In tears, "I should keep the news from you in vain;
Gallant Sigfrid, Lord of Netherland, is slain."

1019   "Now stop your wicked tales," Lord Sigmund spoke,
"For sake of me. This is no time to joke,
Telling someone that his son is slain.
My life would be too short to overcome such pain."

1020   "If you will not believe what I report,
Listen!—you can hear them, queen and court,
Mourning over Sigfrid slain and dead."
Great fear struck King Sigmund then. He sprang from
    bed.

1021   His hundred men rose up, their hands in haste
Upon their long and pointed blades, they raced
Toward the sound of weeping, all distraught.
The thousand also came whom gallant Sigfrid brought.

1022   They heard the ladies weep their great distress.
Some imagined they should even dress
To visit them; their very senses strayed
With so much sorrow. They went, in their deepest hearts
    afraid.

1023   Sigmund came to Kriemhild. "I curse this land
And the trip that brought us here. What murderer's
    hand—
Here among such friends a cruel reward—
Has robbed me of my son and you of your dear lord?"

1024   "If I found out," she cried, "my heart and hand
Would be his enemies until I planned
Mortal hurt for him. His every friend
Would weep and, weeping, know who caused his sudden
    end."

1025   Sigmund the king embraced the prince, his son.
Such sadness then took hold on every one
That palace and hall were filled with a great noise;
The whole town of Worms echoed with their cries.

1026   No one could console Lord Sigfrid's lady.
They now removed the clothes from his fair body
And washed his wounds and placed him on a bier.
In hurt and misery his followers paid dear.

1027   Then cried his men-at-arms from Nibelung lands:
       "He shall be avenged by willing hands.
       The man we want is in this castle here."
       And Sigfrid's warriors ran to get their battle-gear.

1028   Eleven hundred knights with shield in hand
       Approached in force, King Sigmund's whole command.
       He wanted vengeance gained for the death of his son,
       And truly, he had cause enough to wish it done.

1029   They did not know on whom to turn their swords,
       Unless it be on Gunther and Gunther's lords,
       With whom he rode to hunt. For war arrayed
       Lady Kriemhild saw them come. She stood dismayed.

1030   However deep her hurt or great her dread
       She feared still more to see the Nibelungs dead
       At the hands of her brother's men. To thwart this end,
       She warned them out of kindness, as friend to loyal friend.

1031   The wretched woman cried, "What could you do,
       Sigmund, my lord? Oh, if you only knew!
       King Gunther has so many fearless men—
       The knights you send against them will not return again."

1032   Helmets donned, battle was their heart's need.
       And yet the noble queen began to plead
       And even to command that they desist.
       Great her sorrow when it seemed they might insist.

1033   She cried, "Wait until some better time,
       My lord, and you and I shall avenge this crime
       Against my husband. Once I am satisfied
       I know who took him from me, he shall be destroyed.

1034   The Rhineland has its arrogant men—no lack.
That is why I say do not attack.
For they have thirty men to your one.
(God give them just reward for the evil they have done!)

1035   Stay here and share my pain. At break of day,
Men of noble heart, help me lay
My dear lord in his coffin, I beg of you."
The warriors answered, "What you ask, we shall do."

1036   No one could tell you how vast it was, the crowd
Of knights and ladies weeping now—so loud,
The sound of lamentation roused the town,
Whose goodly people all in haste came running down.

1037   They mourned with the many guests their painful loss.
No one yet had told them by what cause
Sigfrid the noble warrior lost his life.
So noblewoman wept, and good burgher's wife.

1038   They ordered smiths, out of silver and gold
To build a coffin, large and strong, and told
The men to make the straps of finest steel.
(How sad at heart his passing made the people feel!)

1039   The night was past, and day, they said, would break.
Then the noble lady bade them take
Her dear lord Sigfrid to the minster square.
They walked, weeping, all the friends he counted there.

1040   They brought him to the church. Bells rang,
And everywhere many priests sang.
Then King Gunther came with his retinue
To join their lamentation—and fierce Hagen, too.

1041   "My dear sister, alas! what pain you bear!"
Said Gunther. "Oh, that something could repair
Our loss! We'll mourn forever that Sigfrid died."
"You have no reason to," the wretched woman cried.

1042   "If you had cared, all this would never be!
I say it now: you gave no thought to me
When I was torn from my dear husband," she said.
"I would to God it had been me, and I were dead."

1043   And now, as Gunther's men cried out denial:
"Who says he has no guilt, submit to trial!
He shall, before this crowd, approach the bier.
For such is the quickest way to make the truth appear."

1044   A mighty marvel, this, which still is done,
For if beside the corpse you see the one
Who bears the mark of murder, the wounds will bleed.
And so it was they knew that Hagen did the deed.

1045   The wounds poured out their blood, as they had before.
Those who once wept greatly now wept more.
And Gunther cried, "I will have this clearly said:
Bandits struck him down. This is nothing Hagen did."

1046   "Well I know who the bandits are," she cried.
"God grant his own good friends be not denied
Their vengeance. Gunther and Hagen, you did this!"
Men of Sigfrid waited battle—in eagerness.

1047   Then Kriemhild spoke, "Help me bear my pain."
And both the men came by where he lay slain,
Her brother Gernot, Giselher the youth.

207

They mourned him with the others in honest **faith and**
truth.

1048   Their tears welled deep for him. Time for mass
Had now arrived, one saw the people pass—
Man, woman, child—to church where they,
For whom the loss was less, wept too for him that day.

1049   Both brothers said, "As you are sister to me,
Take heart in face of death, for this must be.
We'll make amends to you as long as we live."
But solace now was more than all the world could give.

1050   His coffin stood complete by noon that day,
They took him from the bier on which he lay,
And still his lady would not have him buried—
By which the people all were pained and sadly worried.

1051   They wrapped his body in finest silk. I doubt
That any eyes were dry. The queen cried out
In her heart's grief, Uta the nobly born,
Over the handsome knight. Her ladies helped her mourn.

1052   They heard from the minster now the sound of song.
He lay in state. There came a mighty throng—
What offerings they brought for his soul's repose!
He still had loyal friends, here among his foes.

1053   Poor Kriemhild spoke to her chamberlain. Said she:
"Let them take this trouble because of me,
All of those who wished him well and hold
Some love for me. For Sigfrid's soul, give out his gold!"

1054   No child of age to use his wits at all
Was left at home. Before the burial

They sang that day a hundred masses or more.
Crowds of Sigfrid's friends thronged the minster door.

1055 Mass was sung and done, the people gone,
And Kriemhild spoke, "Do not leave me alone,
To watch beside my perfect lord tonight.
All my joy is gone with him, and my delight.

1056 Three days and nights I wish him here in state,
To fill my heart with my sweet lord and mate.
And what if God command that death take me?
That at least would end my wretched misery."

1057 The townsfolk started on their homeward way,
But priests and monks the lady asked to stay,
And all his retinue who served her hero.
The night they spent was troubled, the day was full of
sorrow.

1058 Many stayed with not a thing to eat
Or drink. For those who wished, a lavish treat
Of food was set, proclaimed and all supplied
By royal Sigmund. Nibelung hearts were sorely tried.

1059 For all three days, they say, the clerics there,
Who knew the chants of mass, were forced to bear
The brunt of toil, but their reward was great.
Those who once were poor were now in rich estate.

1060 Needy men who had no gold were sent,
With money from Sigfrid's store, to the sacrament.
Since it was not his lot to live, they told
His treasure out for his soul, thousands of marks of gold.

1061   She granted in usufruct the lands around,
Wherever cloisters were or poor men found;
Silver and clothing she gave to those in need,
Proving her high esteem for him by her gracious deed.

1062   When the third morning came, and matinsong,
The square before the minster seemed to throng
In all its breadth, with weeping folk who brought
Homage even after death, as dear friends ought.

1063   In the space of four days, or so they say,
Thirty thousand marks were given away—
Maybe more—in alms for his soul's rest,
For now his manly beauty and his life lay waste.

1064   When God was served and mass was sung no longer,
Many struggled mightily to conquer
Pain untold. They had his body borne
From church to grave—for those who missed him most
 to mourn.

1065   With loud cries the crowd walked with him there—
No joy in man or woman, anywhere.
Before they buried him they sang and read.
The best of priests was there, for burial of the dead.

1066   Before his wife had reached the grave she fought
With grief so great that often people brought
Fresh water to bathe her face, for this affliction
Sent upon her spirit was harsh beyond description.

1067   It seems a miracle that she recovered,
Though many helped her mourn the loss she suffered.

Cried the queen, "By your fidelity,
Men of Sigfrid, grant this proof and grace to me:

1068 One little pleasure after all my pain,
That I may see his noble face again."
She begged in such a piteous way, so often,
They were forced at last to break his splendid coffin.

1069 They brought the queen to him. She took his head
In her white hands to raise it. Though he lay dead
She kissed him now, noble knight and good.
Because of all her pain, her shining eyes wept blood.

1070 This was their wretched parting. Now they bore
The queen away for she could walk no more
But lay in a deep swoon, his stately wife,
From sorrow that nearly cost her sweet and comely life.

1071 Now that they had buried him, a pain
Beyond all measure fell on every thane
From Nibelung land who had followed Sigfrid there,
And seldom did one see Lord Sigmund free of care.

1072 Some, for sorrow, three days long refused
To eat or drink at all, but so ill-used,
The body could not long endure, and then
Worry gave way to eating, as often it is with men.

✠ EIGHTEENTH ADVENTURE
How Sigmund Returned Home

1073   And then it was that Sigmund chose to come
To Kriemhild, saying: "We are going home.
We seem unwelcome guests here by the Rhine;
Beloved lady, come where all the land is mine!

1074   You and I have lost through breach of faith,
Here in this land, your husband done to death——
Why should you pay for that? I'll be your friend
For love of my son, so let your doubts be at an end.

1075   And you shall also have the power and might
That Sigfrid showed you once, that valiant knight.
Crown and country shall be at your command
And Sigfrid's men to serve you, whenever you demand."

1076   They told the men to ready their departure—
And now a hurried search for steed and charger,
For they were loath to stay with bitter foes.
They ordered maids and ladies to gather up their clothes.

1077   Now that Sigmund wished to be away,
Kriemhild's family pled with her to stay,
Remaining in her mother's company.
The gracious lady answered, "That could hardly be.

1078   How could my eyes endure the constant sight
Of him who hurt me so?" "It is only right,
By reason of loyalty if by no other,
My sister," said Giselher, "to stay here with your mother.

1079 You have no need of those who tried to rend
Your heart with care and grief. You shall depend
On my resources!" "I can't," she said. "The pain
And hurt would kill me if ever I saw Hagen again."

1080 "I'll see that you don't have to, sister dear,
Stay with Giselher your brother here,
And I shall make amends for your husband's fate."
Wretched Kriemhild cried, "Truly my need is great!"

1081 While Giselher in kindly words besought her,
Uta came, with Gernot, to beg her daughter
(As did her loyal friends) that she might stay:
Sigfrid's men were not her kin in any way.

1082 Gernot said, "You and they are strangers.
And no man lives so strong but time or dangers
Bring him down. Dear sister, ease your heart.
Reflect—and stay with your kin; this is the better part."

1083 She promised Giselher that she would stay.
Out the horses came; they were on their way,
Sigmund's men, to the land of Nibelung,
With all the gear of warriors loaded to take along.

1084 The king, Lord Sigmund, went to Kriemhild then
And said to her, "My lady, Sigfrid's men
Wait by their mounts—it is time for us to ride.
Burgundy is not for me." The lady replied:

1085 "The counsel all my loyal kinsmen give
Is to stay with them. I have no relative,
They say, in all the Nibelung domain."
What Sigmund heard from Kriemhild filled his heart
with pain.

1086   King Sigmund said, "Let no one tell you so!
You'll have the crown as before, and the powers that go
With wearing it, in presence of my kin.
I don't want you to suffer for our losing him.

1087   For sake of your boy, my lady, come with us.
You have no right to leave him fatherless.
Your growing son will be a comfort to you.
Meanwhile you'll have knights to serve you, brave and
    true."

1088   "Lord Sigmund, I cannot ride with you," said she.
"I must stay here, whatever happens to me—
Here with my own kin, to help me mourn."
(Words, it seemed to them, not to be lightly borne!)

1089   "Let us say to you," they all agreed,
"That we should feel most pained and wronged indeed
If you decide to stay here with our foes.
Heroes' journey never came to sadder close."

1090   "Go without fear," she said, "in God's kind hands!
Escort shall be yours to Sigmund's lands,
That you may ride in safety. I give to you
My dearest child in trust, believing you are true."

1091   Hearing thus that she would never leave,
All of Sigmund's men began to grieve—
Truly, a wretched parting this, the queen's
And royal Sigmund's, for now he learned what anguish
    means.

1092   "Cursed tourney!" cried the noble king.
"The pleasure of chivalry will never bring

The like on any king or his family.
Never again will you see us here in Burgundy."

1093   Sigfrid's men spoke plainly: "This country yet
May see us on the march if we should get
Certain proof by whom our lord was slain.
They shall not look for foes among his kin in vain!"

1094   Sigmund kissed Kriemhild and spoke in grief,
To know in truth that she would never leave:
"We ride, then, homeward. Our joys are scattered far.
And now at last I know how great my sorrows are."

1095   They rode from Worms to the Rhineland, unescorted.
You may be sure that they were so stout-hearted,
If they were set upon by enemies
They'd well defend themselves—valiant Nibelungs, these!

1096   They did not go to say farewell nor claim
Their leave of anyone. But Gernot came,
In kindness, to see the king, and Giselher.
His loss had touched them—of this they made him well
   aware.

1097   Gernot the prince spoke up, a man well-bred:
"God in heaven knows, though Sigfrid's dead,
I bear not even the blame of having known
Who hated him. To your lament I add my own."

1098   Young Giselher, who gave them good escort,
Led from the land the king and all his court
Of knights, in sorrow home to Netherland.
Little happiness they found in kin or friend!

1099   How their journey fared I cannot say,
But those at home heard Kriemhild every day
Weeping, and solaced by none in heart or mind—
Unless by Giselher, for he was staunch and kind.

1100   Brunhild the fair still held forth in pride.
Little did she care how Kriemhild cried—
For her she had no love or faith to offer.
(At Kriemhild's hands, in later days, she too would
    suffer!)

✠ NINETEENTH ADVENTURE
How the Treasure of the Nibelungs Came to Worms

1101 **W**ith Kriemhild left a widow, Eckewart stayed
At home with her, with all his men, and paid
Daily homage and service, so to afford
His lady help in frequent mourning of his lord.

1102 In Worms, by the church, they built her a building there;
Wide it was and large, costly and fair.
Here with all her suite she dwelt most sadly,
Though often she went to church, reverently and gladly.

1103 She hardly left the place her love was buried.
There in sorrow of heart she always hurried,
Asking the good Lord's mercy on his soul.
This was the hero's mourning—constant and heart-whole.

1104 Uta and her ladies tried to keep
Her spirits high; her heart's wound ran so deep
That nothing came of all their sympathy.
She longed for her beloved more insatiably

1105 Than ever woman for man, before or since.
(In this you see her proven excellence!)
She mourned till the end, as long as life endured,
But what a bold and thorough vengeance she secured!

1106 After the pain of her lord's death, it appears,
She lived alone for three and a half long years,

Never to speak to Gunther; never to see,
In all of that long time, Hagen her enemy.

1107   Said Trony now, "What of some arrangement
Devised to end your sister's long estrangement,
And bring the Nibelung gold to our domain?
If she were well disposed there might be much to gain."

1108   "We'll try," said Gunther. "Let my brothers, who spend
Much time with her, persuade her to be our friend—
Perhaps we'll get it without offending her."
"I do not think," said Hagen, "that such will ever occur!"

1109   He sent to court Sir Ortwin, then, for one,
And Margrave Gere another—which being done,
They brought in Gernot and young Giselher,
Who did their best to urge her, both with a friendly air.

1110   Bold Gernot of Burgundy addressed her so:
"You mourn too long. The King would have you know
It was not he by whom your lord was slain;
And yet we hear you mourn, my lady, in awfullest pain."

1111   "No one accuses him. Hagen got
From me the secret of the fatal spot—
And killed him! How," she cried, "was I to know,
When he came to me, that Hagen hated Sigfrid so?

1112   Else I should never have betrayed his life
And should not now be weeping—his wretched wife!
I'll never forgive the ones who did that deed."
Then the handsome Giselher began to plead.

1113 At last she promised, "I shall see the king."
With that, they saw him come to her and bring
His closest friends, but Hagen did not dare,
For he had done her harm, and the guilt was his to bear.

1114 When she renounced her hate for Gunther, this
(And doubly!) was the moment for his kiss.
Had she not been undone by schemes he laid,
He might have come before her lightly and unafraid.

1115 Never with more tears was peace regained
Among old friends, and still her sorrow pained.
But she forgave them all—all but one!
(Except for Hagen, there'd have been no murder done.)

1116 They so arranged it shortly afterward
That Lady Kriemhild got her treasure-hoard
From Nibelung land and brought it back to Worms.
This was her dowry money, and hers by any terms.

1117 Gernot went to get it, with Giselher.
Kriemhild bade eight thousand men prepare
To fetch the treasure from its hiding-place,
Where Alberich stood guard, and the best of Alberich's
race.

1118 The valiant dwarf soon saw the men of Rhine
Come for the hoard, and to his friends made sign:
"This treasure here we do not dare withhold.
The noble queen will claim it as her dowry gold.

1119 But this would not have happened," Alberich spoke,
"If we had never lost the Magic Cloak,

And Sigfrid, too, by wickedness and crime,
For Lady Kriemhild's lover wore it all the time.

1120   And now he falls a prey to evil thus,
Because he took the Magic Cloak from us
And forced this land to bear him fealty."
With this the steward turned and went to get the key.

1121   Kriemhild's vassals stood by the great hill,
With her several kin. Down to the sea, to fill
The little ships, they bore the treasure in line
And carried it over the waves, up the river Rhine.

1122   Now hear the wondrous measure of the hoard:
All that twelve wagons could load aboard,
In four days and nights, and haul away
From the mountain, each one making three good trips a
  day!

1123   Nothing but jewels and gold! And had they paid
Every person there, it would have weighed
Not less than half a pound, each portion of it.
Such treasure Hagen had no lack of cause to covet!

1124   (The best lay underneath: a wand of gold—
Understand its nature and you would hold
The world in sway and every man therein!)
Now Gernot left, and with him many of Alberich's kin.

1125   When they had got the treasure to Gunther's land
And Lady Kriemhild took it all in hand,
It filled the palace rooms and many a tower.
Never had people known such endless wealth and power.

1126   Yet had there been a thousand times as much—
If Sigfrid were restored to sight and touch,
With empty hands she would have stood at his side.
No warrior ever found himself a truer bride.

1127   She drew to the land, now that she had the treasure,
Unnumbered foreign knights. She gave in measure
So unstinting they never in all their days
Saw such bounty. For merit and worth they sang her
praise.

1128   To poor and rich she now commenced to give
So freely Hagen said if she should live
For any time she'd soon have every stranger
Bound to her in service—for them a mortal danger.

1129   Said Gunther, "Her person is hers, and her property.
Whatever she does with it, don't look to me
To interfere! We two are barely friends.
Forget who shares her silver and gold, and what she
spends."

1130   Hagen said to the king, "A prudent man
Would leave no part of this hoard to a woman who can,
With generous giving, bring about the day
That bold men rue it all—as we of Burgundy may!"

1131   "I swore to her an oath," cried Gunther the king,
"That I would cause her no more suffering.
She is my sister. That oath I'll not disclaim!"
Hagen spoke once more, "Then let me take the blame."

1132   All their oaths were broken. Her vast wealth
They took from her, a widow; Hagen, by stealth,

Got the key to it all. When Gernot learned
The true account of this, a brother's temper burned.

1133   Said Giselher, "Hagen has done my sister wrong.
I should have stopped it! He'd not live for long,
I swear, if he were not blood-kin to me."
Kriemhild renewed her tears. Said Gernot, "Are we to be

1134   Forever weighted down beneath this blanket
Of gold? We'd do better if we sank it
In the Rhine—and let it be no man's!"
The queen had come to her brother; she spoke with a
    piteous glance:

1135   "Dear Giselher, my brother, remember me,
And be my guardian in life and property!"
"It shall be so, I promise," he replied,
"When we come back again. But first we mean to ride."

1136   And now the king and his kinsmen left the country,
And with them rode all the finest gentry,
But Hagen alone, who stayed, for the enmity
He bore the Lady Kriemhild—he did it willingly!

1137   Before the mighty king returned once more,
Hagen had taken all the treasure-store
To Lochheim, there to sink it in the Rhine.
(He hoped to use it later—that was not fate's design.)

1138   The princes now, and their many men, returned,
As Kriemhild with all her maids and ladies mourned
For her great loss; it pained them bitterly.
Giselher would gladly have proved his loyalty.

222

1139   All together said, "He has done great wrong."
But Hagen, evading the princes' wrath so long,
At last regained their favor. They let him be;
But never had Kriemhild hated him more bitterly.

1140   Before the lord of Trony hid the gold
They pledged with mighty oaths that they would hold
The treasure secret till every man was gone—
Never one of them to have it, nor pass it on.

1141   The pain of her husband's death revived and throbbed
Within her breast, as now they even robbed
Her worldly goods. This plaint was never stilled
In all her life, until her span of days was filled.

1142   After Sigfrid's murder, it appears,
She lived in deepest grief for thirteen years,
And never could forget her master's death.
Her faith to him was known the country's length and
    breadth.

PART II

How King Attila Sent to Burgundy for Kriemhild

1143 This was the time when Lady Helke died
And King Attila sought a second bride.
His friends proposed a noble widow who came
From the land of Burgundy—and Kriemhild was her
name.

1144 Since lovely Helke now had left this life,
They urged, "If ever you would win a wife,
The best and noblest any king has won,
Then take this lady, once the wife of Sigmund's son."

1145 The king replied, "I don't see how I can,
For I am unbaptized, a pagan man.
And she who is a Christian will not agree.
What a miracle if that could ever be!"

1146 But his bold knights rejoined, "Perhaps she would;
Because your wealth is great and your name is good.
One ought at least to venture asking her.
Think of the happy feeling so sweet a love would stir!"

1147 The king inquired, "Who among you knows
Land and people where the Rhine flows?"
Good Ruedeger of Pöchlarn spoke, "I've known
That high and gracious queen since she was a girl half-
grown;

1148   And Gunther and Gernot, highborn, worthy lords;
The third is Giselher. In deeds and words
They strive to merit glory and high fame,
And always in the past their forebears did the same."

1149   Attila said, "Tell me this, my friend:
Is she the one to wear the crown in my land?
For if she is as fair as I hear say,
My closest friends and kin will not regret the day."

1150   "In beauty she is like my lady, sir,
Like mighty Helke; none to rival her
Among the queens of all the world around.
Whoever wins her hand—his happiness is crowned."

1151   "Then as you love me, Ruedeger," he cried,
"Take up this task. If ever at my side
The lady lies, I'll give, as best I can,
A fit reward. You will have well fulfilled my plan.

1152   Out of my stores I'll see that they provide
All the clothes you want and steeds to ride,
To keep you happy—and the men of your company.
All this I order done for you on your embassy."

1153   Ruedeger replied, the great margrave,
"Such help would be a shameful thing to crave.
I'll be your messenger to Rhenish lands
At my own cost in goods, which I have from your hands."

1154   Asked the mighty king, "When will you go
For my fair queen? May God in glory bestow
Safety to you on the trip—to my lady, too;
And Fortune grant me this, that she should smile on you."

1155   Said Ruedeger, "Before we leave the land,
The arms and dress we take must first be planned,
To gain from kings respect and dignity.
I want five hundred men to take to the Rhine with me,

1156   That Burgundy, in seeing me and mine,
May then concede: Never were sent to the Rhine
By any king so many men, so far,
Or better fitted out than these of Attila's are.

1157   Not wishing, Sire, to turn your purpose aside—
She was Sigfrid's once, his noble bride—
The son of Sigmund, you have seen him here;
One says but simple truth to make his glory clear."

1158   "What if she was his wife?" the king returned.
"Such was the great distinction Sigfrid earned
That I could never think her of low degree.
And for her loveliness she greatly pleases me."

1159   "I'll tell you then," Ruedeger went on,
"Twenty-four days from now, and we'll be gone.
Soon I shall see my wife and say to her:
Your word shall go to Kriemhild with me as messenger."

1160   He sent to Pöchlarn news for the margravine
That he would leave to sue for the hand of a queen,
A wife for Attila. Sad, yet happy too,
She thought of lovely Helke and the sweet love they knew.

1161   So Gotelind heard of the trip, and sorrow swept
Upon her at the thought. She rightly wept.
What lady could be like her queen before?

Whenever she thought of Helke, her inmost heart was
    sore.

1162   In seven days the margrave rode away
From Hungary. Attila's heart was gay.
There in Vienna town their clothes were made,
So Ruedeger was loath to have his trip delayed.

1163   In Pöchlarn they were waiting, margravine
And margrave's daughter both, the child all keen
To see her father, the men of Ruedeger—
Many lovely girls happily waiting there!

1164   Before the margrave left Vienna behind,
To go to Pöchlarn, clothes of every kind
Were loaded on their beasts. Little wonder,
Escorted as they were, that nothing fell to plunder.

1165   Reaching Pöchlarn now, the lord requested
Shelter for his friends. Soon they rested,
By his kindness, each in a decent room.
Gotelind was glad to see her master home.

1166   And his dear daughter, the young margravine—
For her his coming never could have been
Sweeter than now. And the Huns—with what delight
She met these knights! The maiden cried, her spirits
    bright:

1167   "All welcome to my father and his men!"
She earned a burst of gracious thanking then
From many zealous knights. And Gotelind
Herself was well aware of her master's state of mind.

230

1168   She lay that night at the side of Ruedeger.
With tender questioning, she asked him where
The King of Huns had ordered him to go.
"My lady Gotelind, I shall gladly let you know.

1169   My mission is to seek another bride
For my liege-lord, since lovely Helke has died;
I ride to where the Rhine river runs—
For Kriemhild, who shall be the great queen of the Huns."

1170   "Such favor," Gotelind said, "may God confer!
We hear so many splendid things of her,
We may in time place her in my lady's stead
And gladly see the Hunnish crown upon her head."

1171   The margrave spoke, "My dear, these men who go
To the Rhine with us—to them I beg you show
Your generous wealth and sweet desire to share it.
When heroes travel richly, they travel bright in spirit."

1172   "To every one of them, if he will choose,
I'll gladly give whatever he can use,"
Said she, "before you leave with your company."
The margrave said, "Your kindness greatly pleases me."

1173   What silks they brought from her chambers, splendid furs
In linings neatly sewn from neck to spurs,
And these she gave the knights in generous share,
For they were the men he wanted, the choice of Ruedeger.

1174   They rode from Pöchlarn at dawn of the seventh day,
The host and his knights, well laden on their way
With arms and clothing through Bavarian lands,
Yet they were not attacked en route by robber bands.

231

1175 Within twelve days they reached the Rhine, and word
Of this could not be hid; they soon had heard,
The king and all his men, that guests had come
From foreign lands. The king then asked if there were
some

1176 Who knew these men, that they should tell him so.
The heavy load their sumpters bore would show
That they were men of wealth. They brought them down
Without delay to lodgings in the ample town.

1177 And when they had the strangers settled there
They all began to wonder, most aware
Of these new men, whence they might have come.
The king of the Rhineland asked if Hagen knew their
home.

1178 "I have not seen them yet," said Trony's lord,
"But soon we shall, and I give you my word:
Wherever they came here from, these mounted men,
They must be foreign indeed, to be beyond my ken."

1179 The strangers now were lodged and settled down,
The messenger got dressed in his splendid gown,
His company as well, and rode to court—
Cut by a master, theirs were clothes of the finest sort.

1180 Bold Hagen spoke, "As far as I can tell—
I have not seen this man in a long, long while—
The way they look it might be Ruedeger
Of Hunnish lands, a lord most valorous and fair."

1181 "What?" said the king. "Am I to understand
That Pöchlarn's lord has come to this, my land?"—

A question Gunther the king had barely broached
When Hagen saw indeed that Ruedeger approached.

1182　He and all his friends went out in force,
As five hundred men got down from horse.
Lords from Hunnish lands were welcomed well.
Of clothes more elegant than theirs no man could tell.

1183　Hagen of Trony's words were loud and clear:
"God give welcome to all you warriors here,
Regent of Pöchlarn, men of your company!"
(A greeting for Hunnish heroes, in honor and dignity.)

1184　The king's own next of kin drew near the place
Where Ortwin spoke to Ruedeger, face to face:
"Never in all our days—I swear it's true—
Have we seen guests," he said, "as welcome here as you."

1185　For greetings given now they thanked them all
And with their suite entered the door of the hall.
There they found the king and his company;
He rose up from his seat, in greatest courtesy,

1186　And went to them. What perfect form in greeting!
He and Gernot showed their zeal in meeting
Properly their guest and his noble band.
The king took Ruedeger and led him by the hand.

1187　He brought him to his seat, at his own side
And bade them serve (which they did with pride)
Excellent mead, and the very finest wine
That ever they could find in lands around the Rhine.

1188 Giselher and Gere both appeared.
Dankwart and Folker heard, their hearts were cheered
By news of the strangers there. They came to bring
Their greetings to well-born knights, in presence of the
  king.

1189 Hagen of Trony spoke, and said to his lord,
"Our vassals here should render fit reward
For kindness done us by the margrave's aid.
The husband of fair Gotelind deserves to be repaid."

1190 Gunther spoke, "One thing I must say:
Tell me how it goes with them, I pray—
King Attila and Helke of Hungary."
Margrave Ruedeger spoke, "I'll tell you willingly."

1191 With all his men he rose and left his seat,
Addressing the king, "If it is right and meet
To give me leave, my lord, abandoning
My silence now I'll gladly tell the news I bring."

1192 Gunther said, "Whatever news you have
For me and my men, speak! I give you leave
To tell us—I'll not call my friends in session,
But grant you full respect, to carry out your mission."

1193 Boldly the messenger spoke, "My sovereign sends
His loyal faith to you and all the friends
That you may have, here by the river Rhine.
My mission to you is also a true and faithful sign.

1194 My king has asked that his grievous case be said:
His people joyless, and my lady dead,
Mighty Helke, wife of my noble lord,
And orphaned by loss of her, many a maid, her ward:

234

1195   Children of highborn princes, reared by her hand!
From this the misery stems that fills our land,
For they have none to care and none to tend.
My sovereign's sorrow, I think, will have no early end."

1196   "God's grace to him," said Gunther, "that he sends,
With such good will, to me and all my friends
His pledge of faith. I'm pleased to hear from him.
We hope to merit his regard, my men and kin."

1197   Champion of Burgundy, Lord Gernot, said,
"Helke's death the world may well regret,
With all the excellence that she displayed."
Hagen and others seconded the speech he made.

1198   Said Ruedeger, the noble emissary,
"Since you permit, my lord, the message I carry
From my beloved master I shall speak.
For him, since Helke's dying, everything is bleak.

1199   They tell him Sigfrid is dead, and in his place
Kriemhild has no husband. If this is the case,
And if you grant permission, she shall wear
The crown among his knights. This is the message I bear."

1200   The great king spoke (his manner most refined):
"She'll hear my wishes, if she is so inclined;
Within three days from now I'll let you know.
Before I question her, why should I say no?"

1201   Meanwhile they saw to the comfort of every guest.
So well they served him, Ruedeger confessed
He found good friends in Gunther's men of war.
Hagen was kind to him, as he to him before.

1202   So Ruedeger remained till the third day.
The king requested counsel—the wisest way—
Whether it seemed to his kin a proper thing
That Kriemhild should be married to Attila the king.

1203   All advised him so, but Hagen not.
He spoke to Gunther the king, "If you have got
Your wits about you, this will never be.
And she must be prevented, even if she agree!"

1204   "And why," said Gunther, "should I not concur?
Whatever pleasant thing can come to her
I ought to grant. She is after all my sister.
Whatever serves her greater good we ought to foster."

1205   Hagen replied, "This much and I am through:
If you could know Attila as I do—
Let her marry him as you have said,
And you'll be inviting troubles heaped upon your head!"

1206   "And why?" said Gunther. "I shall take good care
To stay away from him, and need not fear
His enmity, though she should be his wife."
"I'll never agree to that," said Hagen, "in all my life."

1207   They sent for Gernot and Giselher, to see
Whether these two lords would not agree
That Kriemhild ought to wed the mighty Hun.
Hagen still opposed, but not another one.

1208   Spoke young Giselher of Burgundy,
"Now is the chance to show your loyalty,
Friend Hagen; make up to her for all the pain

236

You caused nor grudge her what good fortune she may
gain.

1209 So numerous are the wrongs that you have done
To hurt my sister," Giselher went on,
"That if she hates you, what could surprise you less?
Never was woman robbed of so much happiness."

1210 "One thing I know, and tell you," Hagen said.
"Should she live long enough to go and wed
King Attila, her plotting will bring us harm,
For she will then be served by many a man's strong arm."

1211 In answer to Hagen, valiant Gernot cried,
"It may well not occur until they've died
That we should ever go to Attila's land.
For sake of our noble name, lend her our loyal hand!"

1212 Hagen said, "No man can talk me down.
If ever Kriemhild wears Queen Helke's crown
She'll do us ill, however she may start it.
All you lords would be far better advised to thwart it."

1213 Giselher, Uta's son, in anger gave
His answer: "All of us needn't play the knave.
If honors come to her, our hearts should fill
With joy. I'll serve her truly, Hagen, say what you will."

1214 Hagen listened, in a somber mood.
Gernot and Giselher, proud and good,
And powerful Gunther joined at last to advise
Consent without ill will, if Kriemhild found it wise.

1215   Prince Gere said, "I'll tell my lady this:
Not to take Attila's suit amiss—
Lord in awful liege of many a knight,
Whatever wrong she suffers, he can make it right."

1216   He went to Kriemhild then. In gentle meeting
She received him. "Well may you grant me greeting,"
He cried, "and herald's pay for what I bring.
Good fortune comes to ease you of all your suffering.

1217   For sake of your love, my lady, one of the best
Who ever wore a crown or yet possessed
A king's domain in honor has sent to us
Noble lords as suitors. Your brother informs you thus."

1218   "May God forbid," this wretched woman cried,
"That you or any of my kin deride
My sorrow. What would a man want of me,
If ever his heart enjoyed a good wife's company?"

1219   And so she was opposed. But later came
Her brothers Gernot and Giselher, to claim
That she should be consoled and not demur:
If she were to wed the king, all would be well with her.

1220   That she should ever give a man her love
Was more than they could all persuade her of.
The lords then begged, "To this at least defer,
If nothing else, and deign to see your messenger."

1221   The noble lady said, "I shall not claim
I do not wish to see him, since Ruedeger came,
So excellent a man. If it were not he,
But any other herald, he'd not lay eyes on me.

1222   Tomorrow morning ask if he will be
       At my apartments. He shall hear from me
       My will in this, which I shall then declare."
       And thus it was all renewed, her tears and great despair.

1223   Noble Ruedeger wished for nothing more
       Than to see the gracious queen, for on this score
       He knew himself so skilled, that if she waited
       For his visit, she could surely be persuaded.

1224   Next morning early, after matin-song,
       The noble heralds came, a mighty throng,
       With Ruedeger to court—and what a sight
       To see in such apparel so many a splendid knight!

1225   The gracious Kriemhild, sad of heart, was there
       To wait the noble herald, Ruedeger.
       He found her in mourning dressed as for every day,
       While all her suite was clad in the most expensive way.

1226   She went to meet him, standing by the door,
       Welcoming King Attila's men—no more
       Than twelve in all went in. What courtesies
       Were offered them! She never saw such heralds as these.

1227   Lord and vassals sat, upon her order.
       Standing before the queen, two Counts of the Border,
       Eckewart and Gere, took their place.
       Because of their lady-liege, there was not a cheerful face.

1228   Lovely women sat at her feet, while she,
       In constant plaint, renewed her misery.
       The clothes before her breasts were wet with tears.
       (And none of this escaped the margrave's eyes and ears.)

239

1229   "Child of a noble king," said the messenger,
       "On me and those who came with me confer
       Permission to stand before you and declare
       The tidings we bring to you, for which we journeyed
          here."

1230   "Say what you wish, you have the leave you require,
       Noble herald. Such is my desire
       That I shall gladly hear." But all the rest
       Could clearly sense: she seemed unwilling and distressed.

1231   The prince of Pöchlarn spoke, "A glorious king,
       Noble Attila, loyally bids us bring
       Expression of his regard to you in this land.
       My lady, he sends good knights to ask for your love and
          hand.

1232   He offers you affection, sweet and free
       Of any pain, and pledges constancy
       Such as he had for Helke, his heart's love,
       Whose merit he spends bitter hours thinking of."

1233   The queen replied, "Margrave Ruedeger,
       If anyone knew the sharp pain I bear,
       He would not ask that I should marry again:
       I lost the finest husband a woman could ever win."

1234   "What makes up for pain," the prince declared,
       "But joy of friendship, if one be so prepared,
       And find another one who suits the part?
       For nothing so avails against distress of heart.

1235   And if you deign to wed my noble lord
       The power of twelve great crowns is your reward.

He'll give you thirty princes' share of land,
All of whom were conquered by his most valiant hand.

1236   Many worthy men will acknowledge you
Their mistress, who once were Helke's retinue,
And many ladies born of princely rank,
Over whom she ruled." He spoke on, bold and frank:

1237   "If you consent, my lord the king assures,
To wear the crown at his side, this too is yours:
Of powers that Helke had, the uttermost,
The mighty fealty of all of Attila's host."

1238   The queen replied, "How in all my life
Should I desire to be a hero's wife?
In one, death hurt me so that I shall cherish
In my heart the grievous pain, until I perish."

1239   The Huns spoke up, "Queen of power and grace,
Your life with him will be so full of praise
That you will have great joy, if it comes to be;
For the king has many lords of charm and dignity.

1240   If Helke's maids in waiting and yours could be
Together in a single company,
Heroes' hearts would glory in the sight.
Take our word, oh queen, all things will turn out right."

1241   With perfect presence she said, "Let this be all
Until tomorrow morning, then pay your call,
And I shall give you the answer you ask of me."
(What could gallant warriors do except agree?)

1242   When they had all returned to their quarters there,
The lady sent for Uta and Giselher.
She told them both, her mother and her brother:
The one right course for her was weeping—there was no
    other.

1243   Giselher answered, "Sister, I am told—
And would believe—that all your pain of old
King Attila would banish, once you wed.
I think you should, whatever others may have said.

1244   His power to give redress or aid," said he,
"Extends from Rhone to Rhine, from Elbe to sea.
There is no other king of equal might.
If he espouses you, rejoice, with every right!"

1245   "Brother dear, why give me such advice?
Mourning and tears are far the better choice.
In courtly life how could I carry on?
Perhaps I once had beauty, that is past and gone."

1246   Lady Uta addressed her daughter, too:
"What your brother counsels, dear child, do!
Follow your friends, and see if good may be.
I've seen you live so long in the depths of misery."

1247   She asked and begged of God that he not withhold
The means to be generous: silver, garments, gold,
As it was when he was alive, her lord the prince;
Never had she enjoyed such happy moments since.

1248   She thought in her heart, "Christian as I am,
Can I betroth myself to a pagan man?
As long as I live I'd feel the great disgrace.

Though he gave me all his realm, it is more than I can
   face."

1249   And there she left it. All the night till day
Deep in many thoughts, the lady lay
Upon her bed, her bright eyes never dried,
Until she went to matins again, at morningtide.

1250   They came in time for mass, the kings of the land,
Meaning to take their sister again in hand.
They counselled her to marry the royal Hun,
But all of them found that lady a most unhappy one!

1251   They now sent out to gather Attila's men,
Who wished for leave to go back home again,
With yes or no, however it might be;
Ruedeger came to court, met by his company.

1252   To make the test of the noble prince's mind,
And do it soon—so were they all inclined.
Back home, they said, was a long way to fare.
They found where Kriemhild was and took Lord Ruede-
   ger there.

1253   The knight began to entreat, but gently so,
Begging the noble queen to let him know
What answer to King Attila she would choose.
It seemed that she could still do nothing but refuse;

1254   For she would never love another man.
The margrave cried, "That is the poorest plan!
Why should you want to ruin so fair a life?
With honor and homage still you can be a good man's
   wife."

1255 Their pleading did no good, till Ruedeger
Assured the queen, in trust alone with her:
Whatever wrongs she suffered, he'd requite.
On the darkness of her grief there seemed to fall some
  light.

1256 He said to the queen, "Let this weeping be.
If you had among the Huns no one but me,
Beside my loyal kin, and my retinue,
A man would pay for any harm he did to you."

1257 Her mind was now relieved in good degree.
"Swear me an oath, whatever is done to me,
That you will be the first to avenge my hurt."
The margrave said, "On that, milady, you have my word."

1258 The margrave joined with all his men, in swearing
To serve her loyally for ever, declaring
She would never lack, in Attila's land,
For homage of excellent knights, the pledge of Ruedeger's
  hand.

1259 The faithful woman thought, "Since I have found
So many friends, let people all around,
Who see me wretched, say what they wish to say.
What if my lord's dear life should be avenged some day?

1260 If Attila has as many men as these
And they are mine to command, I'll do as I please;
And surely he's so rich that I can be free
In giving, though evil Hagen took my wealth from me."

1261 She said to Ruedeger, "Could I but know
That he was not a heathen, I'd gladly go,

Following his will, and we'd be wed."
"Speak no more of this, my lady," the margrave said.

1262   "So many of his knights are Christians now,
You'll suffer no remorse with him—and how
If you should bring about that he were christened?
Your reason to marry the king is not in this way lessened."

1263   Her brothers cried again, "Sister, agree,
And let this show of your displeasure be."
They begged so long, until the sorrowful one
Promised in their presence she would wed the Hun.

1264   "Poor queen that I am," she said, "I will comply
And go among the Huns, but I must try
To find some friends to take me to his land."
On this, in heroes' presence, Kriemhild gave her hand.

1265   Margrave Ruedeger spoke, "If you have two,
I have more beside, and that will do
To take you across the Rhine in propriety.
Lady, you should no longer stay in Burgundy.

1266   Five hundred of my men and kin will afford
Good service here, and will at home accord
With every wish, milady, and I the same,
Whenever you remind me, that I may bear no shame.

1267   Have them now prepare your riding gear—
You shall never regret what I counselled here—
Inform the maids you want to take with you;
For excellent knights will join us as we travel through."

1268   They still had jeweled harness they used to use
In Sigfrid's time. In honor, she could choose

Many maids to go, when she was ready.
They found a perfect saddle for every lovely lady.

1269   Whether they ever wore rich clothes before,
They had a plenty now for the trip in store,
Because of the king, of whom all people talked.
They opened boxes now which always had been locked.

1270   No idle hour till nearly the sixth day!
They took from garment bags whatever lay
Within their folds. Kriemhild came to unbar
Her treasury, making Ruedeger's men richer by far.

1271   She still had some of the gold from Nibelung land—
She wished the Huns to have it from her own hand—
More than any hundred horses could hold.
This was Kriemhild's plan, and Hagen heard it told.

1272   "She'll never waste her love on me, that's plain,
So Sigfrid's gold must not leave our domain.
Why should I hand my foes such revenue?
With treasure like this," he said, "I know what she would
do.

1273   If once she got it there, it's plain to see,
It soon would be paid out for hate of me.
Beside, they don't have horses to carry the gold.
Hagen will keep it all—so let Kriemhild be told."

1274   She heard this news; it pained her bitterly.
The same was also told the kings, all three,
Who gladly would have stopped it. This came to naught,
But noble Ruedeger proposed this happy thought:

1275   "Mighty queen, why lament your gold?
Attila has for you a love untold,
And when his eyes shall once behold you there,
He'll give you more than you can ever spend, I swear."

1276   "Good Ruedeger," the queen replied at last,
"No king's daughter ever had so vast
A wealth of riches as Hagen took from me."
But then her brother Gernot went to her treasury,

1277   And set to the door, by royal right, the key,
Passed out her gold, as great a quantity
As thirty thousand pounds, or more, and bade
The guests receive it all. This made Gunther glad.

1278   Lord of Pöchlarn, Gotelind's husband, cried,
"Now if my lady wants it kept aside—
All that was ever taken from Nibelung land—
It need not ever be touched by mine or the queen's own
    hand.

1279   So have it put away, for I want none.
I brought along with me so much of my own
That we shall have, for the road, a good surplus.
Fare for the journey back stands splendidly with us."

1280   Her maids had packed a dozen boxes full
Of golden things, in all this interval—
The best there were; and these they carried thence,
And for the ladies' journey many ornaments.

1281   Stunned by the force of fierce Hagen's works,
She kept as an offering a thousand marks

247

And spent it for her beloved husband's soul,
Playing, to Ruedeger's mind, a loyal woman's role.

1282   Spoke the mourning queen, "Where are my friends,
Who, for me, will live beyond the ends
Of home and ride to the land of Huns with me?
Take my money and buy them horses and livery."

1283   Kriemhild heard the Margrave Eckewart call:
"Since I became your vassal first of all,
I've served you loyally," the warrior cried,
"And will, until the end, continue at your side.

1284   I'll take five hundred of my men, in faith
And trust to grant you service. But for death,
No force shall ever make us separate."
For the words he spoke she bowed to him. Her need was
    great.

1285   Then they brought the steeds, for they were leaving;
One heard their many friends deeply grieving,
Uta the mighty and many a fair maid,
So great was the pain at losing her which they displayed!

1286   A hundred splendid maids she took, attired
In every way as dignity required;
The tears ran coursing down from their bright eyes.
(Attila's court would one day bring her many joys.)

1287   Then, as breeding willed and courtly manners,
Came Gernot and Giselher with their retainers,
On their dear sister's leaving, to give escort.
They brought a thousand handsome men, knights at court.

248

1288   Neither Gere nor Ortwin stayed behind,
Nor Kitchener Rumold either. Night would find
They'd reached the Danube, there to settle down.
(The farthest Gunther rode was just outside the town.)

1289   Before they left the Rhine, they'd sent ahead
The swiftest heralds to the Huns, who said
To royal Attila: Ruedeger had seen
And won as wife for him the high and gracious queen.

✠ TWENTY-FIRST ADVENTURE
How Kriemhild Went among the Huns

1290   Let the heralds ride, and we shall say
     How through this country Kriemhild made her way,
     And where Gernot and Giselher retired,
     Having served her well, as loyalty required.

1291   They rode along to the Danube shore at Pförring,
     There to take leave of her, no longer caring
     To be kept from riding back—except
     That even this must have its cost, and good friends wept.

1292   Said Giselher, a man of bravery:
     "Whenever, sister you have need of me—
     If ever you're in trouble, I shall go
     To Attila's land to help you—only let me know."

1293   Kin of hers she kissed upon their lips.
     Numerous sweet farewells for homeward trips
     There were for Margrave Ruedeger's men-at-arms
     The queen had many maids along, of many charms!

1294   How richly dressed they were, all hundred four,
     In ornate, patterned silks! And warriors bore,
     As they walked along the path, where the ladies were,
     Broad shields in hand; till the gallant lords took leave of
       her.

1295   Down through Bavarian lands their journey stretched,
     News of unknown guests advancing reached

The place where a cloister-house has always been,
Down where the Danube takes the waters of the Inn.

1296   A bishop dwelt in the town of Passau there,
But princely court and burgher's house stood bare,
As people sought their guests, in haste to get
Up to Bavaria, where Bishop Pilgrim and Kriemhild met.

1297   Knights of the land were not annoyed to see
The comely maidens in her coterie—
Their eyes paid court to daughters of high lords.
(They found for these noble guests good lodging after
    wards.)

1298   The bishop rode to Passau with his niece.
They soon informed the burghers of the place
That Kriemhild came, his sister Uta's daughter—
And what a flood of greetings all the merchants brought
    her!

1299   It was the bishop's hope they might remain
But Eckewart said, "That wish is all in vain.
We have to go on down to Ruedeger's lands:
Many lords expect us—the news is in their hands."

1300   Of this the lovely Gotelind was aware,
Who with her highborn child made haste to prepare,
As Ruedeger asked and as to him seemed right:
That they might thus provide the queen with much de-
    light,

1301   Riding out to meet her, with his thanes,
As far as the river Enns. Roads and lanes
On every hand were far from standing idle,
While they went out to meet their guests, on foot or saddle.

1302   By now the queen had come to Eferding.
Bavarian folk, had they a mind to cling
To ancient custom, could have brought the dangers
Of highway robbery and harm upon the strangers.

1303   This the margrave took good care to prevent.
He had at least a thousand knights who went
With him and Gotelind his wife. She, too,
Had many noble thanes in her splendid retinue.

1304   When they had crossed the river Traun and reached
The field beside the Enns, tents were pitched
And awnings, for the guests to spend the night—
Ruedeger provided for his guests' delight.

1305   Fair Gotelind had left her house behind;
Many steeds of noble stature lined
The roads and walked along with jingling reins.
Ruedeger was pleased, their welcome spared no pains.

1306   On either side, riding to merit praise,
Came many warriors, honoring the ways
Of chivalry, in games that maidens attended—
An office of knighthood by which the queen was not
    offended.

1307   When Ruedeger's men came into the strangers' view,
In spirit of knighthood a host of splinters flew
From warriors' hands high in the very skies—
They rode for praise and glory, before the ladies' eyes.

1308   In kindness now these many knights forsook
Their games to greet each other. Then they took

The lovely Gotelind to see Kriemhild,
As men who honored women found every moment filled.

1309 The lord of Pöchlarn rode to see his wife.
That he'd returned unharmed, in health and life,
From the Rhine, was no regret to her, for now
Her sorrow seemed removed, and joy in its place some-
how.

1310 She greeted him. He bade her be dismounted
Upon the turf, with all the women she counted
In her company. For men of birth,
No idle moments—of service to ladies, little dearth!

1311 Now that Lady Kriemhild once had seen
With all her retinue the margravine,
She'd not go on, but drawing her horse's rein,
Asked to be lifted quickly from the saddle again.

1312 Now the bishop, leading his sister's daughter,
With good Count Eckewart as escort, brought her
To Lady Gotelind. With backward steps,
The crowd made way, as Kriemhild kissed her on her
lips.

1313 Said Ruedeger's lady, sweetly, "How I prize
Dear lady, this good fortune that my eyes
Behold you here in this land. Past or present,
Truly, I can think of nothing half so pleasant."

1314 Said Kriemhild, "Noble lady, may God bless you.
If I stay safe and well—and Attila too—
For our encounter you may sometime be glad."
(Neither woman knew what shape the future had!)

1315   Now came, politely meeting, many a maid,
Receiving knightly homage, gladly paid.
Their greeting done, they sat on the clover lawn—
Friends to many now they never before had known.

1316   Wine was served the ladies. The time was noon;
The court would stay no longer. Riding soon,
They came where many spacious tents were ready—
Willing service there for strangers, lord and lady.

1317   They rested through the night, till break of day.
Men of Pöchlarn had to find some way
To shelter all their august visitors.
If little enough was lacking, the credit was Ruedeger's.

1318   Along the walls, the windows stood ajar—
The town was open wide! Guests from afar,
And welcome there, rode in through Pöchlarn's gate.
Their noble host provided shelter in fitting state.

1319   Ruedeger's own daughter went to greet
The queen most graciously, with all her suite.
Her mother, too, the margrave's wife, attended.
How kind a welcome to these maidens they extended!

1320   They took each other by the hand and went
To a most lovely palace of vast extent,
Beneath which flowed the Danube. Here with the breeze
To blow on them they sat and took their pleasure and ease.

1321   What other things they did I cannot say.
The knights of Kriemhild chafed at this delay
Which slowed their trip—it cast their spirits down.
What stalwart men went with them when they left the
town!

1322   The margrave was kind in offer of homage and honor.
     His daughter took what the queen bestowed upon her:
     Lovely clothes and twelve red-gold armbands,
     Gifts as good as any she took to Attila's lands.

1323   Though she had been deprived of the Nibelung gold,
     All who saw her there were soon enrolled
     In her support, for with the little left,
     She gave her host's retainers each a generous gift.

1324   Lady Gotelind in turn conferred
     Such honors on her Rhenish friends one heard
     Of scarcely any guest who did not wear
     Some splendid dress of hers or precious jewel there.

1325   When they had eaten and prepared to go,
     The mistress of the palace came to show
     Most loyal homage to King Attila's bride;
     And she in turn embraced her lovely child, who cried:

1326   "My Queen, whenever you are so inclined,
     I know my dearest father would not mind
     Sending me to you, among the Huns."
     The girl's sincere devotion Kriemhild felt at once.

1327   Their steeds were ready now and stood in view
     Of Pöchlarn's gates. The queen now bade adieu
     To Ruedeger's wife and daughter. Demoiselles
     Of greatest beauty took their leave with sweet farewells.

1328   (Rarely, in time to come, would they behold
     One another!) From Melk, in cups of gold
     Flashing on outstretched arms, men carried wine
     For the strangers on the road—this was their welcome
       sign.

1329   The lord who lived there was Astold by name—
He pointed out the road by which they came
To Austria, down the Danube, toward the spot
Called Mautern. What a royal welcome Kriemhild got!

1330   The bishop parted fondly from his niece.
How eagerly he wished her joy and peace,
And honor there to equal Helke's honor.
Oh, what splendid homage the Huns would shower upon
   her!

1331   They took the strangers to the banks of Traisen,
With Ruedeger's men to guide, till in due season
Came the Huns, riding overland.
There she found what lavish honors they had planned.

1332   Beside the Traisen was a castle-town
Owned by the Hunnish king, widely known
And called Traismauer—where Helke lived before
In perfect merit such as the world would see no more,

1333   Except for Kriemhild, who could give in measure
Such that after all her pain some pleasure
Still was hers—and homage rendered, too,
By King Attila's men, in full and generous due.

1334   Attila's power was granted far around,
Whence at all times in his court were found
The most courageous knights that Christendom
Or heathen countries knew—and all of these had come.

1335   Under his rule (but scarcely any more)
Men lived by Christian faith or pagan lore,
As they might choose. Whatever life each led,
On all alike the bounty of the king was shed.

✠ TWENTY-SECOND ADVENTURE
How Attila Married Kriemhild

1336   At Traismauer she stayed four days as guest.
The dust upon the road was never at rest—
Like smoke from fires swirling, on every hand;
Attila's men came riding through the Austrian land.

1337   The king soon let his happy thoughts dispel
All trace of sorrow, from what they had to tell
Of Kriemhild in splendor crossing the countryside.
Attila hurried out to meet his lovely bride.

1338   Many valiant knights, of many tongues,
Rode the ways before the king in throngs,
Christian men and heathens far and wide,
Coming to his lady in splendor and in pride.

1339   Many men were riding, Greek and Russian;
On perfect mounts they came, in swift procession,
Strong on their steeds, Wallachian and Polish
Warriors playing all their native roles with relish.

1340   Many horsemen rode from Kiev land,
And savage Kangli tribes. And many spanned
Their bows to shoot, for sport, at birds in flight;
Back to the fullest draw they drew their arrows tight.

1341   In Austria on the Danube lies a town,
Its name is Tulln. Customs all unknown
To her before she saw for the first time there,
And many welcomed her, whom later she did not spare

1342   Retainers rode ahead on Attila's way,
In might and cheerful mind, polite and gay,
Great and august princes—twenty-four!
They wished to see their queen, desiring nothing more.

1343   Duke Ramung, with his troop of seven hundred,
From Wallach land—before her eyes they thundered,
Riding as fast as flying birds almost.
Then came Gibech the prince with all his splendid host.

1344   And now Hornbow the brave, with a thousand men
Turned from the king to his queen, raising then
A loud noise, as is by custom done
Within that country. How they rode, those men of the
    Hun!

1345   Then, from Denmark, valiant Haward came;
Iring the bold, free of the traitor's blame,
Fair Irnfrid from Thuringia, sharing the honor
Which came from such a welcome as they urged upon her.

1346   They had twelve hundred warriors in their band.
Attila's brother Bloedel of Hunnish land
With his three thousand warriors now appeared
Where the queen was waiting. In splendor Bloedel neared.

1347   And then Attila came, and Theoderich
With all his friends. High in praise, the pick
Of noble-lineaged knights, a stalwart crowd,
And all of this made Kriemhild's spirit light and proud.

1348   "His Majesty will," said Ruedeger to the queen,
"Welcome you, my lady, upon the scene.

258

Whomever I bid you kiss, so let it be—
You may not greet his vassals all in like degree."

1349 They lifted the gracious queen down from her mount.
Attila now would wait on no account
But with his valiant lords sprang to the ground
And walked toward Lady Kriemhild—the happiest man
around.

1350 The train of the princess' dress, so people say,
Was borne by two great princes on the way,
As King Attila came to her, and she,
In turn, kissed the noble prince most tenderly.

1351 She raised her wimple; her lovely color shone
In all that gold. And many men looked on
And swore that Helke could have been no fairer.
Now Lord Bloedel, brother of the king, came nearer.

1352 To him the margrave said a kiss was due,
And royal Gibech. Theoderich stood there too.
Attila's lady kissed, in all, twelve lords,
And then to many knights extended welcome words.

1353 Attila stood by Kriemhild. The whole time through,
Young knights rode, as people still will do,
In splendid jousts and tilts, both Christian lords
And, after their several ways, men of the pagan hordes.

1354 In true chivalric form, Theoderich's knights
Made lances fly in splinters, over the heights
Of shields from hands of men as fine as live—
Shields the Germans left with holes more like a sieve!

1355   The breaking of lances raised a mighty sound.
All the knights of the land had gathered 'round,
And the royal guests, many noble men.
The glorious king arrived with Lady Kriemhild then.

1356   Beside them stood a pavilion of great expense,
And all the field around was filled with tents,
For men to rest in after all their pains;
There many maids were ushered by stalwart lords and
    thanes.

1357   And there the queen was brought, to take her seat
Upon the tapestried chair; and this was sweet
To Attila's mind; to see how people prized
This throning of the queen his margrave had devised.

1358   Just what Attila said I do not know—
In his own right hand lay her white hand, though,
And lovingly they sat—but Ruedeger
Would still not leave the king alone and free with her.

1359   Then they bade the jousting be suspended;
So in honor all the tumult ended.
Attila's men repaired to the tents; they found
Good lodging for their guests, near and far around.

1360   The day was over now, and rest in store,
Until they saw bright morning shine once more—
And then to horse, and many men were mounted,
Honoring the king with pleasures and games uncounted.

1361   Attila told his Huns to act in manner
Suiting them. They journeyed to Vienna,

260

Leaving Tulln, and found there, well arrayed,
Ladies to greet Attila's bride, and homage paid.

1362   All they needed was there in fullest measure.
Crowds of cheerful knights foresaw with pleasure
All the tumult. Search for lodging started.
Attila's feast began, gay and happy-hearted.

1363   Not all could stay within the city borders.
All but foreign guests should take their quarters,
Ruedeger said, out among the peasants.
I dare say one could find in Lady Kriemhild's presence,

1364   At any moment, Lord Theoderich
And many others. Rest for them was quick
To yield to labor—heartening to see
For all the guests, and sport for the margrave's company!

1365   The celebration fell in Whitsuntide,
When King Attila lay beside his bride
In the city of Vienna. (Did her first wedding
Ever bring so many men to do her bidding?)

1366   By gifts she made herself well known to folk
Who'd never seen her, and many among them spoke,
"We thought that Kriemhild must have nothing left,
And here she works amazing things with every gift."

1367   The celebration lasted seventeen days.
I know of no king winning greater praise
For grander feast—of such we never hear.
And everyone had brought his newest clothes to wear.

1368 I doubt if she had sat with such a host
      Of vassals in Netherland. For all the boast
      Of Sigfrid's power, I think he never won
      The number of noble knights she saw before the Hun.

1369 Nor has any king bestowed so many capes,
      For his wedding feast, in wide and ample shapes,
      With many other splendid clothes, to make
      A sum so large as here was given for Kriemhild's sake.

1370 Both friends of theirs and guests were so inclined
      As not to stint in wealth of any kind.
      They gladly gave whatever people chose,
      Till many stood, for their largess, bereft of clothes.

1371 Her life beside the Rhine she thought of yet—
      Beside her noble husband. Her eyes grew wet
      With tears which she concealed that none might see—
      After so much pain to be honored in such degree.

1372 The merest trifle, all the giving done,
      Beside Theoderich's! What Botelung's son
      Had granted him was spent and given away.
      And generous Ruedeger's hand did wonderfully that day.

1373 By order of Bloedel, prince of Hungary,
      His many traveling chests were emptied free
      Of gold and silver, all of which was spent.
      Attila's heroes lived in joy and merriment.

1374 Werbel and Swemmel, minstrels of the king,
      Got each a thousand marks—if anything,
      I gather, more—upon this high occasion
      When Kriemhild sat with Attila at their coronation.

1375   They left Vienna on the eighteenth morning.
Chivalric practice left their bucklers yawning
Wide with the cut of spears they bore in hand,
Thus King Attila came to his own Hunnish land.

1376   They stayed at ancient Hainburg overnight.
Who could guess the crowd or tell aright
The force with which they rode across the face
Of Attila's land? What beauties graced his native place!

1377   At mighty Wieselburg they had to embark.
The waters there, with horse and men, were dark
As solid ground, as far as the eye progressed.
Women weary of travel now found comfort and rest.

1378   Numbers of sturdy boats were lashed together,
Protected thus from harm by wave or weather,
And over all, their many tents were spanned,
As if they had beneath them open field and land.

1379   The news had come to Attila's fort at Gran,
And everyone there rejoiced, woman and man.
This was the suite where Helke once held sway;
They saw, with Lady Kriemhild, many a happy day.

1380   Numerous highborn maidens waited there,
Who since Helke's death had suffered care
And sorrow; daughters of seven kings she found,
Who graced in beauty all of Attila's land around.

1381   Mistress Herrat had the suite in charge,
Daughter of Helke's sister, her merit large,
Theoderich's betrothed, and royal child
Of King Nentwin, on whom in time great honor smiled.

1382   Her heart was glad to see the strangers come.
Money too stood ready, a mighty sum.
How Attila lived—who could describe the scene?
The Huns had never fared so well with any queen.

1383   As king and wife now rode up from the beach,
Noble Kriemhild heard the name of each,
And so could welcome him with better grace.
(With what a show of power she sat in Helke's place!)

1384   They rendered loyal services untold.
The queen, in turn, gave clothes away and gold.
And gems and silver, all she brought with her
Across the Rhine to the Huns—all this she must confer.

1385   Attila's kin and all his men became
Her subjects soon, to serve in Kriemhild's name;
And Lady Helke never had such power,
Since they were sworn to serve till Kriemhild's dying hour.

1386   Such honored excellence in court and nation,
That everyone found pleasant occupation,
According as his taste and mind might lean—
All for love of the king and of his gracious queen.

✠ TWENTY-THIRD ADVENTURE
How Kriemhild Planned to Avenge the Wrong She Suffered

1387   The truth of the matter is, till the seventh year
They lived together in much splendor here.
And then it was the queen gave birth to a boy.
Nothing else could have brought Attila greater joy.

1388   The queen would not give in till she realized
Her purpose to see Attila's son baptized
In Christian rites, Ortlieb to be his name.
Great was the pleasure reigning in Attila's domain.

1389   Every point of excellence that lay
In Helke's life she strove day after day
To equal, in mastery of manners led
By exiled Herrat, mourning in secret for Helke dead.

1390   She became well known alike to stranger and friend,
Who said no lady ever ruled king's land
So well and generously—this truth was clear.
She lived amid praise of the Huns until the thirteenth year.

1391   She now had seen that no one flouted her
(As any king's retainers still defer
To a prince's wife) and that she had twelve kings
Always before her. She thought of many painful things,

1392   Done to her at home. She also thought
Of the glories of Nibelung land, once hers, all brought

To nothing by Hagen's hand, in Sigfrid's death—
And whether that might once be turned on him in wrath.

1393   "It might, if I could bring him to this land."
She dreamed that Giselher walked, close at hand,
Her brother, and she kissed him all the while,
Often, in gentle sleep. (There would come a time of trial!)

1394   I think the Devil counselled her to break
With Gunther's friendship, whom she kissed for sake
Of peace restored in the land of Burgundy.
But now her hot tears fell and dulled her finery.

1395   Night and day, there weighed on her heart the question,
Why she was forced to love not a Christian
But a pagan, through no fault of her own.
This is what Lord Hagen and Gunther the king had done.

1396   One intention never left her mind:
She thought, "I have power of such a kind,
And wealth enough, to hurt my enemies badly—
This I swear I'd do to Hagen of Trony gladly.

1397   Often my heart cries out for loyalty.
I wish I were near to those who injured me—
Vengeance then would come for my lover's life.
For that I can hardly wait." So thought Attila's wife.

1398   Attila's vassals loved her, every knight
Of Kriemhild's court—which was no more than right.
Eckewart managed her treasure. Thus he made
Good friends for her, and what she willed no one gainsaid.

1399   She held this constant thought: to ask the king
That he, in kindness of heart, might let her bring
Her kin to the land of Huns. Not one man
Among them ever fathomed the queen's malignant plan.

1400   There by Attila's side one night she lay.
He had her in his arms, as was his way,
Embracing his beloved, dear as his life—
When thought about her foes came to his regal wife.

1401   And now she said to the king, "My dearest lord,
By your favor, I'd ask that you afford
Some sign, if I should merit it, to show
If you are truly fond of my family or no."

1402   The mighty king replied in honest mind,
"But I assure you, anything good and kind
That might befall them I'd be happy of,
For never have I gained such friends through woman's
    love."

1403   The queen cried, "That is good of you to say,
But I have noble kin, hence my dismay
That they have never deigned to visit me;
And I am called 'the stranger' among your citizenry."

1404   "Dear wife," said Attila, "if they do not mind
So great a distance, whomever you are inclined
To have as guests I'll ask across the Rhine
To my country here." She heard his wish, and that was
    fine!

1405   "If you would serve me well and truly, my lord,
Send messengers to Worms on Rhine with word

Of what I have in mind, and you shall see
Within our borders knights of high nobility."

1406   He answered, "When you command, so let it be.
Your kin you could not more desire to see
Than I the sons of Uta. Far too long
Have they been strangers to us; I think it very wrong.

1407   And my dear lady, if it pleases you,
This is what I'd be prepared to do:
Send to Burgundy my fiddlers here
To get your friends." He bade his minstrel lords appear.

1408   Soon they hurried where the king was seated
Beside his queen. He told them they were needed
As messengers to Burgundy, and ordered
That as heralds they be splendidly accoutered.

1409   They made up clothes for twenty-four knights, whose task
The king disclosed to them, for they must ask
Most royal Gunther and all his men to ride.
(Lady Kriemhild later spoke to them, aside.)

1410   Then said the king, "I'll tell you what to do.
Wish them fortune and say my heart is true,
And may they not refuse to ride our way!
Rarely have I known such welcome guests as they.

1411   If they would pay my wishes due respect,
These kin of Kriemhild, may they not neglect,
This summertime, to come to my tourney here.
My lady's kin account for much of my good cheer."

1412   Proud Swemmel the fiddler cried, "When is the day
Of tournament time in our land, so we may say
The word to your friends?" King Attila replied,
"Let the date be set at next solstice-tide."

1413   "We'll do as you command us," Werbel said.
The queen gave secret orders they be led
To her room among the chambers of the women,
To speak with them—for many knights no pleasant omen.

1414   She said to both the heralds, "Do my will
In kindly fashion, and earn yourselves a fill
Of worldly goods, with messages home to our lands;
I'll put splendid clothes and riches in your hands.

1415   Whatever kin of mine you two may meet
In Worms by the river Rhine, do not repeat
That you have ever seen my spirits low;
Say this to those gallant knights: to them my greetings go!

1416   Ask that they comply with the king's desires
Freeing me from all that so conspires
To hurt me. I have no friends, the Huns would say.
Oh, if I were a knight, I'd get to them some way!

1417   My noble brother Gernot—tell him too
No one loves him more the whole world through,
And I would have him bring to me the best
Of all our friends to make our greatness manifest.

1418   Tell Giselher that he must not forget:
Never through fault of his have I suffered yet.
And sight of him would please my eyes to see,
I should like to have him here, for his great loyalty.

269

1419   And tell my mother that I live in splendor.
And if Lord Hagen stays, who then shall tender
Escort through these lands? He has known the ways
Here to the Huns ever since his youthful days."

1420   The heralds did not know why this was done—
Why Hagen of Trony should be the very one
Not to be left by the Rhine. They learned it late,
In sorrow; his challenge meant for many a cruel fate.

1421   They had their charge, by letter and spoken word.
They traveled rich in goods and could afford
The best of living, and a splendid show
Of things to wear, for they had royal leave to go.

✠ TWENTY-FOURTH ADVENTURE
How Werbel and Swemmel Carried Out Their Sovereign's Mission

1422 Attila sent to the Rhine his messengers riding
With news that flew from land to land, inviting
(And commanding) by heralds bold and fast
Attendance at his fete—for many to be their last.

1423 Out of the land of Huns his riders went
To the land of Burgundy, where they were sent
For three most noble kings and their retinues,
Asked to Attila's court. They had no time to lose.

1424 First they rode to Pöchlarn, finding there
Unstinted care and service. Ruedeger,
His wife, and child made sure that every sign
Of their respect should go with them to the river Rhine.

1425 They did not let them leave without bestowing
Gifts on Attila's men, so that their going
Might be more pleasant. Ruedeger bade them tell
Uta and her sons no margrave loved them so well.

1426 They sent to Brunhild pledge and kindly word,
Constant faith and friendship. Having heard,
They wished to go forth on their job of herald.
The margravine prayed God to speed them unimperiled.

1427 They had not passed through all Bavaria yet
When Werbel met the bishop. I forget
What message to his Rhenish friends he sent—
Except he gave the heralds gold, which he spent

1428 Out of kindness, and so he let them ride.
Bishop Pilgrim said, "What delight
If I should have them here, my sister's sons!
I cannot go to the Rhine to see them, even once."

1429 I don't know by what route they sought their goal,
Through all those lands to the Rhine; but no one stole
Their clothes or silver, fearing so the anger
Of their noble lord, than whom no king was stronger.

1430 Werbel and Swemmel reached the Rhine, and the spot
Where Worms is, in twelve days. News was brought
To kings and men, of foreign heralds nearing.
Now the lord of the Rhineland Gunther spoke, inquiring:

1431 "Who can tell us from what place they are,
Riding here, strangers from afar?"
No one knew, until Lord Hagen came
And saw them there, at which the king heard him exclaim:

1432 "I want to tell you this, that there will be
Great news. Those are Attila's fiddlers I see,
Sent to the Rhine by your sister. They deserve
A kindly welcome here, for sake of the lord they serve."

1433 That very moment up to the palace they rode—
Such splendor no king's minstrels ever showed!
Now they were met and welcomed by Gunther's suite,
Who stored their clothes and found them places to lodge
    and eat.

1434 Their traveling clothes were rich and so well made,
At court thus dressed they might with honor have stayed

But would not go before the king that way.
"Who wants these clothes?" the heralds cried, "Come and
   say!"

1435   This was the case with many, who were glad
To take what they were given. The guests were clad
In better garments now by far, the sort
A great king's heralds wear for sake of fair report.

1436   By Gunther's leave, Attila's men repaired
Where he was seated. In pleasure, people stared.
Hagen ran, as chivalry requires,
To greet them with affection, thanked by both the squires.

1437   He sought for information—asking how
Attila fared, and his men. "Better than now,"
The fiddler said, "our countries never were,
Nor the people so happy, of that you may be sure."

1438   They sent to the king. The palace now was filled,
For such reception of guests as custom willed,
The kindly welcome to lands of another lord.
(Werbel found a host of knights at Gunther's court.)

1439   Gunther greeted them in courteous words:
"Welcome to you both, minstrel lords
Of Hunnish lands, and to your company!
Did mighty Attila send you here to Burgundy?"

1440   They bowed to him. Said Werbel, "To you we bring
The loyal greetings of our beloved king,
His pledge of service—from Kriemhild your sister, too,
For they have sent us here in all good faith to you."

1441   The great prince answered, "This I am glad to hear.
And how," the king went on, "does Attila fare?
And my sister Kriemhild, far in the land of Huns?"
To this the fiddler spoke, "I shall tell you that at once.

1442   Never yet have people prospered more
Than do these two—be certain on this score—
And all their courtiers, too, kin and man.
We left them very happy, as our trip began."

1443   "My thanks for the loyal greeting he extended
My sister too, since any doubt has ended
That now both king and men live happily—
Because I asked for news with some anxiety."

1444   The two young kings had come, just now aware
Of what had happened. In youthful Giselher
The happy sight of the heralds there awoke
Great joy for love of his sister. With kind regard he spoke:

1445   "You heralds would be very welcome here
Beside the Rhine, if you were to appear
Much more often; you'd find such friends as warm
Your hearts to see, and in our country meet no harm."

1446   "We trust in your high favor," Swemmel spoke.
"Not with all my powers can I evoke
The loving manner of King Attila's greeting—
And your great sister's, whose ways are honored as is
    fitting.

1447   The queen recalls to you your gratitude
And trust, your hearts and persons once imbued

274

With love for her. But first is our command
To see the king and ask that you should ride to our land.

1448   Great King Attila said, at all accounts,
To ask you this, bidding us announce,
If you would not submit to your sister's view,
He then would like to know what he has done to you,

1449   That you shun his land and him. Even suppose
You never knew the queen—your honor owes
At least a visit granted to the king,
Which, if it should occur, he'd find a pleasant thing."

1450   "Seven nights from now," the king replied,
"And I shall let you know what I decide
In council with my friends. Meanwhile repair
To your hostelry, and may you have good resting there."

1451   Werbel answered, "Would you be averse
To our seeing noble Lady Uta first,
Before we seek the comfort of our rooms?"
Said Giselher, with the breeding chivalry presumes:

1452   "No one shall hinder. Seek your audience.
In seeing Uta thus you suit the sense
Of her desire; she'll see you willingly,
For sake of my sister Kriemhild. How welcome you will
be!"

1453   Giselher took them to the queen at once.
Glad to see these heralds from the Huns,
She greeted them sweetly, so fine her character.
The heralds spoke their message, courtly and kind, to her.

1454   Said Swemmel, "My lady sends her loyalty
And pledge of faith to you. And might it be
That she could see you often, believe of her:
No greater joy than this could all the world confer."

1455   Said the queen, "It cannot be, however gladly
I'd see my daughter often; I tell you sadly,
She lives too far away, your great king's wife.
I can only wish for her and the king a prosperous life.

1456   But now before you leave: do let me know
When you return! It never cheered me so
In a long time to see such heralds as you."
This the herald-squires gave their word to do.

1457   Now the Huns went back where they were quartered.
Highborn Gunther, mighty king, had ordered
His kinsmen to him, asking how they inclined
To judge the present matter. More than one opined

1458   That he could well proceed to Attila's land,
Indeed the best among them took this stand,
Except for Hagen (to him, a baleful thing!).
"You call down war on yourself," he whispered to the
    king.

1459   "After all, you know what things we did.
With Kriemhild there, we never can be rid
Of worry and fear. I killed her lord with these hands.
What makes you think we dare to ride to Attila's lands?"

1460   Said the king, "She quit her anger, with a kiss,
And lovingly. What hurt we caused her, this

276

She had forgiven us, before she went—
Unless, my lord, her hate for you is not yet spent!"

1461   "Do not be fooled," said Hagen, "whatever they say,
These heralds of the Huns. You may well pay
For seeing Kriemhild there, with loss of life
And honor both. Revenge is long with Attila's wife."

1462   Adding his word to the council, Gernot cried,
"You fear your death—and that is justified—
But if for that alone we fail to travel
To Hunnish lands to see our sister, our course is evil."

1463   Prince Giselher addressed his knight, to say:
"Then since you know your guilt, friend Hagen, stay
And take good care of yourself! Let those who face
The trip with courage go with us to my sister's place."

1464   Then the lord of Trony was angry. He cried,
"I don't intend that you should take this ride
To court with men of purpose any stronger
Than mine which I'll prove to you, since you will wait **no**
   longer."

1465   Rumold, Master of the Kitchen, spoke:
"Here you can entertain familiar folk
And strangers as you will—with all your stores.
Would Hagen hold you here like captives in the wars?

1466   If you won't listen to him, take my advice;
I'm bound to you by liege, and loyal ties,
And I tell you: stay here for sake of me.
Attila's safe with Kriemhild now—there let him be.

277

1467   How could things be better in all the earth?
       You have protection here when foes come forth;
       Excellent clothes to adorn you, the finest sort
       Of wine to drink, the fairest of charming women to court.

1468   Besides, the food you get is a favor earned
       By no other king on earth—and if it weren't,
       Still you should stay for your lovely ladies' sake,
       Not go and place your lives on a risk no child would take!

1469   And so I say to stay. Your lands are rich;
       Here at home, if you make some foolish pledge,
       We're better set for bail than with the Hun.
       Who knows how things are there? Stay, say I for one."

1470   "We shall not stay," said Gernot. "So kind a word
       From my sister and the king as we have heard,
       Inviting us—why should we fail to come?
       Whoever doesn't want to go, can stay at home."

1471   Hagen answered this: "Whatever you do,
       Don't let what I say appear to you
       A pointless thing. If you would not be harmed,
       I tell you this sincerely, go to the Huns well-armed.

1472   Send for your men, if you won't change your mind—
       Send for the best you have or can ever find,
       Then I shall pick among them a thousand knights,
       And you need not fear the harm her wicked heart incites."

1473   "I'll gladly do as you say," the king replied.
       He sent his heralds far through the countryside,
       Till they brought back three thousand men or more,
       None of whom imagined the fearful hurt in store.

1474 They rode to Gunther's land in great good cheer,
Where they were given steeds and clothes and gear,
All of those preparing to depart
From Burgundy. (And many he found with a willing
    heart!)

1475 Hagen bade his brother Dankwart summon
Eighty of the knights they had in common,
Here to the Rhine. Gallantly, with helm
And clothes and armor they rode, into Gunther's realm.

1476 Valiant Folker came, of noble birth,
A minstrel, with thirty men and clothing worth
A king's wearing. Off to the Hunnish court
He meant to go, and sent to Gunther this report.

1477 I'll tell you more of Folker: nobly born,
A lord of Burgundy, to whom were sworn
In liege some of the best of that domain,
He played the fiddle, too, hence his minstrel name.

1478 Hagen chose his thousand. He knew them well,
The work of their hands where battles rose and fell—
All the many things they had done he knew.
Call them valiant men, no other word will do.

1479 Kriemhild's messengers grew much concerned,
Fearful over their master. Daily they yearned
For leave to go, which was denied to them
By Hagen of Trony. This was a cunning stratagem.

1480 He said to his master, "We should take good care
Not to let them ride till we prepare

To leave for Attila's land, one week hence.
If someone bears us malice, we'll have a better chance

1481   To find it out, and Kriemhild has no time
To turn this plot of hers to someone's crime
Against us—though if that is her intent
She may get hurt. The men we bring are excellent!"

1482   Shields and saddles, clothes, and everything
That they would take to the land of the Hunnish king
Stood ready now for all these valiant men.
They told the heralds of Kriemhild: go see Gunther again

1483   The heralds came, to hear Lord Gernot cry:
"Attila asks and Gunther will comply;
We shall come to his festival and tourney,
And see our sister. Have no doubt, we welcome the
    journey."

1484   Gunther asked them, "Can you say perhaps
When the festival is, what time should elapse
Before we ought to leave?" Swemmel replied,
"The truth is this, it is to be next solstice-tide."

1485   He granted them what never yet had been:
An audience, if they wished it, with the queen,
Lady Brunhild—he would not forbid it.
But Folker held them back, and she was glad he did it.

1486   "My lady's humor is not such of late
That you can see her," Folker said. "So wait
Until tomorrow, then we'll let you pay
Your visit to her." (They went there and were turned
    away.)

1487 In courtesy, the prince, who seemed to hold
   The heralds in good esteem, brought forth his gold,
   For he had much, and the shields they put it in
   Were broad. They also had rich presents from his kin.

1488 Gere and Ortwin, Gernot and Giselher
   Gave proof of their largess. Indeed so fair
   And costly were the gifts that they presented,
   The Huns did not dare take them; fear of their lord
    prevented.

1489 "Great king," declared Lord Werbel the messenger,
   "Keep your gifts in your own country, sir.
   We cannot take them, my master won't permit
   The taking of gifts—and we have little need of it."

1490 The Lord of Rhineland found it most unpleasant
   That they refused so great a monarch's present,
   And so they had to take his gold in hand,
   And clothes, to carry back with them to Attila's land.

1491 They sought the queen before they left again.
   Giselher ushered both the minstrel men
   Before his mother. She sent with them this word:
   By honors paid her daughter her own joy was assured.

1492 The queen presented them with gold and braid
   For Attila's sake and Kriemhild, whom she paid
   Her loving respect. The minstrels had no fear
   To take the gifts from her; her giving was sincere.

1493 And so the messengers had taken leave
   From men and women there, nor did they grieve
   As they rode to Swabia, given escort through
   By Gernot's men—who kept them free of trouble, too.

1494   When those who went to give them escort left,
The power of the Hun made safe their ways—no theft
Of clothes or steeds at anybody's hands.
They made all haste they could to mighty Attila's lands.

1495   Where they had friends, they halted to proclaim
That from the Rhineland men of Burgundy came
To the land of the Huns—and little time to lose!
(Thus did Bishop Pilgrim also hear the news.)

1496   As they rode down the road by Pöchlarn town,
They did not fail to make the story known
To Ruedeger and Lady Gotelind,
Who looked to their visit there, both in a joyful mind.

1497   The minstrels with their tidings hurried on,
Finding Attila in the town of Gran.
They told him the friendly things so many said,
Their many greetings. He flushed with joy, all pleasure-
    red.

1498   When Kriemhild heard in truth that Uta's sons,
Her brothers, were on their way to the land of Huns,
Her heart was light. Her minstrels she presented
With costly gifts—her reputation thus augmented.

1499   "Werbel and Swemmel, tell me both of you,"
She said, "which of my next of kin are due
To come to our feast, of those we asked to this land?
And what did Hagen say, hearing what we planned?"

1500   "He came to council," they said, "early one day,
And very few kind things did he have to say!
When they spoke of coming here and gave their word,
It seemed the name of Death that fierce Hagen heard.

1501   The kings will make the journey, your three brothers,
        High in spirit; as to all the others—
        To tell so great a sum would be too hard.
        But Folker promised to ride with them, the gallant bard."

1502   "Folker," she answered, "I can do without,
        Or the sight of him anywhere about!
        Hagen I like—a man of hero's measure.
        If we are to see him here, my heart is filled with pleasure."

1503   The queen then went to the king. Her words were sweet
        That now she spoke to him. "And do you greet
        This news, my dearest lord, with joy—or how?
        All my will desired will be accomplished now."

1504   "Your will is my delight," replied the king.
        "I should not take more joy in the journeying
        Of kin of mine to my land. Worry ends,
        And cares are banished by the kindness of your friends."

1505   The king's officials set out everywhere
        In hall and palace benches to prepare
        For welcome guests about to pay their call—
        Who soon enough would leave the king no joy at all.

✠ TWENTY-FIFTH ADVENTURE

How the Lords all Traveled to the Land of the Huns

1506   No more of this, of what the Huns were doing.
So proud a sight, of splendid heroes going
To any monarch's land, rarely happens.
They took whatever they chose of armor and of weapons;

1507   The lord of the Rhine equipped his warriors well—
A thousand and sixty knights, so I heard tell,
And nine thousand squires, on their festive way.
(The ones they left at home would later mourn the day.)

1508   Across the courtyard at Worms they took their gear.
An ancient bishop of Speyer encountered here
The lovely Uta: "Our friends will now repair
To the tournament—may God preserve their honor there."

1509   Then the noble Uta spoke these words
To all her sons: "Stay here, most excellent lords!
I had a dream last night, of things I dread
And fear to see: for all the birds in the land were dead."

1510   "He who goes by dreams," Lord Hagen cried,
"Cannot in any rightful way decide
What fully suits his honor and good report.
I hope my lord will go and ask for leave at court,

1511   And we should gladly ride to Attila's land,
Where kings may well be served by hero's hand,
When we have gone to Kriemhild's tournament."
Hagen spoke for a trip he later would repent—

1512   And would have then opposed, had Gernot not,
        In violent words, provoked him with the thought
        Of Sigfrid, Kriemhild's husband. These words he cried:
        "That's why Hagen wants to miss our courtly ride!"

1513   "I do not act from fear," Lord Trony said.
        "Whatever your will, my lords, go right ahead!
        I shall gladly ride with you to Attila's realm."
        (In time to come he shattered many a shield and helm.)

1514   The ships were set, and many men were there;
        They took aboard them all their things to wear.
        Till evening time they had no moment free;
        Soon they would leave their homes in the greatest gaiety.

1515   Awnings and tents they pitched upon the grass,
        Across the Rhine. When that was brought to pass,
        His fair wife came and begged the king to stay—
        Embracing her handsome lord the night of that same day.

1516   The morning came, and flutes and trumpets blew
        For them to leave, which they prepared to do.
        For those who lay in love, one more caress—
        Parted soon by Attila's wife in bitterness.

1517   The sons of lovely Uta had a thane,
        Bold and true; when they would not remain,
        He told the king his feelings secretly.
        He said, "Your trip to court is a cause of grief to me."

1518   This was Rumold, man of mighty hand.
        He spoke, "To whom will you leave people and land?
        Why, my lords, can no one change your mind?
        The good in Kriemhild's plan is more than I can find."

1519   "My lands I commend to you, and my little son,
And serve the ladies well. Let this be done.
Whomever you see weeping, bring him solace.
Great King Attila's wife will do us no deed of malice."

1520   Kings and men, each one found his charger,
And then with tender kisses took departure,
All of them with spirits proud and high.
For many lovely wives there would come a time to cry.

1521   As valiant warriors mounted, one perceived
That many women stood about and grieved.
Their thoughts foretold that being long apart
Would end in awful loss—a balm to no one's heart.

1522   The bold Burgundians set out to ride;
The country stirred with action. On either side
Of the mountains people wept. All unworried
By men and women's lot at home, away they hurried.

1523   With them knights of the Nibelung treasure had come,
In a thousand hauberks. They had left at home
Lovely ladies, never again to be seen.
The hurt of Sigfrid's wound weighed hard upon the
    queen.

1524   They set their course to the Main river then,
Up through East Franconia, Gunther's men,
With Hagen leading (he knew what the route should be).
Dankwart was their marshal, hero of Burgundy.

1525   Riding from East Franconia to Swaleveld
They showed to what high sense of form they held,

Kings and kin—and were so lauded for.
And on the twelfth morning they reached the Danube
    shore.

1526   Hagen of Trony rode the forwardmost,
A help and solace to the Nibelung host.
Dismounting now, upon the river sand,
He quickly tied his charger to a tree, to stand.

1527   The waters were in flood, no boat in sight.
The men of Nibelung worried how they might
Cross the river—it ran too wide a course.
Many a dashing knight dismounted from his horse.

1528   "My lord of the Rhine," said Hagen, "this may be
Ill luck for you; as you yourself can see,
The water is over the bank, the current is strong.
We'll lose good fighters here today, unless I'm wrong."

1529   The king said, "What do you reproach me for?
For good of your name, discourage us no more.
Seek us out the place for fording here,
So we can bring across our horses and our gear."

1530   "I'm not so tired of life," Sir Hagen said,
"That I should want to drown myself in the bed
Of these broad waves. Rather my hand should kill
Men in Attila's land—for that I have the will.

1531   Stay by the water here! I'll follow the river
And look for a ferryman to take us over,
My noble lords, into Gelfrat's land."
Now the sturdy Hagen had his buckler in hand.

1532   Well armed he was! He took a shield along,
And tied his helmet on, bright and strong,
And over his byrnie carried a sword so wide
That it could take a fearful cut with either side.

1533   He looked all around for the boatman. A sudden sound
Of splashing met his ears; he listened and found
Wise sorceresses at a lovely pool,
Who made the noise, bathing there to make them cool.

1534   Hagen saw and crept up stealthily.
At sight of this, they were in haste to flee—
And glad to get away! All their clothing
Hagen took from them, but otherwise did nothing.

1535   He heard Hadeburg, one of the mermaids, cry:
"Noble Hagen, we will prophesy—
If you, bold knight, will give us back our things—
And tell your trip to the Huns, and what that journey
    brings."

1536   Seeing them float like birds upon the water,
He felt they must have magic truths to utter,
So much the more believing what they would tell—
And what he wanted of them, they told him all too well.

1537   She spoke, "Ride on in trust to Attila's land;
On this assurance to you I pledge my hand,
That greater honors never were conferred
On warriors riding to any realm. Believe my word."

1538   Her speech made Hagen in his heart so gay
He gave them back their things without delay.
When they had donned their wondrous clothes anew,
They told his trip to Attila's land—and told it true.

1539   Another mermaid, Sigelind, began,
"I warn you, Hagen, child of Aldrian:
To get our clothes my aunt has lied to you.
If you go to the Huns, you're deluded through and
    through.

1540   While you still have time, turn back again,
And do it soon. You go, as valiant men,
Invited there to die in Attila's land.
Those who make this journey Death will take in hand."

1541   "Don't play tricks on me," came Hagen's reply.
"How could it ever happen that we should die,
All of us there, through anybody's hate?"
Then, more fully now, the mermaids told their fate.

1542   The first of them spoke up, "It must be so.
No single one of you—and this we know—
Except the king's own chaplain shall survive
Unscathed, to come again to Gunther's land alive."

1543   Dauntless Hagen cried, with an angry shout:
"A fearful thing to tell my lords about—
That every man of us in Hun land dies.
Show us the way over the waters, if you are so wise!"

1544   "Since you insist upon your trip," she cried,
"Upstream there stands a house by the waterside,
With a boatman—nowhere else." He had learned enough
From all his questioning now, and quickly broke it off.

1545   She cried as Hagen left, in anger and worry,
"Wait a moment, you're in too great a hurry!
Listen how you cross to the opposite beaches.
A man whose name is Else rules these border reaches.

1546   His brother is Gelfrat, lord in Bavaria land.
In his domains are dangers to withstand.
If you pass through, be on your mettle there.
And as for the ferryman, handle him with care.

1547   Your life is in danger—so fierce his disposition—
Unless you treat him with consideration.
If you want his services, pay him his fee.
He guards this land for Gelfrat in loyal fealty.

1548   If he should take too long, then give a shout
Across the flooding water, making out
You're Amelrich, who left when this became
A hostile land for him. He'll come when he hears the
    name."

1549   Haughty Hagen thanked the women, bowed,
And fell to silence, saying nothing aloud.
He walked by the water, heading upstream more,
Until he found a house that lay on the other shore.

1550   He called with a great voice across the wave:
"Come and get me, ferryman, you shall have
As pay an armband made of gold, all red.
I need this crossing badly—let the truth be said!"

1551   The ferryman had such wealth that it would look
Unseemly for him to work, and so he took
But seldom pay, and his men were men of pride.
So Hagen stood there all alone on the other side.

1552   He called till the water echoed in reply—
So vastly great his power: "It is I,
Amelrich, Else's man; in enmity
I left this country once. Come and ferry me!"

1553   High on his sword he put a ring, to show,
Bright and fair, all gold and red aglow,
That he might ferry him to Gelfrat's land.
The haughty ferryman himself took oar in hand.

1554   Now he was a troublesome man, no easy friend,
And greed for wealth will bring an evil end.
He wanted to earn Hagen's gold, all red,
For this the warrior left him sword-stricken and dead.

1555   Quickly now the ferryman rowed over.
He'd heard a name and now did not discover
The one he thought, but Hagen. His wrath was stirred.
He spoke to the lord before him, anger in every word:

1556   "Knight, maybe Amelrich is your name—
The one I thought of doesn't look the same,
He was my brother—sire the same, and mother.
Since you tricked me, stay on this side, not the other!"

1557   "No, by mighty God," said Hagen then.
"I am a foreign knight, in charge of men.
Take my payment as a friend would do,
For carrying me across. I'll be obliged to you."

1558   The ferryman said, "That cannot be, for these,
The lords I serve and love, have enemies;
I take to this land no strangers any more.
In case you wish to live, step back at once on shore!"

1559   "Not that!" said Hagen. "My heart is full of worry.
Take this gold for love of me, and ferry
Our thousand horse across and as many men."
"That shall not be done," the fierce thane said again.

1560 He lifted a heavy oar, big and broad,
And fetched unhappy Hagen a blow so hard
He fell to his knees in the boat. This was as yet
By far the fiercest boatman Hagen ever met.

1561 To give his haughty guest a better right
To hurt and anger, he swung his pole at the knight,
And broke it over his head; his strength was vast.
But the ferryman of Else suffered for this at last.

1562 In fury Hagen reached for his sheath and took
The weapon he found in it, and off he struck
The boatman's head, which he plunged to the riverbed.
Among the proud Burgundians news was quickly spread.

1563 Just as he hit its pilot, the boat took off
To drift downstream, and he had trouble enough
To bring it back, growing tired and sore
Before he did. Hagen pulled a mighty oar.

1564 With rapid strokes he turned the boat about
Until the great oar in his hand gave out
And broke in two. He wanted to reach his friends,
On shore, but his pole was gone. Swiftly he took the ends

1565 And tied them with a shield-strap, a narrow thong.
He turned now towards a wood and went along
Till he found his liege-lord standing by the shore.
They all came out to meet him, handsome men of war.

1566 The bold lords gave him welcome. Then their eyes
Saw within the boat the warm steam rise
Out of the blood from the wound, cruel and grim,
That slew the boatman. They had questions to ask of him!

1567   And when King Gunther saw the blood, all hot
        And rolling in the boat, he quickly sought
        Answer from Hagen: "Where is our boatman, friend?
        I gather that thanks to your valor he has met his end."

1568   Hagen denied it. "By a wild willow I found
        This vessel here which then my hands unbound,
        But I have seen no ferryman here today.
        No one's been hurt through fault of mine in any way."

1569   Gernot spoke, lord of Burgundy:
        "Thought of dear friends dying worries me.
        We have no boatman and did not prepare
        To get ourselves across; I stand here in despair."

1570   "Servants, lay our harness on the grass.
        By the Rhine, as I recall, I used to pass
        For the best by whom a boat was ever manned.
        I trust I can ferry you," said Hagen, "to Gelfrat's land."

1571   To get across the river fast they struck
        The horses and drove them in. They had good luck:
        In swimming, the great waves failed to make them
            founder.
        Some drifted far—with their weariness, it was little
            wonder.

1572   They took to the boat all their clothes and gold,
        Determined to go no matter what they were told.
        Hagen managed things. To the opposite sand
        He brought them, all the powerful knights, to a foreign
            land.

1573 First he ferried over fifty score
Of splendid knights, and then his own, and more:
Nine thousand men he took across the way—
The gallant lord of Trony was busy enough that day!

1574 When he had got them over safe, he thought
(Fearless lord) of strange tidings brought
To his ear before, told by a wild mermaid,
For this the royal chaplain's life was all but paid.

1575 He found the priest among his chapel gear,
Leaning on his hand, with the altar near.
Little good it did him! When Hagen saw,
It meant great harm for him, poor servant of God's law.

1576 He threw him out of the boat—it was quickly done.
And many cried, "Grab him, men, hold on!"
Young Giselher was angered and annoyed,
But Hagen would not stop till the chaplain was destroyed.

1577 Gernot spoke, "Hagen, what profit to you
Is the chaplain's death?—which if another should do
Would make you angry with him at the very least.
What reason did you have to turn against the priest?"

1578 The cleric tried hard to swim: he might pull through
If someone helped, but that no one could do—
With Trony fierce and angry there, no wonder!
But all of them stood aghast when Hagen pushed him
under.

1579 Now that the poor priest saw no help in store,
With great travail he turned about once more.

He could not swim, and yet by God's own hand
He still came out, unhurt, back again to land.

1580 There the poor priest stood and shook his clothes.
And thus did Hagen see no force could oppose
The things he heard the mermaids prophesy;
And Hagen thought to himself, "All these men must die."

1581 When they had emptied the boat and took the things
They had aboard, these men of the three great kings,
Hagen smashed it and threw it on the wave.
They all were taken aback, bold as they were and brave.

1582 "Why did you do that, brother?" Dankwart cried.
"How shall we cross from Hun land when we ride
Back from the Rhine to home and family?"
(Later Hagen told him this could never be.)

1583 Said Trony's hero, "I did it in this hope,
If on our journey now we have to cope
With any coward who wants to run in fear,
That he should meet his shameful end, by the waters here."

1584 They had with them one lord from Burgundy,
A man of deeds, called Folker. Eloquently,
The fiddler spoke, stating in full his view,
And all that Hagen did he gave approval to.

1585 Their steeds were ready, the pack-horse train
Was loaded well. The journey brought no pain
Or hurt for any but the chaplain to meet.
He had to go back to Rhineland on his own two feet.

✠ TWENTY-SIXTH ADVENTURE
How Gelfrat Was Slain by Dankwart

1586   Now they all had come to the waterside;
And Gunther asked, "Who is here to guide
Our travel through this country, lest we miss
The proper way?" Said Folker, "Let me take care of this."

1587   "Stop, all of you," said Hagen, "squire and knight!
You follow friends in trust, and that is right.
But this is an awful thing to hear from me:
Never again shall we return to Burgundy.

1588   Two mermaids told me early this very day
We'll not come back. But here is what I say:
Warriors, arm yourselves, stay clear of hurt!
Our foes are powerful here; ride on, and keep alert.

1589   I thought to catch them lying, wise as they are.
They said not one of us would get as far
As shore again, except the chaplain alone.
And that," he said, "is why I wished to see him drown."

1590   From company on to company went the tale,
And valiant heroes, in their pain, turned pale,
To think of bitter death upon the way
To Attila's court. They had good cause for their dismay.

1591   At Mehring, where the boatman's life was lost
(Else's man), there they all had crossed.
And Hagen spoke once more, "Since I have made
Enemies en route, we'll doubtless be waylaid.

1592 I killed the ferryman early this very day,
   As well they know. Prepare, without delay—
   If Gelfrat and Else choose this time and place
   To hit our forces, let them see what losses they face!

1593 I know these men have courage; they'll not forget.
   So make your horses march more slowly yet—
   Let no one think we use these roads to flee."
   "This word," said Giselher, "is good enough for me!"

1594 "Who shall guide us overland?" they cried.
   "Let Folker! Road and byway, far and wide,
   The gallant minstrel knows." They'd not expressed
   But half the wish, when there before them fully dressed

1595 In armor stood the fiddler, his helmet fastened.
   The colors of his battle-garments glistened;
   He fixed a red device upon his lance.
   (He and the kings were soon to fall on evil chance.)

1596 The boatman's death had come by true account
   To Gelfrat. Mighty Else too had found
   What happened there; they both were pained and angered.
   They summoned their knights to readiness—and no one
    lingered.

1597 I tell you this, the time was very brief
   Before they came a-riding. Monstrous grief
   And hurt they caused, when mighty war was made.
   Seven hundred or more had come to Gelfrat's aid.

1598 As they rode to meet the savage foe they faced,
   Their masters led. They were in too great haste,
   Seeking such valiant guests, to vent their wrath.
   For this they lost a goodly toll of friends in death.

1599   Now Hagen, lord of Trony, well had planned
(Could hero better guard his friends?) to stand
At the army's rear on watch with his allies,
And with his brother Dankwart, too. This course was wise.

1600   The light of day was spent, there was no more.
He feared for his friends great pain and hurt in store.
Across Bavaria they rode, shields up-drawn
And held at ready. Shortly they were set upon.

1601   On either side of the road and close behind
They heard the beat of hooves—a foe inclined
Too much to haste. "They mean to strike us here.
Fasten your helmets on! The need for that is clear."

1602   Thus spoke Dankwart. As it must, the stream
Of travel ceased. They saw through dusk the gleam
Of shining shields. Hagen could not sit by:
"Who hunts this road for us?" Gelfrat had to reply,

1603   The margrave and Bavaria's overseer:
"We look for foes, and we pursued them here.
Who killed my boatman today, I do not know—
A stalwart hero, his loss has left my spirits low."

1604   "And was the boatman yours?" his answer came.
"He would not ferry us. Mine is the blame,"
Said Hagen. "I killed him, but it had to be;
Your champion's hands were very nearly the death of me!

1605   To reach your land I offered him in payment,
To ferry us over, milord, gold and raiment.
That so angered him he struck me a blow
With a heavy pole—at which my gall began to flow.

1606   I got my sword and settled his angry whim
With a mighty wound, and that was the end of him.
I'll make amends to you, as you think right."
Their hearts were set and hard. It ended in a fight.

1607   "When Gunther and his men came riding along,"
Said Gelfrat, "I knew that we should suffer wrong
From Hagen of Trony, and he shall not go free.
For the boatman's death, this man shall be our surety."

1608   Lance over shield they lowered for the thrust,
Gelfrat and Hagen; each one had a lust
For meeting the other. Dankwart and Else were curious
Who was braver. They rode in splendor; the fighting was
    furious.

1609   How could ever lords compete as well?
A mighty charge, and over backwards fell,
Unhorsed, valiant Hagen, at Gelfrat's hand.
His martingale was broken; he came to understand

1610   What fighting is. The sound of lances shivered
Rose from their armies. Hagen had recovered,
Who before had fallen, thrust to the earth.
He thought of Gelfrat, I dare say, with little mirth!

1611   I do not know who took their steeds in hand,
But now they both were down, upon the sand,
Hagen and Gelfrat, charging. Either knight
Had friends to help him—and show the others how to
    fight.

1612   Hagen sprang at Gelfrat, fierce and wild,
And yet the noble margrave struck from his shield

A mighty piece, and made the fire dance,
And Gunther's vassal almost died from this mischance.

1613   He called upon Lord Dankwart, "Help, dear brother!
This man who set upon me is no other
Than a hero. He'll never let me go."
Bold Dankwart cried, "Let me decide if that is so."

1614   He sprang up close and struck him a blow so hard
He lay there dead, victim of his sharp sword.
Else wanted vengeance for him, but he—
And all his troops—left there in hurt and injury.

1615   His brother was slain, and he had many wounds.
Eighty of his knights had passed the bounds
Of bitter death. Thus compelled to flee,
Their master turned and ran from Gunther's company.

1616   As the Bavarians fled the battleground
One could hear close after them the sound
Of awful blows, as knights of Trony chased
Foemen eager not to suffer, all in haste.

1617   Lord Dankwart raised his voice in their flight, to say:
"We ought to turn and ride the other way,
And let them go, for they are soaked with blood.
Let's hurry to our friends. This word of mine is good."

1618   When they came back where all the hurt took place,
Hagen of Trony spoke, "Men, let us trace
What friends are missing here, or whom we've lost
In this engagement, counting what Gelfrat's anger cost."

1619   Four were lost, but there is an end to pain,
And they were well atoned, for they had slain

300

In turn a hundred Bavarians—perhaps more yet;
The shields of the knights of Trony were dark with blood
   and wet.

1620   The bright moon broke a moment from the cloud.
   And Hagen said, "Let no one say aloud
   To my good masters what we managed here.
   Let them go along till morning, safe from fear."

1621   When they who fought caught up with all the rest,
   Fatigue had left their ranks so much oppressed
   That many asked, "How long are we to ride?"
   Bold Dankwart answered, "What shelter can we provide?

1622   You all must ride till daybreak." Folker the bold,
   In charge of the servants, sent one whom he told
   To ask the marshal, "What place tonight affords
   A rest for all our mounts, and my beloved lords?"

1623   Brave Dankwart answered, "How am I to say?
   We cannot rest until the break of day.
   We'll camp whatever grassy spot we find."
   They heard this news, and more than one was sad in mind.

1624   And so, the red of warm blood undisclosed,
   They stayed till over hills the sun proposed
   Its brilliant light to morning, and the king
   Perceived that they had fought. He said an angry thing:

1625   "What's this, my friend? It seems that you disdained
   My company when coats of mail were rained
   With soaking blood. Who did this thing to you?"
   Said Hagen, "Else did, before last night was through.

1626   We'd been attacked because of all the bother
Over his boatman. Gelfrat fell to my brother,
Else fled us, forced by his awful plight:
A hundred of his and four of us lay dead in the fight."

1627   Where they camped, we have no information;
Later, word reached all the population
That highborn Uta's sons were on their way,
To visit at court. Passau received them well that day.

1628   Bishop Pilgrim, uncle to all three
Of these high kings, was filled with joy to see
His nephews come to the land with a complement
Of so many knights. His kindness soon was evident.

1629   Friends ran out in welcome along the way.
Passau could not provide a place to stay,
They had to cross the water, where they found
A field to set up tents and shelters all around.

1630   They stayed there one whole day, till night had ended.
The treatment they received was truly splendid.
Then it was time to leave for Ruedeger's land.
The margrave had the tidings soon enough in hand.

1631   Travel-weary men had found their rest.
Onward toward the Hunnish land they pressed,
And there at the border found a guard, asleep.
Hagen of Trony took his mighty sword to keep.

1632   This same good knight was called Sir Eckewart;
But he was now oppressed and sad at heart
To lose his sword to this heroes' expedition.

302

(The watch on Ruedeger's border they found in poor condition!)

1633 "Oh, the shame!" he cried. "I rue the cost
Of this Burgundian journey. When I lost
My lord Sigfrid, my days of joy were through.
Alas, Lord Ruedeger, what have I done to you?"

1634 When Hagen saw his doleful circumstance,
He gave him back his sword and six gold bands.
"Take these, milord, in kindness! And may you own
Yourself my friend—you're bold to stand this border alone."

1635 "May God repay your gift of rings," said he.
"And still your trip to the Huns disquiets me.
You killed Sigfrid, and you are hated here.
Be on your guard, I tell you—believe that I'm sincere."

1636 "The Lord watch over us!" said Hagen then.
"The only thing that much concerns these men
Is a place to stay, for king and squire and knight—
Where in these domains we spend the present night.

1637 Our steeds have come to ruin on such far ways;
Our food is gone. And where does one buy who pays?
What we need is a host," Hagen said,
"Who for his good name tonight would give us bread."

1638 "I'll show you a host," Lord Eckewart exclaimed,
"And you will rarely be so entertained
As guest in any land, as you will fare
If you bold men will come and visit Ruedeger.

1639 He lives beside the road, the finest host
That ever owned a house. His heart may boast
Such virtues as, in sweet May, the grass does flowers.
He spends, in heroes' service, his most happy hours."

1640 "Will you bear my message," Gunther cried,
"To see if for my sake he will provide
For all my kin and our men?—and I'll repay
My good friend Ruedeger for this, as best I may."

1641 Eckewart spoke, "I'll gladly bear your message."
With willing spirit he set out on passage,
To tell Lord Ruedeger what he had heard.
Not in a long, long time had come such pleasant word.

1642 He ran to Pöchlarn, first identified
By Ruedeger. "That's Eckewart," he cried,
"A vassal of Kriemhild, hurrying along."
(He thought at first that enemies had done him wrong.)

1643 He went before the gate where he espied
The herald undoing his sword to lay aside.
The news he had to bring was not concealed
From either host or kin of his, but soon revealed.

1644 He said to the margrave, "They who ordered me
To find you here are Gunther of Burgundy,
And Giselher his brother; Gernot, too,
Each of whom has pledged his high regard for you.

1645 From Hagen you hear the same, Folker as well,
In loyal zeal. But I have more to tell.
The royal marshal sends this word by me;
His excellent squires need your hospitality."

1646   Ruedeger said with a laugh, "What welcome news
That these most noble, gracious monarchs choose
To seek my service—which shall not be slighted.
If they will visit my house, I am pleased and most de-
    lighted."

1647   "The marshal, Dankwart, asked that you be told
How many—and whom—your house was asked to hold:
Sixty valiant champions; in rank of knight,
A thousand, and nine thousand men." This was his de-
    light.

1648   "What luck for me, these guests," said Ruedeger.
"These champions here in my house! The times are rare
That I have any chance to nobly treat them.
Kin and men of mine, ride out now to meet them!"

1649   They hurried to their chargers, squire and knight,
For what their lord commanded seemed most right.
They sped their service, eager not to be slow.
(Gotelind, in the ladies' suite, still did not know.)

✠ TWENTY-SEVENTH ADVENTURE
How They Arrived at Pöchlarn

1650 The margrave went to where the ladies waited,
His wife and daughter, quickly then related
The pleasant news which he had taken to mean
That they should have as guests the brothers of their
      queen.

1651 "Dear love," said Ruedeger, "go, in kindness meet
These highborn, gracious monarchs and their suite
As soon as they approach our court and castle.
Greet with kindness also Hagen, Gunther's vassal.

1652 With them comes a lord called Dankwart—he,
And one named Folker, models of gallantry.
You and my daughter too shall grant these six
Your kisses and in gentle courtesy shall mix

1653 Among the champions." This they gladly vowed.
They chose from boxes garments costly and proud
To wear in meeting the knights when they went out.
How eagerly the lovely women hurried about!

1654 These ladies had but little make-up on.
Upon their heads, golden chaplets shone,
Costly garlands, lest breezes disarray
Their lovely hair. (The simple truth is all I say.)

1655 There let us leave the women occupied—
Here the margrave's friends made haste to ride
Out where the princes were, across the plain.
They found a good reception in Ruedeger's domain.

1656 When valiant Ruedeger saw them coming near,
The margrave called aloud in great good cheer,
"Welcome, lords, and all your retinue,
Here in my land! What pleasure I have in seeing you!"

1657 In homage free of hate the champions bowed.
He loved them well, and this he freely showed.
Hagen he knew, and greeted specially,
And did with Folker likewise, knight of Burgundy;

1658 And gallant Dankwart, too, who came to ask,
"If you give aid to us, whose is the task
To care for the men we brought, our retinue?"
The margrave said, "I promise a good night's rest to you.

1659 And I shall place such guard on all the force
You brought with you to my land, armor and horse,
That nothing shall be ruined, nor incur
So much as the loss to you of one single spur.

1660 Servants, out to the field, erect the tents!
And any loss you have, I'll make amends.
Let the horses free, remove the reins!"
Seldom before had host of theirs taken such pains.

1661 And the guests were glad of this. When all was done,
The lords rode off, the servants every one
Lay down in the grass and rested in comfort there.
I doubt if they had on all their trip such kindly care.

1662 Now with her comely daughter the margravine
Came before the palace, where were seen,
Beside her, winsome ladies, fair and tender
Maidens wearing many rings and clothes of splendor.

1663   How far the gems of their costly garments shone!
        How fair of form they were! Riding on,
        The guests had now arrived and soon dismounted.
        In men of Burgundy, true courtesy abounded.

1664   Thirty-six maids and many matrons too,
        Figures as lovely as one could wish for, flew
        To meet them there, and valiant lords attended.
        What kindly welcome the noble womenfolk extended!

1665   The margravine's daughter kissed the kings, all three
        (As did her mother). And Hagen—there was he.
        Her father said to kiss him, but she thought,
        Staring at him: he seems so fearsome, I'd rather not.

1666   Still her lord commanded, so she must.
        Her color changed; by turns she paled and blushed.
        She also kissed Lord Dankwart; the minstrel, too.
        For valor and mighty prowess, this greeting was his due.

1667   The youthful margravine took by the hand
        Giselher the prince of Burgundy land;
        As did her mother, Gunther the gallant peer.
        And so they left with the heroes, full of the greatest cheer.

1668   The host, with Gernot, entered a spacious hall,
        Where knights and ladies sat. Now came the call
        To have for all their guests good wine obtained.
        Never were any heroes better entertained.

1669   Loving glances fell from many eyes
        On Ruedeger's child, her beauty so fair a prize
        That in his fancy many a knight embraced her—
        As was her merit, too; highest spirits graced her.

1670   (Let them think as they would, it could not be.)
Much the glancing, back and forth, to see
The maids and ladies, in such a multitude,
The noble fiddler paid the host his gratitude.

1671   By custom then they went their different ways,
Knights and ladies each to a separate place.
They set the tables in the ample hall,
Nobly serving guests they had scarcely known at all.

1672   For love of her guests the margravine had deigned
To come to table. Her daughter, though, remained
Among the maidens, her proper place to sit.
The guests, unable to see her, did not like this a bit!

1673   After they had drunk and eaten all,
They led the lovely women back to the hall.
There was no lack of merry small talk there,
Of which the gay and gallant Folker did his share.

1674   Loud and plain the noble minstrel cried:
"Most powerful margrave, God has not denied
His grace to you, in giving you a wife
Of such great beauty—and this as well: a blessed life.

1675   If I were a prince, sometime to wear a crown,
Then I should want your daughter for my own
To be my wife—suiting my wish and mood,
For she is sweet to look at, nobly born, and good."

1676   "What chance is there," Margrave Ruedeger cried,
"That any king could ever want as bride
My darling daughter? We live afar, exiled,
My wife and I. What good is beauty to the child?"

1677   Gernot answered this, a man of breeding:
        "If I could have a lover truly meeting
        My every wish, I'd be most satisfied
        With such a wife." And Hagen cordially replied:

1678   "After all, Lord Giselher must marry.
        She comes of so noble a line hereditary
        That few of us would grudge the margravine
        Our service in Burgundy, should she become our queen."

1679   What he said seemed good to Ruedeger
        And Gotelind, and pleased their hearts to hear.
        With this, the nobles soon arranged her marriage—
        Befitting Giselher as a king and man of courage.

1680   Who can hinder what is bound to be?
        They bade the maiden join their company
        And promised him this lovely girl as bride.
        He vowed in turn to keep her lovingly at his side.

1681   She was granted palaces and land,
        Secured by oath and the noble monarch's hand.
        And Gernot's too, that this would soon be done.
        The margrave spoke, "Castles, I have not a one.

1682   I pledge you the love and loyalty I hold,
        And give my daughter dowry of silver and gold
        As much as a hundred loaded sumpters carry,
        To suit this hero's kin, their sense of honor and glory."

1683   They formed a circle and bade them enter it,
        For that is the custom. Standing opposite,
        There was a group of youths—their cares were few,
        And they let their fancies play, which young men like to
            do.

1684   They asked if she would have him. Much embarrassed
Though she was at this, still she cherished
Thoughts of him as husband. So for shame
The maiden blushed (as many have) when the question
    came.

1685   Her father counselled her that she say yes,
And that she gladly take him. Soon the press
Of his white hand, and there he stood beside her,
Giselher—though joy of him would be denied her.

1686   "High and mighty kings," the margrave cried,
"When, as custom has it, you shall ride
Home to Burgundy, I'll give to you
My child to take along." This they vowed to do.

1687   After their noise, silence was now in order.
The maiden was asked to go to the women's quarter,
The guests to sleep and rest until the day.
Then he fed them again, their host, in his generous way.

1688   When they had eaten they wished for leave to go
To the land of Huns. "I would not have it so!"
Their noble host declared. "Stay here with me,
For rarely have I gained such pleasant company."

1689   "That surely cannot be," Lord Dankwart said.
"Where would you get the food, the wine and bread,
With all these many men you'll need it for,
Even tonight?" The margrave answered, "Say no more!

1690   Dear lords and friends of mine, do not refuse.
I'd give you all the food that you could use
In two week's time, for all your company.
Little indeed has Attila taken away from me."

1691   They had to stay (much as they would not yield),
       Until the fourth morning. Their host revealed
       Such generosity, men spoke of his deeds
       Far and wide. He gave his guests both clothes and steeds.

1692   But this could last no longer; they must go.
       And still Lord Ruedeger could never slow
       His generous hand. Whatever anyone wanted—
       One had to humor him—ask and it was granted!

1693   The servants brought their steeds, with saddles set,
       Before the palace gate, where they were met
       By many foreign knights, with shield in hand,
       For they were eager to ride, off to Attila's land.

1694   The margrave urged his gifts on each and all,
       Before his noble guests could leave the hall—
       A generous man, his ways were honored there.
       His lovely daughter he had given to Giselher.

1695   He gave to Gunther, champion nobly praised,
       What he could wear with honor undisgraced,
       Rarely as he took gifts: an armor suit.
       Gunther bowed to Ruedeger's hand in gratitude.

1696   Then he gave to Gernot a noble sword,
       With glory borne in battles afterward—
       Generous giving which pleased the margrave's wife.
       Yet Ruedeger, by the gift, was doomed to lose his life.

1697   Now Gotelind—rightly, since even the king
       Accepted presents—offered some loving thing
       As gift to Hagen, lest with no favor from her
       He leave for the festival. At first he'd not concur.

312

1698   But then he said, "Of all I have chanced to see
       I wish for nothing more to take with me,
       Except that shield which hangs upon the wall.
       That I'd like to have when we pay the king our call."

1699   These words of Hagen fell on Gotelind's ears
       And turning her mind to sorrow, led to tears.
       She thought of her love for Nudung, whom Witich slew—
       And from whose loss her pain and lamentation grew.

1700   She said to Hagen, "I will give you the shield,
       Would God that he whose once it was to wield
       Were still alive! In battle he was killed—
       For me, poor woman, a cause for tears and never stilled."

1701   The margravine arose from where she sat
       And took the shield in her white hands; with that
       She brought it to Hagen, who took it in his hand,
       A gift of honor given and placed at his command.

1702   A cover of brilliant silken cloth concealed
       Its color, bright with jewels—a better shield
       The sun has never seen. Should one desire
       To buy it, its worth would be a thousand marks or higher.

1703   Hagen ordered the shield carried away.
       Now Dankwart came to court, receiving that day
       Costly clothes the margrave's child presented,
       Which later he wore among the Huns, proud and
          splendid.

1704   All these many gifts they took, which never
       Would be theirs without their host's kind favor,

Who freely proffered all. (So hostile to him
They became one day, that in the end they slew him.)

1705   Folker came with his fiddle, having his mind
On courtly form, to stand by Gotelind
And play her his sweet tunes and sing a lay—
Saying farewell to Pöchlarn as they turned away.

1706   The margravine now had them bring a casket.
(This is a tale of friendly giving—ask it,
And you shall hear!) From this she took twelve rings
And wound them on his wrist. "I want you to take these
    things

1707   To Attila's land with you, to wear at court
For sake of me, that I may have report,
When you return, what deeds of service you did
At this high feast." How well he accomplished what she
    bid!

1708   The host announced, "Travel at ease the more
As I shall escort you, making very sure
That no one does you damage on the road."
His train of sumpters soon was ready with its load.

1709   He too prepared. Five hundred men, with steed
And dress for each, were set to follow his lead,
Off to the festival the Huns were giving,
Gay at heart. Not one returned to Pöchlarn living.

1710   Their host took leave with a loving kiss, likewise
Lord Giselher, heeding his heart's advice.
They held their lovely women in arms' embrace—
A thing for many maidens to mourn in coming days.

314

1711   On every hand were windows opened wide.
Host and men were ready to mount and ride.
I think their hearts foretold some awful woe,
For all these ladies and charming maids lamented so.

1712   Many longed for friends they'd never see
In Pöchlarn town again; yet cheerfully
They rode away, down by the sand where runs
The Danube in its valley, far to the land of Huns.

1713   Cried noble Ruedeger, the merry knight,
To the men of Burgundy, "It is not right
To keep from the Huns news of our visit in store.
Attila never received a message to please him more."

1714   Down through Austria a herald hastened,
Telling everywhere as people listened—
Attila's court was never so gratified—
How knights were come from Worms, on the farther
    Rhenish side.

1715   Heralds ranged ahead to tell their story:
Nibelung men in Hunnish territory!
"Greet them well, Kriemhild, this you must do.
Your loving brothers come in honor and homage to you."

1716   Lady Kriemhild stood in a window watching,
As friends will do, for her kin. She saw them marching,
Men from her father's land. This came to the king,
Who when he heard it smiled as at some pleasant thing.

1717   Kriemhild cried, "How sweet is my delight!
My kinsmen bring new shields, and hauberks white
And shining. Whoever has a wish for gold,
Recall my pain. My gratitude will be untold."

✝ TWENTY-EIGHTH ADVENTURE

How the Burgundians Came to the Castle of Attila

1718   And so the Burgundian warriors entered the land—
News which soon had reached old Hildebrand.
He told his lord of Verona, who grieved to hear it
But said to welcome them, as men of valor and spirit.

1719   Wolfhart, quick of courage, got their steeds.
There rode with Theoderich men of mighty deeds;
Out to the fields and the place of welcome they went,
Where men were packing on horses many a splendid tent.

1720   When Hagen of Trony saw them far ahead,
He called his lords, in courtly manner said,
"Men of courage, I'll tell you what to do:
Get up and go to meet these men who welcome you.

1721   There rides a troop that I know well," he said,
"Sturdy Amelung warriors, they are led
By the lord of Verona, men of spirit and pride.
Whatever service they offer should not be turned aside."

1722   All of them dismounted, as was right,
Theoderich and many a squire and knight,
And went where the guests, like heroes, took their stand.
They gave an affectionate welcome to men of Burgundy
land.

1723   Theoderich spoke. (You may be curious to hear
This warrior's words, as he saw them drawing near,

These sons of Uta, whose journey here he dreaded.
Lord Ruedeger knew the truth, he thought, and could
  have said it.)

1724   "Gunther and Giselher, welcome, my lords, to you!
To Gernot and Hagen welcome, and Folker, too,
And Dankwart the bold! But are you informed so ill
You do not know that Kriemhild weeps for Sigfrid still?"

1725   "She can weep a long time, can't she?" Hagen said.
"That man has lain for years, slain and dead.
She ought to save her love for the Hun she married.
Sigfrid won't come back. He is dead and long since
  buried."

1726   "Let us speak no more of Sigfrid's death.
Harmful things can happen so long as breath
Is in her body," cried Verona's lord.
"Prince and shield of the Nibelung host, be on your
  guard!"

1727   The great king answered, "What should I watch out for?
He sent us heralds—should I inquire more?—
And brought us word that we should not refuse
To ride to Attila's land; and my sister sent good news."

1728   Said Hagen again, "In this I counsel you well:
Ask Theoderich and his knights to tell
Their story in more detail, that you may find
The truth from them: what Lady Kriemhild has in mind."

1729   The great kings went, conferring privately,
Gunther and Gernot, Theoderich, all three:
"Excellent lord of Verona, be so kind

And tell us what you know of the queen's true state of
   mind."

1730   The lord of Verona spoke: "What more should I say?
I hear the wife of Attila every day,
Her heart in misery, weeping and crying the love
She had for stalwart Sigfrid, to mighty God above."

1731   A valiant man, Folker the fiddler, cried,
"What we have heard cannot be turned aside.
Ride to court and let us see what fate
For gallant men like us among the Huns may wait."

1732   And so to court the brave Burgundians came,
With all the splendor due their country's name.
Hagen of Trony, among the Huns, could strike
The wonder of many valiant men—what was he like?

1733   Reason enough: because their ears were filled
With tales of him by whom Sigfrid was killed,
That warrior peerless in strength, their queen's first lord,
So Hagen was the cause of many questions at court.

1734   A man of heroic build, truth to say:
Broad in the chest, his hair all streaked with gray;
His legs were long; a look that terrified
Flashed from his face; he walked along with a splendid
   stride.

1735   They found a place for the knights of Burgundy
And put up Gunther's servants separately—
This was the work of the queen, whose heart was filled
With hate for which the men in the inn would soon be
   killed.

1736   Dankwart, Hagen's brother, was marshal there.
The king assigned the servants to his care,
That he might be their guard, supplying their needs.
He was well disposed to them, and a man of noble deeds.

1737   Kriemhild the fair, taking her retinue, went
To welcome the Nibelungs—with false intent.
Giselher she kissed and took by the hand;
Hagen of Trony saw—and tightened his helmet band.

1738   "After a greeting like that," Hagen cried out,
"Men of valor have some cause to doubt.
For kings and men their welcome seems to differ.
Our trip to this tournament has little good to offer."

1739   "Have welcome from someone to whom your sight is
       dear!"
She cried. "Not as a friend do I greet you here.
Tell me what you bring from Worms on Rhine
That you should merit any welcoming of mine."

1740   Said Hagen, "If I had known that this was the way—
That vassals should bring you presents, I dare say
I'm rich enough—had I given this more thought,
There would have been some gift for you I could have
       brought."

1741   She cried, "There's more I want to know from you:
The treasure of Nibelung—what did you do
With that which was mine, as well you understand?
You should have brought it here to me, to Attila's land."

1742   "I assure you, milady, many days have passed
Since I was guardian of that treasure last.

My lords had it sunk in the Rhine, all the way
To the bottom, and there it must remain till Judgement
   Day."

1743   To this the queen replied, "That's what I thought.
It's very little for me that you have brought,
Though it's all mine and once was in my power.
For this my days are filled with hour on wretched hour."

1744   Said Hagen, "The devil a lot I'll bring to you,
To carry my shield is all that I can do,
And my byrnie here, my helm, with its brilliant hue.
The sword I have at my hand I'll never bring to you!"

1745   The queen cried out to the warriors one and all:
"No weapons shall be carried in this hall.
Hand them over to me, my lords, I'll see
That they are stored." Cried Hagen, "That will never be!

1746   Kind lady and prince's love, I do not mean
To covet such honor—that you, who are a queen,
Should carry my shield and armor to the inn.
That's not what my father taught me. I'll be chamberlain."

1747   Then Kriemhild cried, "Oh, the pain of it!
Why will my brother and Hagen not permit
Their shields to be stored? Some warning has been spread,
And if I knew the one who did it I'd see him dead."

1748   Theoderich answered, in his voice was anger:
"I am the one who warned these kings of danger—
And Hagen their vassal of Burgundy. Go to it,
Evil woman, you're not the one to make me rue it."

1749   At this, Attila's wife was struck with shame
And bitter fear of Theoderich. Quickly she came
Away from them and had no more to say,
But looked upon her enemies in a baleful way.

1750   And then two men shook hands, Hagen the one,
The other Theoderich; which being done,
The lord of light heart spoke in words well bred
And gallant: "I'm deeply sorry you came to the Huns," he
    said,

1751   "The way the queen has talked." Said Trony's knight:
"We'll see. Things may still turn out all right."
Thus they spoke together, two brave men.
This King Attila noticed and inquired then:

1752   "I'd surely like to know who that might be,
The knight to whom Theoderich courteously
Is giving welcome. He's proud and confident—
Whoever his father was, a knight most excellent!"

1753   One of Kriemhild's thanes replied, "That man
Was born of Trony, his father was Aldrian.
He's fierce enough, however gay he acts.
You'll see that what I say are the plain and simple facts."

1754   "You say he's so fierce, but how am I to know?"
Still the king was unaware what woe
The queen had plotted for her kindred ones,
Such evil that, living, none of them should leave the Huns.

1755   "Aldrian I knew, from early days,
A vassal who gained with me both honor and praise.

I made him a knight, and granted him my gold,
And faithful Helke loved him more than could be told.

1756 So I know Hagen well, and his career.
Two handsome boys I had as hostage here,
They grew to manhood, he and Walter of Spain.
Walter ran off with Hildegund, Hagen I freed again."

1757 He thought of long ago and what occurred,
Recognizing his friend of Trony, his ward,
Who served him well as a youth—and now by whom,
A man full grown, beloved friends would meet their
doom.

✠ TWENTY-NINTH ADVENTURE

How Kriemhild Accused Hagen and How He Did not Rise when She Approached

1758   So they parted, two knights whom all men praised,
Theoderich and Hagen. Gunther's vassal gazed
Over his shoulder then, looking around
For one of his companions, whom he soon had found.

1759   There stood Folker, master of minstrel-song,
By Gunther's side. He asked him to come along,
His spirit of fierceness in mind, and he was right.
He was in all respects a brave and perfect knight.

1760   Their lords still waiting in the courtyard there,
These two set off alone across the square
To go before a far-off, spacious palace—
Knights of the highest order, fearing no man's malice.

1761   Down they sat on a bench in front of it,
With the rooms of Lady Kriemhild opposite,
Their garments gleaming so brightly as to show them
In all their splendor. Many who saw them were eager to
    know them.

1762   The Huns were gaping as if each haughty knight
Were some wild beast. Attila's wife caught sight
Of both of them through her window, a sight designed
To sadden and trouble deeply lovely Kriemhild's mind.

1763 Recalling her sorrow and pain it made her cry.
Attila's men began to wonder why.
What, they asked, had cast so deep a pall
Upon her heart? "Brave heroes, Hagen did it all!"

1764 They asked her, "How is that? A moment ago
We surely saw you happy. But tell us so—
Bid us avenge it, and no man lives so brave
Who, if he did this to you, shall escape the grave."

1765 "Whoever avenged my wrong I should repay
With all he wished, and gladly. Pleading, I lay
Myself at your feet." Thus cried Attila's wife.
"Give me vengeance on Hagen, that he may lose his life."

1766 Sixty valiant men, for Kriemhild's sake,
Got ready, swift to venture out and take
The life of brave Lord Hagen and his friend
The fiddler, too; and this was done with base intent.

1767 But when the queen perceived her troop so small,
She came to the warriors, full of wrath, to call:
"You'll miss the mark in what you hope to do—
You'll never take the measure of Hagen with so few!

1768 Whatever may be Hagen's valor and power,
Folker the fiddler at his side will tower
Higher than he in strength—a dangerous man.
You'll not fight them with ease, and do not think you can."

1769 Hearing this, more men came on the scene,
Four hundred stalwart lords. The gracious queen
Was bent on causing harm and spared no pains.
Serious trouble was in store for all these thanes.

1770   Seeing her brave retainers armed and ready,
She spoke to the warriors thus, the royal lady:
"Wait a while, do not break your rows;
With crown upon me I shall go before my foes.

1771   Then hear what he did, and what reproach I throw
At Gunther's vassal, Hagen. This I know,
That he is proud beyond denying it.
What happens to him in turn I do not care a whit."

1772   The fiddler, gallant bard, was now aware
Of the noble queen descending by a stair
That led from the building. Folker the valiant man
Turned to Hagen his friend and, watching this, began:

1773   "Look, friend Hagen, there she comes, the one
Who asked us here—in poor faith that was done.
I never saw king's wife accompanied
By so many men with sword in hand, warlike indeed.

1774   Have they something against you, Hagen my friend,
Do you know? If so, I say you'd best attend
To life and honor—a sound idea, I find.
Unless my eyes deceive me, they come in an angry mind.

1775   And some of them are rather broad in the chest—
If one would be on guard, it might seem best
To do it soon; I think they wear bright mail
Beneath their silk. For whom they mean it I cannot tell."

1776   Then Hagen the fearless answered angrily:
"I know that all of this is meant for me,
The shining weapons they carry there in hand—
For all of them, I'd still get back to Burgundy land.

1777   Tell me now, my friend, do you stand with me,
If I am set upon by this company
Of Kriemhild's men? As you love me, let me know,
And you shall have forever the loyal thanks I owe."

1778   "I'd help you just as surely," the minstrel said,
"If I saw here a king approach at the head
Of all his knights; there is, while I may live,
No inch I yield in fear, no help I will not give."

1779   "God bless you, noble Folker! If they fight
Against me here, I need no other knight,
Since you will help me as you said you would,
Let them come this way, and may their guard be good!"

1780   "Let's get up from this seat," the minstrel said,
"She is a queen—and let her come ahead,
Showing our respect for her noble birth,
And thus enhancing both of us in fame and worth."

1781   "Over my dead body," Hagen said.
"These thanes would think I acted out of dread
And apprehension here, if I retreated.
Not for one of them would I rise, when I am seated.

1782   Better indeed by far if we did not.
Why give honor when hate is all I've got?
That I never will, while I have life.
What do I care for the malice of King Attila's wife?"

1783   Across his knees the arrogant Hagen laid
A shining weapon from whose pommel played,
In light as green as grass, a jasper stone.
Kriemhild knew at once that it was Sigfrid's own.

1784   She saw the sword—how heavy her sorrow weighed!
The hilt was made of gold; the sheath, red braid.
It called to mind her pain, and all this ended
With her weeping—just, I think, what Hagen intended.

1785   There on the bench, bold Folker drew to his side
A mighty fiddle-bow, long and wide,
Much like a sword, sharp and heavily made.
And there the merry warriors sat, unafraid.

1786   They thought themselves so much without a peer
That they would not arise from their seat in fear
Of anyone. Before their very toes
Stepped the highborn queen, and greeted them as foes:

1787   "Tell me, Hagen," she said, "who sent for you,
That you ride to this country—which you dare to do,
Knowing well what you have brought on me?
If you had any sense, you would have let it be."

1788   "No one sent for me," said Hagen. "There came
An invitation for three who are by name
My lords in liege, and I by this same token
Am their vassal. No trip with them have I forsaken!"

1789   She cried, "Go on and tell me why you did
The deed by which my hate is merited.
You killed Sigfrid, my lord and beloved one—
Sufficient cause to weep until my days are done."

1790   "Why go on? We've talked enough, I'm through.
I am Hagen still, the one who slew
The mighty hero Sigfrid. How he suffered
For the slur on Brunhild's name that Kriemhild offered!

1791   Mighty queen, there shall be no denying:
All the guilt is mine, for doom and dying.
Woman or man, avenge it whoever will.
Either I lie to you, or I have done you ill."

1792   "Listen, my lords, hear this man confess
All my hurt! What happens to him for this,
Men of the king, that is my least concern."
And now the haughty warriors looked at each other in
    turn.

1793   If someone had started fighting, what ensued
Would have brought the two men fame and praise re-
    newed.
In battle, they would have made their merit clear.
The Huns laid plans in pride, they gave them up in fear.

1794   One of their warriors cried, "Don't look at me.
I intend to go back on my guarantee,
And not to lose my life for anyone's gift.
Great King Attila's wife would cast us all adrift."

1795   "The same for me," another one near him said.
"Give me towers of solid gold, all red,
I wouldn't fight this fiddler, just for the grim
And terrible look I see upon the face of him.

1796   Also, I've known Hagen since he was young,
And I don't need to hear his merit sung.
On twenty-two occasions I've seen him fight,
In battles where women's hearts were left as dark as night.

1797   They took the road on more than one campaign
Here with Attila, he and the knight of Spain,

328

When they fought so well for the honor of the king.
Credit rendered Hagen is only a rightful thing.

1798   Then he was just a child in years but they
Who once were young with him are now turned gray,
And he is a man mature, a fearsome lord.
Besides he carries Balmung, his ill-gotten sword."

1799   That was the end of it, no one would start
The fighting now. The queen was sick at heart.
The heroes turned about, fearing to die
At the hands of the fiddler. Well they knew the reason why!

1800   "Now we have clearly seen," said Folker the bold,
"That we find enemies here, as we were told.
The kings are in court, and we had best go back
And keep our masters safe from any new attack.

1801   A man will often neglect a thing from fear;
Just so will friend aid friend, if his mind is clear,
And in his friendship do nothing of the kind.
Hurt to many a man is saved by presence of mind."

1802   Said Hagen, "I'll follow you and go along."
They went where brilliant warriors stood in a throng
At court reception. To his lords in the crowd
Folker the valiant knight began to call aloud:

1803   He said, "How long do you mean to stay and let
Yourselves be surrounded. Go to the court and get
Straight from the king's own mouth his state of mind."
Now you could see brave warriors move, in pairs aligned.

1804   The ruling prince of Verona took by the hand
Mighty Gunther, lord of Burgundy land,
And Irnfrid, valiant Gernot; also there
Was Margrave Ruedeger, off to court with Giselher.

1805   However they were paired in going to court
Folker and Hagen never drew apart—
Till once in battle when their end was come;
And that was many women's tearful martyrdom.

1806   People saw the kings on the way to the castle.
A thousand bold retainers, liege and vassal,
Sixty champions, too, who made the ride,
Recruits of dauntless Hagen from his own countryside.

1807   Haward and Iring, two men beyond compare,
Walked along with the kings, a friendly pair,
And Dankwart with Wolfhart (a worthy man was he),
Each impressing the others with his dignity.

1808   The lord of the Rhineland entered the palace gate.
Mighty Attila would no longer wait;
Seeing him, he ran from where he was seated.
No man has been by any king so nobly greeted.

1809   "Gunther my lord; Gernot, and Giselher,
Your brothers, welcome! I sent—and did not spare
Good faith or zeal—my pledge of service to you,
To Worms on Rhine. And welcome to all your retinue!

1810   To you two knights a special welcome word,
Folker, man of valor, and Hagen my lord,
From me and my lady too, upon your entry
Into our land. She sent you heralds to Rhenish country."

1811   Hagen replied, "I've heard that more than once.
Had love of my lords not brought me to the Huns,
In homage to you I'd have ridden to your land."
The highborn host now took his dear guests by the hand,

1812   And led them to sit where he himself was sitting.
They poured for their guests—with eagerness most fit-
ting—
Vessels of wide gold full of wine and mead
And mulberry drink, making the strangers welcome in-
deed.

1813   Said King Attila, "I would have you know:
No greater pleasure could this world bestow
Than you have given me in coming here.
You've made the queen's great burden of sorrow disappear.

1814   For I have wondered what I did to you—
Seeing my many noble guests who do—
That you have never cared to visit here.
Now that I see you before me, the end is joy and cheer."

1815   Said Ruedeger, man of pride and confidence,
"Well may you welcome them! A noble sense
Of loyalty has always been the forte
Of my lady's kin. What handsome knights they bring to
your court!"

1816   The lords had come the eve of solstice-tide
To the court of mighty Attila. Far and wide,
No welcome ever heard of matched their greeting.
Soon came dinner; he sat with them at table, eating.

1817 No host has sat with guests more splendidly.
They gave them all they wished, in quantity,
Of food and drink—most gladly, for they had heard
About these heroes, long ago, most wondrous word.

✠ THIRTIETH ADVENTURE
How Hagen and Folker Stood Watch

1818   Now the day was done and night drew near,
And travel-weary men began to fear
Lest they might have no rest nor get to bed.
Hagen talked of this; word was quick to spread.

1819   Gunther cried to his host, "God save you, sir!
We wish to have our sleep. If you prefer
We'll come tomorrow morning. So give us leave."
The king and his guests were parting; there seemed no
    cause to grieve.

1820   But now the guests were being crowded 'round,
And valiant Folker cried to the Huns, "Give ground!
How dare you come and tread on our very toes?
If you don't stop you'll have your share of pain and woes.

1821   My fiddle-bow will fetch you a blow so smart—
If you have one loyal friend, it'll break his heart.
Get out of our way—you'd better! They share the name
Of warrior, all of them—but their hearts are not the same."

1822   And when the fiddler spoke so angrily,
Valiant Hagen turned around to see.
"That's good advice you hear our minstrel give.
Go back, you men of Kriemhild, back to where you live!

1823   No one will do what you are counting on.
If you want trouble, come back tomorrow at dawn.

333

Tonight, let us as strangers rest in peace.
Men of such a mind as yours do that at least."

1824 They took their foreign guests to a spacious hall
Prepared for courtly taste with beds and all,
Long and wide and splendid. But there the queen
Had plotted them the bitterest woe the world has seen.

1825 There were many quilts of Arras, skillfully made
Of shining satin cloth, with covers laid,
Of very best Arabian silk, thereon;
And all around the edges lovely bindings shone.

1826 Some had coverlets of ermine fur
Or black sable, under which they were,
That night, supposed to sleep till light of day.
No king or king's retainers ever slept that way.

1827 Young Giselher cried, "Alas for this night we spend,
For those who came with us, our every friend!
Think of the kindly things my sister said—
And yet because of her I fear we'll soon lie dead."

1828 Hagen the warrior spoke, "Do not take fright.
I myself will stand shield-watch tonight.
I think that I can keep you safe till dawn—
Have no fear. Tomorrow—let him who can live on!"

1829 They bowed in thanks to him, and off they went
To seek their beds. Little time they spent,
These handsome lords, before they all had gone
Sound asleep. Bold Hagen put his armor on.

334

1830 Folker the fiddler spoke, "If you're not scorning
Offers of help, I'll stand with you till morning,
Hagen, taking my share of tonight's watch."
For this the chivalrous hero thanked Lord Folker much:

1831 "The Lord in Heaven bless you, Folker my friend,
I wish for no companion but you to spend
My anxious moments with, when trouble is near.
I'll pay you back, unless my death should interfere."

1832 Then they both put on their shining clothes
(Taking each his shield in hand) and rose
And left the house, to stand before the door
And guard the guests—out of the loyalty they bore.

1833 Valiant Folker took his trusty shield.
Leaning it by the palace wall, he wheeled
And went inside, to get his fiddle there.
Thus he served his friends, for this was his rightful care.

1834 Beneath the doorway, seated on the stone,
The boldest of fiddlers played, and when the tone
Rose sweetly from the strings, out of the ranks
Of warriors far from home Lord Folker had his thanks.

1835 His strings were loud, and all the hall resounded,
For in this man both valor and art abounded.
He began to play more sweetly and softly then,
Lulling to sleep upon their benches anxious men.

1836 When he could see that they were sleeping fast
He took his shield in hand again and passed
From out of the room, to stand before the tower,

And guard the homeless wanderers from Kriemhild's
    power.

1837   No earlier than the middle of the night,
    I think, bold Folker saw the play of light
    From helmets in the darkness. (All too gladly
    Would Kriemhild's men have reached their guests and
      used them badly.)

1838   The fiddler said, "Hagen, my friend, this trouble
    Might be better borne if we bore it double.
    I see men in armor by the palace.
    So far as I can judge, they mean to fight and kill us."

1839   "Quiet then," said Hagen. "Let them near.
    There'll be helmet-cases jolted here,
    By our two swords in hand, before we're seen.
    We'll send them back in poor condition to the queen."

1840   Suddenly one of the Huns had looked about:
    The door was guarded! He was quick to shout,
    "What we thought of doing cannot be.
    Someone's standing watch—that's the fiddler I see.

1841   On his head he has a helmet, shining,
    Bright and hard, of sound and strong designing,
    His mail is glowing like a fire reflected—
    And Hagen by his side! Our guests are well protected."

1842   When Folker saw the men retrace their path,
    He turned to his companion, full of wrath:
    "Let me leave the house and follow behind,
    And speak to Kriemhild's men—I have questions on my
      mind!"

1843   "No," Lord Hagen cried, "for my own sake!
        Leave the house, and these brave men would take
        Their swords to you. Such trouble they'd have you in,
        I'd have to help you, though it cost me all my kin.

1844   If both of us went out, to wage this war,
        In no time two of them, or maybe four
        Would rush the hall together. The havoc wrought
        Among our men asleep would never be forgot."

1845   Said Folker, "One thing at least we should do then:
        Let them know I saw them. Kriemhild's men
        Shall never have the chance to go about
        Denying the treachery they hoped to carry out."

1846   Folker shouted at them, "How does this happen,
        That valiant men of Kriemhild come, a weapon
        In every hand?—riding out to rob?
        You need my friend and me to help you with the job!"

1847   No one answered that. His anger grew;
        The hero spoke, "You worthless cowards, you!
        While we were sleeping, you'd have murdered us?
        Not often have such worthy men been treated thus."

1848   The queen was duly told her messengers
        Had failed their mission. Greatest grief was hers.
        Fierce of heart, she thought of other ways.
        For this, courageous lords would perish in coming day.

1849   "My armor," Folker said, "is cooling fast.
I do not think this night has long to last.
I can tell by the breeze, day is about to dawn."
They went to wake the rest, still sleeping soundly on.

1850   Now bright morning came for the guests in the hall.
Hagen went to the knights and woke them all,
And would they go to church and hear mass sung?
According to Christian custom, many bells were rung.

1851   (Clearly, they did not sing in harmony,
Christian and pagan, there seemed no unity.)
Gunther's heroes wished to be up and gone
To the minster now, and rose from where they slept, as
one.

1852   The knights got dressed in clothes the like of which
Heroes never brought (they were so rich)
To any king's land—hard for Hagen to bear.
"Warriors," he said, "these are not the clothes to wear.

1853   There's more than one among you here who knows.
Carry a sword in your hand, and not a rose!
And take your solid shining helm in lieu
Of jeweled chaplets. We know what evil she means to do.

1854   And we must fight today, I give you my word.
Wear your hauberk instead of a silken shirt,

Take your good broad shield and not your cape.
If anyone raises trouble, be in fighting shape!

1855 My dear lords, kin, and men, do not be loath
To go to church—your sorrow and trouble both
Complain to mighty God! Let this be clear
In all your minds: the hour of our death is near.

1856 Do not forget the things that you have done,
And stand in earnest before the Almighty One,
For I will warn you this, my splendid men,
Without God's special help, you'll never hear mass again."

1857 To go to the minster, princes and vassals rose
But valiant Hagen stood within the close
Sacred to God and bade them stop and thus
Remain together. "Who knows what the Hun will do to
us?

1858 My friends, place your shields before your feet,"
Said Hagen. "If anyone should basely greet
Your presence here, repay with the fatal sword.
There's my advice!—so act that praise be your reward."

1859 Ahead of the others Folker and Hagen went
In front of the wide minster, with this intent:
To be quite sure the queen must crowd in past,
In order to enter. The rage within their hearts was vast.

1860 Now came the lord of the land, in company
Of his lovely wife. Adorned in luxury
Were the knights one saw with them, walking along.
A cloud of dust rose high from all of Kriemhild's throng.

339

1861   Great King Attila, seeing them armed this way,
The kings and their retinue, was quick to say,
"What's this I see? My friends with helmets on?
I honestly regret if any harm's been done.

1862   And I will make amends as they see fit,
For hurt to mind or heart because of it,
To make it clear to them how bad I feel.
Let them but ask, and I shall answer their appeal."

1863   Said Hagen, "No one's done a thing to us.
My lords by custom go in armor thus
For three full days at any festival.
Hurt to us would be relayed to you in full."

1864   Clearly Kriemhild heard what Hagen spoke,
And cast at him a hostile look that broke
From lowered brow; yet she would not declare,
Well as she knew it from Burgundy, the custom there.

1865   However fierce her hate for them, or bitter,
Had someone told the king the truth of the matter,
He might well have stopped what yet occurred.
In their great arrogance, they told him not a word.

1866   A crowd came with her. A space but two hands wide
Was more than these two men would stand aside.
This was what the Huns felt wary of,
As there was nothing left to do but push and shove.

1867   Attila's chamberlains did not approve.
They would have gladly gone ahead to move
These knights to wrath—which they hadn't the courage
    for,
With Attila there. They jostled about and nothing more.

1868   When church was over and time had come to go,
The Huns made for their steeds—and were not slow.
Maidens stood by Kriemhild, fair to see,
And seven thousand thanes rode in her company.

1869   There by the windows with the mighty king,
She sat with her maids—for him a pleasant thing—
To watch at riding lords of such good cheer.
How many foreign knights rode in the courtyard here!

1870   Dankwart the bold, as marshal, now came back
With the serving-men. He had been keeping track
Of all the staff of the king of Burgundy.
Horses were fitly saddled for Nibelung chivalry.

1871   Now that kings and men were all on horse,
Folker the strong proposed they joust in force
As was their custom at home. This gave the tip
To all the heroes to show their brilliant horsemanship.

1872   So he proposed what they were not against.
The jousting and the noise were soon immense,
As many men approached the spacious court.
Kriemhild and King Attila turned to watch the sport.

1873   Six hundred thanes arrived, drawn by the tests—
Theoderich's knights who came to face the guests
And share the fun with the men of Burgundy.
Had he allowed, they would have done so willingly.

1874   What knights rode after them! The eager news
Was passed to Theoderich; he did not choose
To let them vie with Gunther's retinue.
He worried for his men and had good reason to.

1875 Now that the knights of Verona had left the field,
Ruedeger's men from Pöchlarn, under shield,
Five hundred strong, approached the front of the hall.
The margrave himself would rather they had not come
 at all.

1876 He rode through the ranks of his men, wise and cautious,
Saying they must have noticed how ferocious
Gunther's warriors were, their anger stirred,
And he'd be pleased if they'd not ride in this behourd.

1877 And when these merry knights had left them, then,
Our story runs, there came Thuringian men,
And a thousand valiant lords from Denmark entered,
Brandishing spears; and pieces flew from lances splintered.

1878 Irnfrid and Haward rode to join the melee.
The Rhinelanders waited in their stately way
To offer joust to the men of Thuringia and give
Such thrusts that many a splendid shield was left a sieve.

1879 Bloedel and his three thousand men approached.
The king and Kriemhild saw him, as they watched
The scene before them, the games of chivalry.
The queen was pleased at this, for the hurt of Burgundy.

1880 Shrutan and Gibech, Ramung and Hornbow joined
In jousting, for so the Huns are always inclined,
Facing the men of Burgundy, heroes all.
Shafts went whirling, high as the royal palace wall.

1881 (All this was nothing more than sport and sound.)
The crash of shields made house and halls resound

Loud with the echoing noise of Gunther's lords.
His retinue was first in glory and high awards.

1882　So fast and violent did their pastime get
That through the saddle cloths the shining sweat
Ran from the fine horses the heroes rode.
They tried their luck with the Huns, in an overbearing
　　mood.

1883　The minstrel cried, "It seems these men would rather
Not attack us now. From what I gather,
They bear toward us some hateful prejudice.
Well, there never was a better time than this!"

1884　And Folker went on, "Have our chargers led
Back to quarters. We'll ride toward evening instead,
Whenever the time is ripe. What will you bet
The queen must give the prize to men of Burgundy yet?"

1885　No man could match in pomp one of the chaps
Whom they saw riding up. He had, perhaps,
A sweetheart on the parapet, to ride
In clothes so elegant, just like a knight's new bride.

1886　Folker cried, "How can I let that go?
This lady's man deserves a whacking blow.
Let no one hinder me, he pays with his life;
And what do I care if this should anger Attila's wife?"

1887　"No, for my sake don't," said Gunther in haste.
"If we should launch the attack, we'd stand disgraced
In people's minds. Let the Huns, as is more fitting."
Attila still was there with his queen, quietly sitting.

1888   Hagen said, "I'm going to join the battle.
Let these lords and ladies see the mettle
Of our riding. This is the best we can do—
They won't give any prizes to Gunther's retinue."

1889   Folker the valiant rode behourd again,
Destined soon to be a cruel bane
To many women, for his spear impaled
That wealthy Hun, at which both maids and ladies wailed.

1890   Hagen and his men, with sixty thanes,
Rode off in a mighty rush, taking pains
To follow the fiddler where the games were run.
Attila and the queen saw clearly what was done.

1891   The kings were loath to let their minstrel go
Without protection there among the foe,
So a thousand heroes rode to show their skill,
Doing all as they pleased, with a proud and haughty will.

1892   Now when the rich and mighty Hun was slain,
His kinsmen all were heard to weep and complain.
And those of his household asked, "Who struck the blow?"
"That was the minstrel Folker, man of the fiddlebow!"

1893   They shouted for their swords and shields at once,
The kinsmen of this margrave of the Huns,
Wishing the death of Folker. Leaving his post
In the window niche he rushed to the scene, their royal
host.

1894   All the people raised a great to-do.
By the hall the kings leaped down, with their retinue.

Burgundians too had pushed their horses back.
Attila intervened lest either side attack.

1895 Nearby, a friend of the Hun happened to stand.
Attila snatched a weapon from his hand
And beat them back, for he was very mad.
"What a way to ruin the welcome these knights have had!

1896 If you should kill this minstrel before me here,
What a wicked thing! My view was clear;
I saw the way he rode when the Hun was humbled.
That was no fault of Folker's; it happened because he
    stumbled.

1897 You'll have to leave my guests in peace," he said,
And gave them his protection. Now they led
Their horses back to the inn; servants there
Stood in readiness to give them zealous care.

1898 The host and all his friends entered the palace;
And he'd allow no further show of malice.
They set out tables, serving them water on these—
But here the men of Rhine had many enemies.

1899 Before they all were seated, a long time passed.
Fear of Kriemhild's plotting held them fast.
She cried, "Prince of Verona, I seek your aid,
Your guard and counsel. I'm in peril and afraid."

1900 Answered Hildebrand, a worthy lord,
"The man who kills the Nibelungs for reward
Need not count on me. He may regret
The step he takes. These knights have not been conquered
    yet."

1901   Theoderich added, a man of courteous air:
"Mighty queen, do not renew that prayer.
Your valiant kin have done no wrong to me,
That I should turn on them in open enmity.

1902   Your wish does you little credit—as the wife
Of a noble prince, to plot against the life
Of your own kin. In trust they sought this land.
Sigfrid will have no vengeance from Theoderich's hand."

1903   Finding Theoderich free of perfidy,
She gave vast marches once in Nudung's fee
In pledge to Bloedel's hand—her move was swift!
(Dankwart slew him soon, and he forgot his gift.)

1904   She said, "Help me, Bloedel! Here in this house
Are foes of mine, by whom my lord and spouse
Lord Sigfrid died. Whoever helps me get
Revenge for that, to him I stand in constant debt."

1905   Bloedel answered, "Lady, this is a fact:
I dare inflict on them no hostile act,
Because of the king. He loves to see them here,
And he would not forget if I should interfere."

1906   "Not so, Lord Bloedel, you'll always have my aid.
I'll give you silver and gold in pay, and a maid
Of greatest beauty, Nudung's bride intended,
A charming maiden in whose arms you'll be contented.

1907   Land and castles, everything I'll give,
Most noble knight, to you that you may live
In joy forever, if you become the heir
Of Nudung's march. I'll keep in faith, what now I swear."

1908   Now that Bloedel had his pay revealed
And found that in her beauty she appealed
So much to him, he thought in war and strife
To win her love. For this he soon would lose his life.

1909   "Go back to the hall again," he said to the queen.
"And I shall raise the alarm before you're seen.
Hagen will pay for what he did to you.
I'll hand him over, bound and tied, when I am through."

1910   He turned: "Now arm yourselves, men of mine,
We go to our foes in the inn, by her design
From which she will not release me, Attila's wife.
That is why each one of us must risk his life."

1911   Leaving Bloedel in spirit battle-fit
The queen now went to table, there to sit
With Attila and his warriors, all of them.
She had devised for her guests a fearful stratagem.

*C1963**

    The princes at long last were seated all
And now began to eat, when into the hall

---

* Here the translation follows manuscript C. B reads:
    Since otherwise the fighting would not start—
    Her ancient pain deep buried in her heart—
    Kriemhild brought to table Attila's son.
    No woman has sought revenge through a deed more cruelly done.
These verses are a holdover from sources in which Kriemhild not only has Ortlieb thus brought to sacrifice, but incites the youth to strike Hagen, who then kills him. In the *Nibelungenlied* Ortlieb is obviously too young to fit into this pattern, and the poem has besides a more reasonable if less traumatic occasion for the outbreak of war: Dankwart's report of the death of all the squires. With this the version of C is in accord, while B's strophe is gratuitous. In affectionate tribute to its grisly impact, B apparently kept it anyway.

To join their party entered Attila's child—
For which the mighty king would grieve, unreconciled.

1913 Quickly, four of Attila's vassals there
Went to bring Ortlieb, his son and heir,
To the princes' table, where also Hagen sat.
There was murder in his hate—the child would die for
that.

1914 And when the great king saw his son, he cried
To all his kin-in-law, in kindly pride:
"Look, my friends, here is my only son,
And your sister's too, a sign of good for everyone.

1915 A valiant man, if he takes after his race,
Rich and noble, strong, and fair of face!
If I shall live to give them, twelve whole lands
Shall all be his. You'll be well served at Ortlieb's hands.

1916 So I am pleased to ask, dear friends of mine,
That when you travel home, back to the Rhine,
You take your sister's son with you, and ever
Let the boy be granted your most gracious favor.

1917 And rear him in the ways of excellence,
Till manhood. Should anyone do violence
In your dominions, he will help you repay it,
When he is grown." The wife of Attila heard him say it.

1918 Cried Hagen, "These knights might well give him their
trust
If he should grow to manhood, yet it must
In truth be said the prince has a fated air.
The times I'll come to this young prince's court are rare."

1919 Attila looked at Hagen. The words had hit.
A cheerful man, he did not speak of it,
And yet his heart was sad, and grave his mind.
This was no jest, not so was Hagen's will inclined.

1920 The princes, like their king, were shorn of joy,
At what Lord Hagen said about the boy,
Annoyed that they must take it—still not knowing
All of what was yet to come of that man's doing.

✠ THIRTY-SECOND ADVENTURE
How Dankwart Killed Bloedel

1921 Bloedel's knights stood ready. All aligned
In a thousand hauberks, they set out to find
Dankwart at table with the squires' train.
There, among heroes, awful hate began its reign.

1922 For when Lord Bloedel came where they were seated,
He was met by the marshal, and duly greeted:
"Welcome, sir, to this house. And yet I doubt
If I fully understand—what is this all about?"

1923 "You need not greet me," Bloedel said. "I came,
But my coming means your end—for this the blame
Is your brother Hagen's, by whom Sigfrid was slain.
You'll pay the Huns for that, with many another thane."

1924 "Oh no, Lord Bloedel," said Dankwart. "We should
    clearly
Regret our journey then. But I was merely
A youth and no more, when Sigfrid lost his life.
Tell me, what cause of reproach am I to Attila's wife?"

1925 "I tell you this, and this is all I know:
Your kinsmen Gunther and Hagen did it. And so,
Outcast men, on guard! There is no path
To safety here; you'll be my lady's bond in death."

1926 "If you will not relent," Dankwart declared,
"I rue my pleading. It were better spared."
Up from the table leapt the valiant lord
And drew his mighty blade, his sharpened sword,

1927   And struck Lord Bloedel such a violent blow,
His head rolled off and lay at his feet below.
"Now let that be your dowry," Dankwart cried,
"For the one whose love you hoped to win, for Nudung's
    bride!

1928   Marry her tomorrow to another—
We'll do the same for him, if he wants to bother
For his dowry." (It seems he'd been apprised
By loyal Huns of the terrible harm the queen devised.)

1929   Bloedel's men, seeing their master slain,
Could not forgive their guests or bear such pain.
Their swords held high, they rushed with fierce intent
Upon the pages, a step which many would soon lament.

1930   Loudly Dankwart cried to the household hands,
"Good squires and pages, you see how your future stands.
On guard, my outcast men! Our need is clear.
And yet most noble Kriemhild sweetly asked us here."

1931   Some had no swords; they reached beneath the table,
Seizing the long footstools—now unable
Longer to bear the great affront they felt.
Even through helmets those heavy chairs could raise a
    welt.

1932   How fiercely the youths resisted this attack!
The men in armor soon were driven back
Leaving within a good five hundred dead.
All the serving men were drenched with blood and
    red.

1933 This fearful piece of news was soon made plain
   To Attila's knights (causing them bitter pain):
   That Bloedel himself was killed, and all his crew,
   Which Hagen's brother did, with men of the retinue.

1934 Before the king found out, two thousand or more
   Of the Huns made ready, and for the hate they bore,
   Fell on the squires—for so their doom took shape.
   Of all of these retainers they let not one escape.

1935 The traitors brought to the hall a mighty host.
   Bravely the foreign squires stood their post.
   What good their valor? Their death was now ordained.
   In all too short a time, most frightful havoc reigned.

1936 Now your ears shall hear both wonders said,
   And monstrous things. Nine thousand men lay dead,
   Besides a dozen knights of Dankwart's own.
   He himself stood up, among his foes, alone.

1937 The din of battle stilled, the tumult died.
   Looking over his shoulder, Dankwart cried,
   "Alas for all the friends I had to lose;
   Now sadly I must stand alone among my foes."

1938 Swords fell heavy on him. (Women would weep
   For this in time.) In order now to keep
   His shield up higher, he set his enarmes low.
   On many suits of mail he made the wet blood flow.

1939 Cried Aldrian's son, "Alas, this pain and despair!
   Step back, you Hunnish men, and give me air.
   The breeze shall cool my battle-weary frame."
   They watched him come ahead, and splendidly he came.

1940   Out of the house, battle-worn, he sprang.
And how the fresh swords on his helmet rang!
They rushed upon the lord of Burgundy land—
Men who had not seen the wonders done by his hand.

1941   "Would to God above I had a herald
To tell my brother Hagen how, imperilled,
I stand and face these knights," Lord Dankwart said.
"He'd help me get away or lie beside me, dead."

1942   Hun lords cried, "Herald? There'll be no other
But you, when we carry you before your brother,
Dead. Gunther's vassal then will know
At last what pain is, for you have hurt Attila so."

1943   "Stop the threats," he said, "and stand aside!
I'll keep the armor yet from getting dried
On some of you. I go myself to reveal
The truth at court and tell my lords the grief I feel."

1944   He soon was such a bane to Attila's lords,
They did not dare resist him with their swords.
They hit his shield with their spears, in number so great
He had to set it down for all the added weight.

1945   They thought to conquer him, now that he bore
No shield in hand, but what deep wounds he tore
Through helmets then! Heroes sank before him.
What a harvest of praise Lord Dankwart's valor bore him!

1946   They rushed him from either side, but of these some
Who joined the fray had been too quick to come.
He faced his foes, like a wild boar held at bay
By dogs in a forest. Could he be braver in any way?

1947   Once again his very path was wet
With steaming blood. Lone warrior never yet
Has better fought against his foes than he.
Hagen's brother strode to court, and splendidly!

1948   Bearers of wine and stewards heard the sound
Of swords at work, and cast their drinks to the ground,
Their food for the court, which they were about to bear,
And—foemen savage enough—met him at the stair.

1949   Said the weary man, "Stewards, what's amiss?
You ought to take much better care than this
Of all your guests, and feed those lords good things—
Letting me tell my tale to my beloved kings."

1950   On those who in their courage blocked the stair
He swung his sword so fiercely through the air
That they moved higher up the steps in fear.
With strength and courage he accomplished wonders here!

✠ THIRTY-THIRD ADVENTURE

How the Burgundians
Fought the Huns

1951   Valiant Dankwart stepped inside the door,
Making the Huns move back a little more.
His clothes were run with blood. He took his stand,
Holding a mighty weapon naked in his hand.

1952   Dankwart shouted loud to all the throng:
"Hagen my brother, sir, you sit too long.
To you and God above I cry our doom.
Our knights and all our squires lie dead in the hostel
    room."

1953   "Who did it?" Hagen shouted back again.
"Bloedel did it, Bloedel and his men.
I tell you this, he's paid a heavy fine,
For I struck off his head with these two hands of mine."

1954   "Little harm in that," his brother said.
"People say that if a man be dead,
And if it be at the hands of some great hero
So much the less excuse for lovely women's sorrow.

1955   But tell me, brother Dankwart, why so red?
You seem in pain from all the blood you shed.
If he who did it is still in this countryside
There'll be his life to pay—or the devil save his hide."

1956   "You're looking at a healthy man, this wet
Is blood from others' wounds. That's what I get

For all the men that I have killed today.
How many I left dead, I swear I could not say."

1957 "Dankwart, watch the door, and look about!
Do not let a single Hun get out.
I'll have a word with them," Lord Hagen said.
"We have no choice but this. Our guiltless men lie dead."

1958 Said he, "If I'm to be the chamberlain,
Why, I know how to serve such worthy men,
And I shall tend the stairs as suits my fame."
To Kriemhild's thanes more gloomy tidings never came.

1959 "I wonder here," said Hagen, "what the Hun
Is whispering about? I gather it's the one
Who stands by the door, the one who brought us the news.
They'd not mind getting rid of him, if they could choose.

1960 They tell the tale of Kriemhild—I've known it long—
That she was one to nurse her heart's wrong.
Now drink a toast for the dead and pledge the wine!
The scion of the Huns shall be the first in line."

1961 He struck the boy Ortlieb, Hagen the lord;
Down to his hands the blood ran on the sword.
And the head flew straight to the queen's lap.
Bitter murder broke about like a thunderclap.

1962 With his two hands he launched a blow that caught
Off guard the man by whom the lad was taught.
By the table there, his head rolled to the floor.
That was the wretched fee he paid to the tutor's score.

356

1963   Before King Attila's table he saw a bard.
Hagen dashed across—his heart was hard—
Straight from the fiddle severed his right hand.
"Take that for your message next when you go to
   Burgundy land!"

1964   "Oh Lord, my hand!" cried Werbel. "What shall I do?
Hagen of Trony, what have I done to you?
I came in all good faith to your masters' land.
How shall I play my songs, now that I've lost my hand?"

1965   Little Hagen cared if he ever played.
In mortal rage and savage hurt he made
His way through Attila's house and host and slew
Great numbers of them. Enough were dead when he was
   through.

1966   Up from the table leapt Folker the strong.
The bow in his hand gave out its noisy song—
Harsh the fiddle play of Gunther's bard.
He earned his fill from the Huns of hate and ill-regard.

1967   The three great kings got up and came at a run
To stop the fight before more harm was done,
But all their wise restraint had no effect,
While Folker and Hagen both poured out their rage
   unchecked.

1968   When Gunther saw the fight could not be stopped,
The lord of the Rhine drew sword himself and chopped
Wide wounds through the bright mail of his foe—
A hero with his hands, as he gave them all to know.

357

1969 Now the sturdy Gernot joined the fray,
And many Huns lay dead from his swordplay
With the sharp blade, his gift from Ruedeger.
He dealt the knights of Attila hurt beyond repair.

1970 Uta's youngest son sprang to the battle;
His sword rang through helmets, in glorious mettle,
Upon King Attila's knights from the land of the Hun—
Where, by Giselher's hand, amazing things were done.

1971 Of kings and men, whatever show of daring,
Giselher stood forth, beyond comparing,
Against the enemy—an excellent man.
Many he felled there, wounded, into the blood as it ran.

1972 Bitterly the Hunnish side fought back.
One could see the foreign warriors hack
With shining swords, a path through Attila's hall.
And soon one heard sounds of moaning over all.

1973 The men without would join their friends inside—
A poor reception waited when they tried.
The ones within were not contented there,
But Dankwart let no one go up or down the stair.

1974 By the towers at the door was such a crowd,
And the sound of sword on helmet grew so loud,
That Dankwart found himself in perilous straits.
His brother showed his concern—as loyalty dictates.

1975 "Comrade, do you see," he shouted back
To Folker there, "my brother under attack,
Before the Huns, with heavy blows to bruise him?
My friend, go save my brother for me, before we lose him!"

358

1976   "Trust me," the bard replied. "It shall be so."
He played his way through the hall with his fiddle-bow.
(A tempered sword made music in his hands.)
They paid their thanks to him, knights of Rhenish lands.

1977   Dankwart heard courageous Folker say,
"I see you've had no easy time today.
Your brother said that I should help you out.
So I shall stand within, if you will watch without."

1978   Brave Dankwart stood outside the entry there
And barred the way to all who approached the stair
(And you could hear the sound of weapons plied
By heroes' hands), while Folker did the same inside.

1979   Over the heads of the crowd the minstrel talked:
"Hagen my friend, this hall is shut and locked.
Attila's door is barred, and it will hold
By the swords in two men's hands, which bolt it a
    thousandfold."

1980   When Hagen saw such a guard upon the door,
He put his shield behind him, squaring the score
With greater fury now, for what they'd done.
His foes had not a hope to see the light of sun.

1981   When now Verona's governor perceived
How many helmets mighty Hagen cleaved,
He rose upon a chair, and they heard him call:
"Hagen here serves out the bitterest wine of all!"

1982   The host was worried now, and no surprise.
So many friends were lost before his eyes—
And a bare escape the best that luck could bring!
He sat, an anxious man. What good that he was king?

1983 Mighty Kriemhild begged the noble lord,
"Theoderich, protect me with your sword,
For all the princely glory in Amelung land!
If Hagen gets me now, my death is near at hand."

1984 "How shall *I* help *you*?" Theoderich said.
"When I have worries enough on my own head,
Oh queen, with Gunther's men in such an anger,
Right now I can't protect a single soul from danger."

1985 "No, Theoderich, no, great knight of merit
And high birth—prove your noble spirit
By helping me escape, or I am dead."
In worry over this the queen was struck with dread.

1986 "I will try to see what help may be.
But not in a long, long time did my eyes see
In such a bitter rage so many lords.
Here is blood, burst from helmets, by force of swords!"

1987 And he began to shout, the nobly-born,
His voice resounding like a bison horn,
Till the great castle shook through all its length
By dint of him—a massive thing, Theoderich's strength!

1988 Gunther heard him call, through all the row
And battle din around. He listened now,
And spoke, "Theoderich's voice rings in my ear.
Our men have done away with one of his, I fear.

1989 I see him on the table, waving his hand.
Friends and kinsmen here, of Burgundy land,
Call off the fighting now; let's hear and see
Just what this lord's complaint against my men may be."

1990   They carried out what Gunther asked them for,
And held their swords at rest, in midst of war.
This was greater power: that no one fought.
He lost no time in asking what Theoderich sought.

1991   "My noble lord," he said, "what have my friends
Done to you? I promise to make amends
And pay the bill in full and willingly.
Any harm to you is deepest grief to me."

1992   Lord Theoderich spoke, "No harm is done.
Let me leave this house, and everyone
Of my command, with guarantee of peace,
From this ferocious war. My thanks will never cease."

1993   Said Wolfhart, "Why so quick to plead? This knight,
The fiddler, hasn't barred the door so tight
We couldn't open it to let us through."
"Quiet!" Theoderich said. "Devil a lot you do."

1994   King Gunther spoke, "This much I grant to you:
Take them out as you will, many or few,
But not my enemies. They shall stay.
They've done me bitter wrong among the Huns this day."

1995   Hearing that, on one protecting arm
He took the queen, who feared for further harm,
And led upon the other Attila then.
Out with Theoderich went six hundred handsome men.

1996   Now the noble margrave Ruedeger cried,
"If any more may make their way outside,
With gratitude to you, then tell us that news.
Loyal friends deserve the firmest pledge of truce."

1997 Answered Giselher of Burgundy:
"Since you and all your men in loyalty
Stand firm and true, we here proclaim our peace.
You may therefore withdraw—and all your worries cease."

1998 As Ruedeger the knight now left the hall,
Half a thousand followed him in all—
These the men of Pöchlarn, thane and friend,
From whom King Gunther drew great sorrow in the end.

1999 A Hunnish warrior saw his monarch come,
With escort which he tried to profit from—
But Folker struck him such a fiddle-beat
As made his head fly off and fall to Attila's feet.

2000 Once the lord of the land had got outside,
He turned and, looking back at Folker, cried:
"My curse upon these guests—a thing of dread,
A scourge is this, that all for them my knights lie dead.

2001 And a curse upon this feast," Attila swore.
"There's a man in there who fights like a wild boar—
By name, Folker; by work, a bard no less!
I thank my lucky stars I fled this devil's mess.

2002 His song has an evil sound, his bow is red;
His melodies have left my warriors dead.
What reason had this bard to be distressed?
I never had such bitter fill of any guest!"

2003 All they ever would they'd now let out.
Within the hall arose a mighty shout.
For what they had suffered the guests would now exact
Their full revenge. How many helmets Folker cracked!

2004   The sound attracted Gunther's notice soon;
      He cried, "Hagen, do you hear the tune
      Our friend is fiddling for the Huns who head
      To the doorway now? The rosin he puts on his bow is
        red."

2005   Said Hagen, "This I rue beyond all measure,
      That while he fought I sat here at my leisure.
      I was his good friend, and he was mine.
      And so we'll be again, if ever we see the Rhine.

2006   My king, Folker is staunch and true; behold!
      How zealously he earns your silver and gold,
      And what hard steel his fiddle-bow will slice
      And how it will crush a helmet's shining bright device.

2007   I never saw a minstrel yet display
      The splendid courage Folker has shown today.
      Through shield and helm his music fills the air.
      For this he should ride good steeds, and have the best to
       wear!"

2008   Whatever Huns had been within the hall,
      There now was not a person left at all.
      The sound was quiet now of their discord.
      Cheerfully the valiant men laid down the sword.

✟ THIRTY-FOURTH ADVENTURE
How They Threw the Corpses Out

2009   The men sat down to take what rest they could.
Folker and Hagen left the hall and stood,
Leaning on their shields, haughty lords,
Both with much to say, in proud and mocking words.

2010   Giselher of Burgundy addressed
His men and said: "My friends, we cannot rest—
Not yet. Let's get these dead men out of here.
We'll have to stand and fight again, let that be clear!

2011   They must not lie around here under foot.
Before the Huns destroy us we shall put
Our swords to work, letting their wounds renew
Our cheerful spirits. That's what I intend to do."

2012   "For such a king," cried Hagen, "praise to Heaven!
This advice that my young lord has given
Is of the kind that only heroes voice.
For this you men of Burgundy may all rejoice!"

2013   They did as they were counselled, casting in all
Seven thousand bodies from the hall,
To lie by the castle steps, where they were thrown.
And from their friends and kinsmen rose a wretched
    moan.

2014   So minor were the wounds of some that fell,
With gentler care they might have gotten well.
Instead, by this high fall, they all were killed—
Due cause for all the grief with which their friends were
    filled.

2015   Shouted the fiddler Folker, cheerful knight:
"Now I see that what they say is right,
About the Huns: What cowards! They are wailing
    More like women, when they should help their hurt and
      ailing."

2016   One took him at his word, a margrave who found
A kinsman fallen in blood; he bent to the ground
To pick him up and save him from his foes.
    The warrior minstrel shot and killed him as he rose.

2017   The others saw. With that began the flight,
And as they fled they cursed the fiddler-knight.
He seized a spear, a sharp and tempered one
    Which had been hurled at him up there by a certain Hun.

2018   He shot it across the courtyard, over the welter
Of fleeing people, pointing safer shelter
To the men of Attila, not so close to the hall.
    They feared the fiddler's violent prowess most of all.

2019   Many thousand stood before the building.
Folker and Hagen spoke, not withholding
Anything they felt from the Hunnish chief,
    Great King Attila, much to their later fear and grief.

2020   "It would seem," said Hagen, "the place for the People's
      Shield
Is in front of the people, first on the battlefield,
And this is the place no king of Burgundy shuns.
    Helmets they hew; their swords fall—and the blood runs!"

2021   The bold king seized his shield. Cried his wife:
"Be careful, Sire, take no risk with your life!

Offer your warriors gold, in shields to the rim.
If Hagen catches you, you'll have your death from him."

2022 So dauntless was the Hun, he would not yield
In his intent, until by the strap of his shield
They held him back—such valor now a thing
Most rare in princes. And yet fierce Hagen mocked the
king:

2023 "A distant sort of kinship, this," he said,
"That Attila shares with Sigfrid! Kriemhild's bed
Was his before she ever looked at you,
Oh coward king, why plot for me the evil you do?"

2024 The great king's wife had heard his calumny.
Incensed that by his daring she should be
Before the king's own court thus vilified,
She tried once more her scheme against the guests. She
cried:

2025 "There is Hagen of Trony. Whoever will kill
That man and bring me his head, for him I'll fill
Attila's shield to the rim with good red gold,
And give him many lands and castles in freehold."

2026 "What are they waiting for?" the minstrel cried.
"I never saw more soldiers stand aside,
Craven, at the offer of such high pay.
Attila has no cause to praise his men today—

2027 Thankless eaters of the king's own bread,
False in his great need, full of dread,
I see them skulk around, assuming the name
Of valiant men, this to their everlasting shame."

✠ THIRTY-FIFTH ADVENTURE
How Iring Was Slain

2028   "I've always," Danish margrave Iring cried,
       "Aimed at excellence in all I tried.
       When armies fought, my deeds were of the best.
       Bring my armor—I'll put Hagen to the test."

2029   "I counsel you, don't do it," Hagen cried.
       "Or tell your Hunnish thanes to stand aside!
       If any of you rush the hall—in pairs,
       Or three at a time—I'll send you aching down the stairs."

2030   "I'll not stop for that," rejoined Lord Iring.
       "I've attempted things as awe-inspiring.
       I'll take you on alone, in a test of swords.
       What good will be your vaunting, all of which is words?"

2031   Iring was swiftly armed. There came along
       Thuringia's bold young Irnfrid and Haward the strong
       To join him, with a thousand men beside.
       They wished to stand with him, whatever Iring tried.

2032   Now the fiddler looked and saw the swarms
       That came along with Iring, all in arms,
       With many handsome helmets tied and ready.
       Valiant Folker could not keep his temper steady.

2033   "Look, friend Hagen, here is the Iring who vowed
       To meet you alone, with swords. Are knights allowed
       By custom to lie? This I must deplore:
       He has with him, in armor, a thousand knights or more."

367

2034   "Don't make a liar of me!" cried Haward's thane.
"I mean to do as I vowed. I'll not refrain
Out of apprehension. I take for granted
Hagen is fearsome—still I'll meet him singlehanded."

2035   He fell to his knees, begging men of his own,
Retainers and kin, to let him fight alone
Against proud Hagen. They would not willingly,
For well they knew that arrogant knight of Burgundy.

2036   He begged so long, it happened. His retinue,
Perceiving his intent, and that his view
Was all on honor, let him go ahead.
And what a battle both men waged, fierce and dread!

2037   Iring, worthy knight of Denmark, held
His spear on high; covering with his shield,
He dashed at Hagen, up to the palace door.
And now the heroes raised a mighty clash and roar.

2038   With violent hands they hurled their spears to sail
Through solid shield and strike the shining mail;
The shafts went spinning. Both the mighty lords
(Fiercely bold they were) reached now for their swords.

2039   Though valiant Hagen boasted strength unbounded,
When Iring hit him, all the house resounded;
Towers and palace echoed with their blows,
And still the knight could not accomplish what he chose.

2040   He left Lord Hagen standing there, uninjured,
And rushed at the fiddler-knight, for Iring ventured
To think his savage blows might lay him flat.
But handsome Folker knew the right defense for that!

2041 The fiddler swung his sword, the buckles scattered
   From the shield that Folker's arm had battered.
   Iring left him—too hard a man was he!—
   And next he ran at Gunther, King of Burgundy.

2042 Each of them was fierce enough in war,
   Yet all the blows that both of them could score
   Brought no flow of blood from any wound—
   Prevented by their armor, which was strong and sound.

2043 He left King Gunther now, off to assail
   Lord Gernot, striking from his coat of mail
   Sparks of fire, and yet the valiant Dane,
   Meeting the savage Gernot there, was nearly slain.

2044 He sprang away from the prince—oh, he was fleet!—
   And quickly slew four knights of the noble suite
   Of Burgundy, from Worms on the Rhenish shore.
   Young Sir Giselher was never angered more.

2045 The prince cried out, "The Lord in Heaven knows,
   Lord Iring, you will pay to me for those
   Who here and now lie dead!" In his attack,
   He struck the Dane a blow which stopped him in his track.

2046 He fell to the ground before him, into the blood.
   They all assumed that in the battle-flood
   He'd strike no further blow of any sort—
   But Iring lay at the feet of Giselher unhurt.

2047 What with clangor of helm and crash of sword,
   His wits had gone all faint, the valiant lord;
   He lay unconscious, like a lifeless one.
   This the strength of mighty Giselher had done.

2048   The ringing in his head, which he had got
From the mighty blow, subsided now. He thought:
"I'm still alive—not wounded anywhere!
But now I really know the strength of Giselher."

2049   He heard his foes, on either side of him.
And had they known the truth, how much more grim
Would be his fate! And he heard Lord Giselher.
How could he flee his foes and get away from there?

2050   Out of the blood he sprang, like a man possessed,
And he could well give thanks that he was fast.
He ran from the hall, meeting Hagen again.
Savage blows fell from his powerful arm like rain.

2051   "You are meant for death!" Hagen thought.
"Unless the foul fiend saves you, you are caught."
Yet Iring, striking straight through Hagen's casque,
Wounded him with his good sword which men called
    Waske.

2052   When noble Hagen felt the sudden pain,
The sword in his hand thrashed wildly. Haward's thane
Gave way to him and had to turn in flight,
Down the stairs, in full pursuit, came Gunther's knight.

2053   Bold Iring swung his shield over his head,
And if these stairs had been three flights instead,
Hagen would not have let him strike a blow
In all that way. The red sparks made his helmet glow!

2054   Still, Sir Iring got to his friends unhurt.
When Lady Kriemhild heard the true report

Of what he did to Hagen in that affray,
The queen gave him her thanks in the very fullest way.

2055   "God reward you, Iring, worthy knight!
In heart and mind you comfort me with the sight
Of Hagen's armor, red with the blood he spilled."
The queen herself, for joy, took from his hand the shield.

2056   Said Hagen, "Keep your thanks on a modest plane.
It would better suit a hero to try again.
Call him a valiant man, should he return.
He wounded me, but little the profit you will earn!

2057   To have you see the rings of my armor red
Has set me hungering for many dead.
Now I am really mad at Haward's knight—
And all the hurt he's done me up to now is slight."

2058   Iring of Denmark turned to face the breeze,
To cool himself in his coat of mail and ease
His helmet straps. And all the people cried
That his strength was great, which filled the margrave's
    heart with pride.

2059   Again said Iring, "Friends, I want you to know
That you must arm me soon. I mean to go
And force, if I can, this haughty man to yield."
Since his was hacked to bits, they brought him a better
    shield.

2060   Soon he was fully armed. In hostile mind
He seized a vicious spear and went to find
Lord Hagen once again and force the fight.
There, in anger, waited a mortally savage knight.

2061 He ran at Iring—Hagen was past restraining—
Ran with thrusting spear and sword blows raining,
Down the flight of stairs, their whole length.
His rage was great. Small joy to Iring, all his strength.

2062 Through shields they smote until it blazed and roared
Like winds of red fire. Hagen's sword
Dealt out a mighty wound to Haward's thane,
Through shield and byrnie, from which he never rallied
again.

2063 He raised his shield—when he felt the wound at first—
Up to his chin-strap, thinking this the worst
In way of hurt that he had had in store,
But royal Gunther's man was soon to hurt him more.

2064 He seized a spear from the ground where it had lain
Before his feet, and shot at Iring the Dane,
And there the shaft protruded from his head.
Hagen had wrought his bitter end; he'd soon be dead.

2065 Iring fled to the Danes. Before they could take
His helmet from his head they had to break
And pull the spear; and now his death drew near.
His kin began to weep—the cause for that was clear.

2066 And now the queen stood over him to mourn
For mighty Iring, and for the wounds he'd borne.
It was bitter pain to her. Once bold and gay,
That warrior now addressed his kinsmen there, to say:

2067 "Leave your mourning, glorious queen! What use
Is all your weeping now, for I must lose
My life from the wounds I have, and death no more
Will let me serve the king and you, as I have before."

2068 To the men of Thuringia, too, he spoke, and the Danes:
"Let each of you be sure his hand refrains
From taking the queen's reward, her gold, bright red.
If you encounter Hagen, men will see you dead."

2069 The color had fled his face, and Iring had
The sign of death upon him. Their hearts were sad,
And Haward's knight was doomed to lose his life.
With this the Danes were all compelled to join the strife.

2070 Irnfrid and Haward rushed in front of the hall
With a thousand knights or more, and over all
There rose a violent noise, monstrous and vast.
They fell on Burgundy—what mighty spears they cast!

2071 Irnfrid ran at the minstrel—but he would gain
At Folker's hands the greatest hurt and pain.
The fiddler struck the landgrave such a blow
As split his solid helmet; he was a savage foe.

2072 Then Sir Irnfrid struck at Folker so hard
The rings of his coat of mail burst apart,
Spraying his byrnie with a fiery red.
Yet soon the landgrave fell before the fiddler, dead.

2073 Haward and Hagen met; and he who saw,
Saw marvels done. With heroes' hands to draw,
Swords fell fast indeed and furiously.
But Haward perished, slain by the lord of Burgundy.

2074 When Danes and Thuringians saw their master slain
Before the hall came strife and fearful pain,
Until, with valiant hands, they gained the door.
Shields and helms were hacked to pieces by the score.

373

2075   "Back!" Lord Folker cried. "Let them come on,
And what they think to do will be undone;
Once inside the hall their time is short,
And they must perish—and reap in death the queen's
    reward."

2076   They entered the hall, proud and insolent,
But many a warrior's head was lowly bent,
And under fearful blows he perished there.
(King Gernot fought with glory, as did Sir Giselher.)

2077   A thousand and four of them went into the hall.
One saw the glowing swish of sword-blades fall,
And every man of them was soon struck down.
What marvels one could tell, to Burgundy's renown!

2078   There came a silence, as the noise subsided.
Through the drains and down the gutters glided,
Everywhere, the blood of warriors killed.
Thus was the valor of the men of Rhine fulfilled.

2079   Burgundians sat down to rest and laid
Their shields and arms aside. And still he stayed
Before the door, the valiant minstrel-knight,
And watched to see if others came to join the fight.

2080   Bitterly the king and queen lamented.
Women scourged themselves, their hearts tormented.
Death, I think, at last had sworn their doom.
The strangers' toll of knights was fated to resume.

✠ THIRTY-SIXTH ADVENTURE

How the Queen Caused the Hall to be Set Afire

2081 "Take your helmets off," Hagen said.
"My friend and I will stand you watch, instead;
If Attila's men have in mind returning,
As quickly as I can, I'll bring my lords the warning."

2082 Many a worthy knight now bared his head,
As they sat on the maimed bodies lying dead
In blood before them, work their hands had done.
The guests had gained the angry notice of the Hun.

2083 They made another try before night fell,
Spurred by the king and by his queen as well,
Who before their eyes had still the sight
Of twenty thousand Huns—now compelled to fight.

2084 The storm rose hard upon the strangers then.
Hagen's brother Dankwart, best of men,
Left his lords and ran to the door to face
His foes—and death, they thought. Unhurt, he reached his
place.

2085 The savage fighting lasted till the night
Prevented more. As was for heroes right,
They fought against the Hun the summer-long day.
How many valiant warriors they were fated to slay!

2086 This awful slaughter came one solstice-time
When Kriemhild took her vengeance for the crime

That pained her heart, against her closest kin
And many more—which Attila took no pleasure in.

2087   The day ran out. Their fears were newly stirred.
They thought swift death a thing to be preferred
To long and tortured wait for awful pain.
Proud lords of highest spirit longed for peace again.

2088   Asked to seek the king and bring him back,
Heroes red with blood and tarnished black
Left the palace, three most splendid kings.
They knew not whom to blame for all these bitter things.

2089   Attila soon appeared, and Kriemhild too.
The land was theirs, and so their numbers grew.
Attila spoke, "What do you want of me?
If you have hopes of peace, that can scarcely be.

2090   For this great hurt you caused me (which shall give
No profit to you while I still may live),
For my child you slew, my kinsmen killed—
Your hope of peace and respite shall never be fulfilled."

2091   Gunther answered, "Greatest need compelled
The deeds we did. My men lay dead, all felled
By yours at their lodgings. Did this deserve to be?
I came to you in trust, thinking you honored me."

2092   Young Giselher spoke, "Whom are you reproving,
Men of Attila, you who still are living?
Why is it me? What have I done to you?
I rode to this land of yours as a friendly man and true."

2093   "My palace is full of your kindness, wretched woe
        Is in our land. If we could have it so,
        We'd wish you had never come from Worms on Rhine.
        You and your brothers leave my land to an orphaned line."

2094   Warlike Gunther answered angrily,
        "Turn this bitter hate to amnesty
        For us, exiled—a favor all around.
        For what Attila does to us he has no ground."

2095   The lord of the land replied, "My pain and yours
        Are most unlike. The insult done, and worse,
        The injury that here has been my lot—
        For that no one of you, alive, shall leave this spot."

2096   Mighty Gernot spoke to the king of the land,
        "Then may you act as a friend by God's command.
        Kill us, your foreign guests, but let us come down
        To the open court with you. That would suit your renown.

2097   Whatever may be our fate, let it be brief.
        You have fresh troops. We have had no relief
        From the storms of battle. Our hope of living fails
        If they attack. How long shall we suffer these ordeals?"

2098   In this Attila's men almost concurred,
        And let them leave the palace. Kriemhild heard,
        Bitterly distressed, and they were driven
        Soon to end the truce these outcast men were given.

2099   "No, Hunnish lords, this thing you plan to do,
        In faith I counsel not to carry through.
        Let those vengeful killers out of the hall,
        And you and all your kin will suffer mortal fall.

2100 Suppose no one were left but Uta's sons,
   My noble brothers—let the breezes once
   Cool their coats of mail, and you are fated!
   Never in all this world were braver men created."

2101 Young Giselher replied, "Fair sister of mine,
   How poorly I placed my trust when over the Rhine
   You asked me here to face these perils! And why,
   By what offense to the Huns, do I deserve to die?

2102 I always brought you friendship, never hurt.
   In this good faith I journeyed here to court:
   That, noble sister, you held me in some regard.
   Think mercifully of us—all other hope is barred."

2103 "I feel no mercy; I am merciless!
   Hagen caused me pain and bitterness
   Which shall be unforgiven all my life,
   And all of you must pay," answered Attila's wife.

2104 "Hagen alone as hostage I ask you give,
   And I may not refuse to let you live
   But try to make these warriors reconciled,
   Since I am sister to you, and one mother's child."

2105 "God in Heaven forbid," Lord Gernot said.
   "If we were a thousand here, we'd all lie dead,
   Kin of your blood, before we'd give to you
   One single man as hostage. That we will never do."

2106 "We die," said Giselher, "but none prevents
   Our fighting here like knights, in self-defense.
   Whoever longs for battle, here we are!
   And I have never left a loyal friend so far."

378

2107 It wasn't right for Dankwart not to speak:
   "My brother is not alone. Those who seek
   To thwart the peace may suffer for it, too.
   We'll give you proof of that, truly I promise you."

2108 Cried she, "Men of spirit, move along
   Up to the steps with you, avenge my wrong!
   I promise the recompense your actions merit.
   The price of Hagen's pride is high, and he shall bear it.

2109 Let no one leave the building there at all!
   At the four corners I shall have the hall
   Set on fire, avenging my every wrong."
   Attila's men were ready; it did not take them long.

2110 The ones that stood outside they drove back in
   With sword and spear, making a mighty din,
   But prince and man they could not drive apart.
   One would not leave the other, out of loyal heart.

2111 Then she had the building lit, a pyre
   To torture warriors' bodies in its fire.
   The house was burning soon, with the breeze that blew—
   The greatest terror, I think, an army ever knew.

2112 There were many cries within of "Help!" and "Woe!"
   "Much better die in fighting than perish so.
   May God have pity how we all are lost!
   She takes her anger out on us, at fearful cost."

2113 A man cried out inside, "And so we die.
   What good the words that we were welcomed by?
   By thirst and this awful heat I am so punished,

379

That in these perils, I think, my life will soon have
    vanished."

2114   Hagen of Trony spoke, "Great lords and good,
If you are plagued by thirst, drink this blood—
In heat like this, finer than wine by far;
At least you'll not do better now, the way things are!"

2115   One of the warriors went where a man lay dead,
And kneeling by the wound, untied from his head
The helmet-case, and drank the flowing blood.
Strange though it was to him, it seemed exceedingly good.

2116   "God bless you, Hagen," said the tired knight,
"For teaching me to drink with such delight.
Rarely have I been served a drink so fine.
And should I live a while, I'll thank you for this wine."

2117   After the others heard he found it pleasing,
Many more drank up, the blood increasing
The strength of all who did so—for which perished,
In return, men whom lovely ladies cherished.

2118   Now fire was falling on them all around.
They used their shields to ward it to the ground,
Smarting from the awful smoke and heat.
Did heroes ever have more wretched fate to meet?

2119   Hagen of Trony cried, "Stand close to the wall,
Do not let your helms be hit when firebrands fall,
Kick them with your feet where the blood is deep.
This is an evil feast the queen would have us keep."

2120   In misery like this they passed the night.
       Still before the house the minstrel-knight
       And his companion Hagen, the valiant ones,
       Leaned on their shields, waiting more harm from the
          Huns.

2121   The fiddler spoke, "Let's go back in the hall.
       The Huns will think that we have perished all,
       Dead from the torment done us. We shall greet them
       With the sight of men of battle, come to meet them."

2122   Giselher spoke. "Signs of day are growing,"
       Said the prince, "there is a cool wind blowing.
       May God above see fit to let us live
       To better times. A wretched fete for my sister to give!"

2123   Another man remarked, "I see the day.
       Since we shall fare no better anyway,
       Put on your armor, men, and think on life!
       She'll be here far too soon for us, Attila's wife."

2124   The king had thought his guests must soon expire
       From their ordeals and from the dreadful fire.
       Six hundred gallant men were living yet
       Within the hall, as good as any king could get.

2125   The guards who watched the guests had noted well
       That they were still alive, despite the hell
       Of pain and hurt, alike to man and lord.
       They saw them in the room, sound and well restored.

2126   Many men survived, they told the queen,
       But she asserted that could not have been,

That any man survived that fire. She said,
"I find it far more likely that all of them are dead."

2127   Men and princes would have liked to live,
If anyone was willing there to give
The gift of mercy—but not in the Hunnish land!
So they avenged their death with more than willing hand.

2128   Toward morning then they paid them their respects
In bitter battle, a thing which came to vex
Heroic men. Heavy spears were hurled
Against the bold defense of the bravest knights in the
    world.

2129   Excitement hurried through Attila's ranks,
To earn the gifts and pay of Kriemhild's thanks
And carry out their king's command in war.
Quick death it was that many had to settle for.

2130   What tales of gifts and offers could be told!
She had them bring on shields her red gold
And gave to whoever would take it. Such an amount
Has never yet been paid against a foe's account.

2131   Then did a host of men in arms appear
And gallant Folker said, "We still are here!
I never saw heroes come more willingly
To fight, taking the king's gold for our injury."

2132   Many called to the warriors, "Closer, friend,
And quickly, let us bring this to an end.
No one falls but who is doomed to die."
Soon their shields were stuck with spears, towering high.

2133   What more can I say? A good twelve hundred Huns
       Attacked repeatedly, but the foreign ones
       Dealt them wounds enough to cool their ardor.
       Neither side prevailed, and so the blood flowed harder

2134   From all the many wounds, that cut life-deep,
       For friends now lost they all were heard to weep.
       Slain were all the stalwart men of the king,
       And loving kin were filled with bitter sorrowing.

How Margrave Ruedeger Was Slain

2135   The foreign knights kept up the fight till dawn.
Then it was that Gotelind's lord had gone
To court, to find great hurt and misery
On either hand. The loyal man wept inwardly.

2136   "Alas," said Ruedeger, "that I was born!
Alas that no one has the power to turn
This evil aside. I want to try for peace—
But not the king, who sees his many woes increase."

2137   Ruedeger sent to Theoderich to see
If they together might save the royal three.
The lord of Verona sent word: "We're all too late.
The king will not let any of us arbitrate."

2138   A man saw Ruedeger standing thus, some Hun—
His eyes were moist from all the weeping he'd done—
And cried to the queen, "Now see how he stands there;
He has of all King Attila's power the greatest share,

2139   And holds in liege all this—land and vassals.
Why does Ruedeger have these many castles,
Of which the king permits him so great a show?
In all our fighting yet he's struck no worthy blow.

2140   I'd say he doesn't care what goes on here,
He has his fill of all that he holds dear.
They say he's braver than any man could be.
We've had poor proof of that in our great misery!"

2141   Sad at heart, the loyal margrave sought
A glimpse of the man who said these words. He thought:
"You'll reap the harvest! You say fear has me cowed.
But you have told this tale of yours in court too loud."

2142   He tightened his fist and ran at him and hit
The Hun so hard a blow, by force of it
He lay in a second dead before his feet—
One more grave misfortune for the king to meet.

2143   "Down, you bare-faced coward!" said Ruedeger.
"I have pain and hurt enough for my share.
Why rebuke me that I do not fight?
I'd be sworn the foe of these guests, with every right;

2144   And everything I could, I should have done,
Except I brought them here, and was the one
Who gave them escort to my master's land,
And so I must not raise against them my wretched hand."

2145   Attila spoke to Margrave Ruedeger:
"So this is how you help us, noble sir!
With so many doomed men here, we have no need
Of any more, and you have done an evil deed."

2146   Said the noble lord, "He made me ill at ease,
Slandering all the honors and properties
I have from your hand and in such generous portion—
Which worked out rather to that lying man's misfortune."

2147   Then Kriemhild came, and she had also seen
What for the warrior's rage his fate had been,
Her eyes were moist and bitterly she lamented:

385

"Through what fault of ours," she said, "have you aug-
    mented

2148   My suffering and the king's? Always before,
    Oh noble Ruedeger, you vowed and swore
    To risk for us your life and honored fame.
    And I've heard many knights who greatly praise your
    name.

2149   I bid you recall your pledge of favor when,
    Urging the choice of Attila, best of men,
    You swore to serve me till one of us should go—
    Help that I, poor woman, never needed so."

2150   "That I do not deny, great king's wife.
    I swore to risk for you both honors and life,
    But not to lose my soul—I've never sworn.
    I brought to your tourney here these warriors, royally
    born."

2151   "Remember, Ruedeger, your loyalty,
    Your constant faith, and the oath you gave to me
    To avenge my hurt and all the pain I bore."
    The margrave answered, "I have not refused before."

2152   But then great King Attila joined her pleas.
    They both fell down before him on their knees;
    And one could see the margrave's sad distress,
    As now the faithful knight spoke in his wretchedness:

2153   "Unhappy man, that I should live to see
    My honors forfeit, my inner loyalty
    And the decent breeding God enjoins—surrendered!
    This, oh Lord in Heaven, I wish my death had hindered.

2154   Whichever course before me I reject,
To do the other, I've done a cursed act.
If I do neither, I face the people's wrath
And their reproach. Counsel me now, who gave me
    breath!"

2155   They pled with force, the monarch and his wife—
For this, in time, knights would lose their life
At Ruedeger's hands, who also perished there.
Listen, you will hear his deeds of great despair.

2156   Foreseeing harm and awful suffering,
He would most gladly have refused the king,
And his queen as well. Of this his fear was great:
If he killed one of the guests, the world would bear him
    hate.

2157   The brave man cried to the king, "Your Majesty,
Take back everything you gave to me,
Land and castles; let all I had be vanished.
I will go on foot to foreign countries, banished."

2158   "Who would help me then?" Attila cried.
"I'll give you your castles and your lands outright,
If you'll bring vengeance on my enemy.
You'll stand beside me then—a mighty king like me."

2159   "How can I do that?" Lord Ruedeger said.
"I asked them home to my house. Drink and bread
I offered them in kindness, and I gave
My gifts to them. How can I send them to the grave?

2160   How easy for men to think that I'm afraid!
But I refused no single service, no aid

To noble prince or man. The very bond
Of kinship we concluded makes me now despond.

2161   I gave to royal Giselher my daughter.
No match in all the world could so have brought her
Trust and manners, honors, and property.
I never saw a young prince so perfect in chivalry."

2162   Kriemhild cried, "Most noble Ruedeger,
Take pity on the hurt we both must bear,
The king and I, and think: no country's master
Ever gained from guests such harvest of disaster."

2163   The margrave spoke again to the king's high wife:
"Today the cost is paid with Ruedeger's life.
The kindness you and my lord have done to me—
I now must die for that. What cannot wait, must be.

2164   I know this very day my towers, my land,
Must all revert to you through someone's hand.
My wife and children I commend to your care,
And the many men of Pöchlarn, now left lordless there."

2165   "May God reward you, Ruedeger," said the king,
He and the queen no longer sorrowing,
"Your people shall be safe in our loyal care,
And I trust you too will live, as I count on my own
     welfare."

2166   He placed upon the balance soul and life.
Then it was she wept, Attila's wife.
"What I have vowed," he said, "I must fulfill.
Alas for my friends whom I must fight, against my will."

2167   They saw him leave the king, sad of eye.
        He found his warriors standing there, close by:
        "Arm yourselves, my men. I now must leave
        To fight the bold Burgundian knights—for which I
            grieve."

2168   They had men hurry out for armor and bring
        Their helmet or their shield, whatever thing
        Each warrior needed, squires brought it here.
        What proud Burgundians heard was news of little cheer.

2169   Five hundred men were armed, with Ruedeger,
        And twelve more knights he found to help him there,
        Fighting to gain renown in peril of war.
        They did not know the truth: that death lay close before.

2170   The guests saw Ruedeger, his helmet on,
        The margrave's vassals with their sharp swords drawn,
        Bright broad shields in their hands. When he perceived
        This sight before his eyes, the fiddler greatly grieved.

2171   Giselher watched his father-in-law as he went,
        Walking with helmet fixed. What other intent
        Could he imagine but help in fullest measure?
        At this the youthful prince's heart was filled with pleasure.

2172   "Thank God for such good friends and kin," he cried,
        "As we have gained on our journey. Now my bride
        Will bring us great good fortune. Take my word:
        I am more than glad our wedding feast occurred!"

2173   "I don't know where you get your comfort from,"
        Said Folker. "When have you seen heroes come

For peace with helmets fixed and sword in hand?
The margrave means to use us to earn his towns and
　　land."

2174　Before the fiddler finished speaking, there,
In front of the hall, stood noble Ruedeger.
And set his good shield down before his feet,
Facing the friends he now could neither serve nor greet.

2175　The noble margrave shouted into the hall:
"Look to your defense, Nibelungs all;
I ought to bring you good, I bring you bad.
We once were friends. I now revoke the bond we had."

2176　These tidings left the troubled men dismayed,
For there was little comfort here or aid,
If he would fight them, whom they thought a friend.
Their foes already had caused them trials without an end.

2177　"Now God in Heaven forbid," Lord Gunther shouted,
"That your devotion to us should be thus flouted,
The trust which after all we assumed of you.
But I prefer to think that this you would never do."

2178　The brave knight cried, "I cannot help it now.
I have to fight with you because of a vow,
So on your guard, brave lords, if ever life
Means much to you. I'm held to this by Attila's wife."

2179　Gunther answered, "Your challenge comes too late,
Ruedeger, God's repayment would be great
For the loyal love you gave, if in the end
It were more tempered by the action of a friend.

2180   We'd owe you thanks for what you deigned to give,
        My kin and I, if you would let us live—
        Your splendid gifts, when in good faith you brought
        Our men to Attila's land: my lord, give that your thought!"

2181   Said Ruedeger, "How I wish this could be granted,
        And I could give you presents, openhanded,
        With such good will as I had hoped to show!
        For then I should not bare myself to censure so."

2182   Gernot spoke: "Noble sir, refrain!
        No host has ever thought to entertain
        His guests with kindness such as you prepared
        To welcome us. Reward is yours if we be spared."

2183   "Gernot, would to God," Lord Ruedeger said,
        "That you were by the Rhine and I were dead,
        In some degree of honor, since now by force
        I fight you. Never have heroes' friends treated them
           worse."

2184   "For these rich gifts of yours," came his reply,
        "God bless you! I regret that you must die,
        And that such excellence of mind must perish.
        Your weapon which you gave me, here in my hand I
           cherish.

2185   For me it never yet has failed its pledge
        In all this trouble. Dead beneath its edge
        Lie many knights. Sound and true, no stain—
        So fine a gift I think no knight will give again.

2186   If you won't end your plan to interfere—
        Kill one single friend I still have here,

And with your very sword I'll take your life!
I pity you, Ruedeger, and pity your lovely wife."

2187   "Sir Gernot, would to God we might fulfill
Here and now the tenor of your will,
And all your friends might be returned to life.
Now both must look to you, my daughter and my wife."

2188   Spoke fair Uta's child, of Burgundy,
"Why do you do this? Those who came with me
Respect you, sir. You do an evil thing—
You plan for your lovely daughter too quick a widowing.

2189   When you and all your knights take up offense
Against me here you give poor evidence
Of why, above all men, I trusted you,
And why I took your daughter's hand in marriage too."

2190   "Most noble king, remember your loyalty,"
Cried Ruedeger, "if here God set you free,
And let my poor young daughter not incur
What blame is mine. As you are good, be kind to her!"

2191   "That I should rightly do," Giselher cried.
"But any of my high kinsmen still inside—
If they should die at your hand, all ties must end,
Joining you and your daughter as kin of mine or friend."

2192   "Then God have mercy on us," the brave lord said.
They lifted up their shields, about to head
For battle with the guests in Kriemhild's hall,
When loudly down from the stairs they heard Lord
    Hagen call:

2193 "One moment more, most noble Ruedeger, stay!"
   (Thus spoke Hagen.) "We have more to say,
   My lords and I, from dire necessity.
   What good to Attila could our wretched dying be?

2194 And I am in perilous straits," Hagen went on.
   "The shield that Gotelind gave me to bear is gone,
   Hacked to bits by the Huns in my very hand,
   And as a friend I brought it into Attila's land.

2195 If only God in Heaven," he said, "would deign
   To let me carry such a shield again
   As you have now on your arm, oh Ruedeger,
   In storm of battle I should need no hauberk to wear."

2196 "I'd gladly offer my shield as a favor to you.
   Because of Kriemhild, that I dare not do—
   But take it, Hagen, wear it at your hand,
   And may you bring it back with you to Burgundy land!"

2197 When he offered him so willingly the shield,
   Eyes were red with hot tears unconcealed.
   This was the very last gift under the sun
   That Ruedeger of Pöchlarn gave to anyone.

2198 As fierce as Hagen was, his heart as hard,
   He still was moved by the gift that noble lord
   Had made with the moments left to him so brief.
   Many noble warriors joined with him in grief.

2199 "God in Heaven bless you, Ruedeger,
   There'll never be one like you anywhere,
   To give to outcast men so great a favor.
   May the good Lord grant your virtues live forever!

393

2201* And noble Ruedeger, I'll repay that gift.
       However these knights treat you, I'll not lift
       My hand against you here in enmity,
       Even though you kill the whole of Burgundy."

2202   Courteous Ruedeger bowed, and warriors wept
       On every side, that peace could not be kept
       Among these wounded spirits—woe most dread!
       The model of chivalry would lie in Ruedeger dead.

2203   Down from the hall there came the minstrel's voice:
       "Since my comrade Hagen swears you peace,
       You have the same assurance from my hand.
       You earned it well enough when first we came to this
           land.

2204   You shall be my herald, noble margrave.
       These are the red arm-rings your lady gave,
       Telling me to wear them at the feast.
       You can see them now and be my witness at least."

2205   "Would to Heaven," Margrave Ruedeger cried,
       "The margravine might grant you more beside!
       I shall give my beloved wife your word,
       If ever I see her safe, of that much be assured."

2206   And as he promised this, he lifted shield,
       Unleashed his rage, and would not wait nor yield,

---

* Following C, the translation omits what is in effect an interruption of his
own speech by Hagen. B's strophe 2200 reads:
       "Now this is a wretched turn," Lord Hagen spoke.
       "With all the grief of which we bear the yoke—
       God help us if we must fight with friends and kin."
       The margrave answered him, "What pain this leaves me in!"

But fell on the guests, a hero upon his foe,
The mighty margrave striking blow on fearful blow.

2207   Folker and Hagen stood aside, these two.
They'd given him their promise so to do,
And still he found by the doorway men of mettle
Great enough to cause him worry in this battle.

2208   With will to slay, they let the margrave past,
Gunther and Gernot, men of heroic cast.
Giselher turned away—how sad this made him!
He hoped to live; with Ruedeger there, he must evade him.

2209   Then the margrave's men attacked their foe.
After their master, as true warriors go,
In their hands sharp-cutting swords to wield.
Helmets burst apart, and many a splendid shield.

2210   Weary men lashed out, savagely felling
The knights of Pöchlarn, deep their blows and telling,
Cutting clear through shining armor rings
To the lifeblood. Their battle deeds were glorious things.

2211   Now came all of Ruedeger's retinue,
But Folker and Hagen rushed up quickly too,
And granted no one peace, except one man.
Their hands were busy; down through helmets the red blood ran.

2212   Within, the many swords made awesome sound,
And many shield-bands sprang from the clasps around,
Their jewels falling, scattered, in the blood.
Warriors never fought so fiercely—nor ever would.

2213   Back and forth went Ruedeger, well comparing
        On that day with any man of daring,
        At his best in battle. Thus he gave
        Full proof that he was a knight, worthy of praise, and
            brave.

2214   Here stood warrior Gunther, Gernot the knight.
        They slaughtered many heroes in that fight!
        Dankwart and Giselher let nothing weigh
        Upon their minds, ushering men to their final day.

2215   Ruedeger proved he was strong, valor-filled,
        And nobly armed. What numbers of men he killed!
        A king of Burgundy saw, was moved to wrath,
        And thus began the course of noble Ruedeger's death.

2216   Gernot summoned the bold margrave and cried,
        "Great Ruedeger, you would have their life denied
        To all these men of mine. My heart is sore
        Beyond all measure. I can stand to see no more.

2217   Your gift may end by bringing you injury
        For all the many friends you took from me.
        Come over here, highborn and gallant man,
        I'll set upon your gift the highest price I can."

2218   Before the margrave forced his way clear through,
        Bright rings were doomed to turn a darker hue.
        They rushed upon each other, men who ventured
        All for glory, each on guard lest he be injured.

2219   Nothing withstood, so sharp was each man's sword.
        Through flint-hard helmet Ruedeger the lord

Struck Gernot, and the blood ran down from the blow.
This the gallant knight repaid, and was not slow.

2220   Wounded to death, he still had strength to lift
And swing with both his hands the margrave's gift,
Cleaving the shield to where the helm-straps lie,
A blow from which fair Gotelind's lord was doomed to die.

2221   Never did splendid gift bring worse reward.
Gernot and Ruedeger fell, slain each lord,
Alike in battle, by the other's hand.
Such damage done was more than Hagen's wrath could stand.

2222   Trony cried, "We bear a heavy cross.
In both of them we suffer such a loss,
The end for lands and people will never be.
But we, the outcasts, have his men as surety."

2223   "My poor brother! Death has had free rein.
These times bring me no news but that of pain.
Ruedeger's death is also grief to me;
The loss is on both sides, and the terrible injury."

2224   When Giselher saw his own brother dead,
It was for those inside a thing most dread.
Death looked about for his retainers then,
And not a one survived of all of Pöchlarn's men.

2225   Giselher and Gunther, Hagen too,
Dankwart and Folker, excellent knights, walked through
To where they found the two great heroes lying.
And now there rose the sound of knights in sorrow crying.

2226   "Death robs us cruelly," spoke young Giselher.
      "Now end your weeping, let us go where the air
      Will cool the rings of our mail; we're tired with strife.
      I doubt if God will leave us much more time for life."

2227   Some sat, and others leaned; many a thane
      With idle hands once more, for they lay slain,
      All of Ruedeger's knights. The din had turned
      To silence lasting so long Attila grew concerned.

2228   "What kind of service is this?" exclaimed his wife.
      "Not loyal or true enough to cost the life
      Of any of our foes by Ruedeger's hand!
      He's trying to get them back again to Burgundy land.

2229   We gave him all he wanted, everything.
      What good? Our knight has done us wrong, great king.
      He who should avenge us must have tried
      To sue for peace!" To this the handsome Folker replied:

2230   "That, great queen, I regret is not the case.
      Dared I cast the lie in so noble a face,
      I'd say that you had played him a fiendish ruse.
      For Ruedeger and all his men there is no truce.

2231   He did with such a will what Attila said,
      That he and his retainers lie here dead.
      Look around you, Kriemhild! Where is a friend
      To give commands to? Ruedeger served you till the end;

2232   And if you won't believe it, you shall be shown."
      And so to her heart's sorrow it was done.
      They carried him out, cut down, for the king to see.
      Attila's thanes had never known such misery.

2233   And when they saw the margrave borne in death—
       This frantic sorrow no man's pen or breath
       Could ever describe, this grief of women and men,
       Which in their heartfelt sadness they gave vent to then.

2234   Attila's pain was such, the great king's voice
       Thundered out, as with a lion's noise,
       In the cry of his anguished heart—joined by his wife.
       They mourned without restraint for noble Ruedeger's
           life.

✠ THIRTY-EIGHTH ADVENTURE
How All of Theoderich's Knights Were Slain

2235   So loud were the cries of mourning all around,
That tower and palace echoed with the sound.
A man of Verona, Theoderich's servant, heard,
And he was quick to pass along the dreadful word.

2236   He ran and told his prince: "Hear, my chief!
With all I've lived through, this is past belief—
Such lament as just now struck my ear.
King Attila himself has come to harm, I fear.

2237   What else would plunge them so in grief and pain?
The king or Kriemhild, one of them is slain
By strangers overbold in their enmity.
Handsome knights are weeping uncontrollably."

2238   "Beloved men," said Verona's hero son,
"Do not be hasty! Whatever they may have done,
These foreign knights, they had urgent cause indeed.
Do not begrudge them now the truce I guaranteed."

2239   Brave Wolfhart offered, "I shall be the one
To go and ask the truth of what they've done
And then to you, beloved lord, present
What I find to be the cause of this lament."

2240   Theoderich said, "If men anticipate
Hostility and someone comes to state

A question rudely, heroes may turn in fury.
Wolfhart, you are not the one to put this query."

2241   Quickly then he bade Lord Helfrich go
And find out all that Attila's men might know—
Or the guests themselves—about these last events.
No one had seen a people whose grief was so immense.

2242   The herald came and asked, "What happened here?"
Said one among them, "All our joy and cheer
In the land of Huns is lost beyond regain.
Here, at Burgundy's hands, Ruedeger lies slain.

2243   Of those that came with him, not one is left."
Never had Helfrich felt so greatly bereft,
And never so loath to say what he had to tell.
Theoderich's herald returned, and from his eyes tears fell.

2244   "Warrior, what have you found out for us?"
Theoderich asked. "Why are you weeping thus?"
"If I mourn," replied the knight, "it is only fair.
Burgundians have slain most noble Ruedeger."

2245   "May God forbid!" the lord of Verona spoke.
"That would be awful vengeance, a mocking joke
For the devil's laughter. What has he done to owe
Such debt to them? He liked these strangers, that I know!"

2246   Wolfhart answered this: "Their lives should pay
If they did that. Let them get away
With such a thing, and all of us shall stand
Disgraced and shamed. We've been well served by
    Ruedeger's hand."

2247   Theoderich asked for news more certain still.
       Despairingly he sat at a window sill,
       Sending out Sir Hildebrand to face
       The strangers there and ask them what had taken place.

2248   Bold in battle, Master Hildebrand,
       With neither shield nor weapon in his hand,
       Prepared to meet them, courteously and mild.
       For this the knight was chided by his sister's child:

2249   Fierce Lord Wolfhart cried, "If you remove
       Your armor to go, don't think men won't reprove.
       Your trip returning you will make in disgrace.
       Go there armed, and that will keep them in their place."

2250   So wise man armed at headstrong youth's behest.
       Theoderich's men, before he knew it, dressed
       And had their swords in hand—to his distress,
       For Hildebrand would gladly have avoided this.

2251   He asked them where they headed. "We'll join you there.
       Maybe then Lord Hagen will not dare
       Address you with his usual scorn and jest."
       Hearing what they said, the warrior acquiesced.

2252   Brave Folker saw them come, these many lords,
       Theoderich's men of Verona, girt with swords,
       Nobly armored, bearing shield in hand.
       This he told his master, king of Burgundy land.

2253   The fiddler spoke, "Theoderich's men I see
       Are coming here in open enmity:
       Armed and helmeted for war they come.
       I think an evil turn awaits us, far from home."

2254 Meanwhile, as he spoke, came Hildebrand;
He set his shield at his feet, there to stand,
And put his question to Gunther's retinue:
"Good lords, alas, what did Ruedeger do to you?"

2255 Theoderich sent me to ask if this is true—
Whether the hand of one among you slew
The noble margrave here, as we were told—
Pain so great that we shall never be consoled!"

2256 "The word you have is true," Hagen cried.
"I'd gladly grant you (had your herald lied)
For love of Ruedeger, that he might keep
That life which now forever men and women weep."

2257 Hearing beyond a doubt that he was killed,
They mourned him as their true devotion willed.
Bitter tears rolled down on beard and chin
Of all Theoderich's men, for the sorrow they were in.

2258 Cried Sigestab, Duke of Verona, "Ended thus
Is all the aid and comfort given us
By Ruedeger, after the days of our pain.
The joy of men in exile lies at your hands slain."

2259 Vassal lord of Amelung, Wolfwin, said,
"And if today I saw my father dead,
I could feel no greater pain than for his life.
Alas, and who shall now console the margrave's wife?"

2260 Cried, in anger of spirit, Wolfhart the thane:
"Who now will lead our warriors on campaign,
As the margrave did so often? Woe to the day,
Most noble lord, that you were lost to us this way!"

2261 Wolfbrand and Helfrich, Helmnot, and all their kith
And kindred fell to mourning for his death.
Sobbing, Hildebrand could ask no more.
He cried, "Do now the thing my master sent me for.

2262 Warriors, bring Lord Ruedeger from the hall,
Dead, and give him to us—the final fall
Of all our joy in woe—we'll not ignore
The loyal things he did for us and many more.

2263 For we are exiled men, like Ruedeger—
Why make us wait like this? Let us bear
His corpse away, after death now giving
Homage to him that we should rather grant him living."

2264 "No service is so worthy," Gunther replied,
"As friend may do for friend when he has died.
I call it constant and loyal so to do.
Well may you honor him, he was a friend to you!"

2265 "How long are we to beg?" said Wolfhart the thane.
"Since you have left our greatest solace slain—
Which sadly is no longer ours to have—
Let us take him away and find for him a grave."

2266 "No one will give him to you!" Folker cried.
"Come and get him where he lies, inside,
In the blood, with deep and deadly wounds, where he fell.
Do that if you would really serve Lord Ruedeger well."

2267 "Minstrel," valiant Wolfhart cried, "God knows
We need no provoking! You've brought us enough woes.
If I dared, in my lord's presence, you'd be inviting
Strife and trouble. But no! He said hold back from fight-
    ing."

2268 The fiddler answered, "He fears more than he ought to,
Who stops whatever someone tells him not to.
I can't call that heroic." Good and right,
To Hagen's thinking, were the words of his fellow knight.

2269 "Don't ask for proof of that," Lord Wolfhart cried.
"Or I'll tangle your fiddle strings so when you ride
Back to the Rhine, you'll have a tale to recite.
I can't, for my good name, endure your haughty sight."

2270 "If you untune my strings of melody,"
The fiddler said, "your shining helm will be
A duller shade by far for work of my hand,
Whether or not I ride back to Burgundy land."

2271 Wolfhart was set to spring, but Hildebrand
His uncle stopped him, seizing him by the hand.
"You seem to lose your head, in youthful anger.
Believe me, you would have my liege's grace no longer!"

2272 "Release the lion, Master, he's so grim
And fierce!" cried Folker. "Let me get hold of him—
Had he slain the world and all, he'd get a beating
Such to put the tale, for him, beyond repeating."

2273 The hearts of all the men of Verona were filled
With terrible rage. Bold Wolfhart seized his shield
And most like a savage lion raced ahead,
And all his friends were quick to follow where he led.

2274 As fast as he sprang to reach the building there,
Old Hildebrand outran him to the stair—
He'd not let Wolfhart be the first who fought!
They found among these foreign warriors what they
sought.

2275   Hildebrand fell on Hagen, clashing swords
Resounding in the hands of both these lords,
And one could see how they were stirred with ire.
From their two swords there came a wind all red with fire.

2276   But they were forced apart in the battle-surge,
As warriors of Verona felt the urge
To deeds of strength. When Hildebrand turned back,
Wolfhart fell on gallant Folker in fierce attack.

2277   He struck the fiddler's helm, the sword blade edge
Cleaving its way down to the metal ridge.
The fearless bard paid back his valor's due,
Striking Wolfhart till the sparks of fire flew.

2278   Mighty hewers of fire from rings of chain—
The hatred each one bore the other plain!
Verona's Wolfwin forced the two apart—
And he could not have done it without a hero's heart.

2279   Champion Gunther welcomed with ready hand
Lords of highest praise from Amelung land;
And Giselher the king—where helmets shone,
He left great numbers of them with the wet blood on.

2280   Hagen's brother was a man enraged.
All that Dankwart had done, in battles waged
With Attila's knights before, was but a flurry,
Now bold Aldrian's son fought in awful fury.

2281   Ritschart and Gerbart, Helfrich and Wichart, these
Were fighting men who never took their ease,
Proof of which they gave to Burgundy.
Wolfbrand strode about in battle, gloriously.

2282 Old Hildebrand fought like a man possessed.
At the hands of Wolfhart many of the best,
Struck dead by swords, in blood lay fallen there.
Thus Theoderich's knights avenged Lord Ruedeger.

2283 Lord Sigestab fought, true to his valiant standard.
His foes in battle found their helmets sundered
By Theoderich's nephew, his sister's son.
No greater feats of war could Sigestab have done.

2284 When Folker of savage power came to look
Upon bold Sigestab and the bloody brook
He hewed from hardened rings, his anger rose.
He rushed at him, and life moved swiftly to its close

2285 For Sigestab, at the fiddler's hands, who taught him
Such a lesson in his art as brought him
By Folker's swordsmanship, to deathly pallor—
But this old Hildebrand avenged, urged on by valor.

2286 "Alas for the loss of so beloved a lord,"
He cried, "as here lies dead by Folker's sword.
Now the fiddler shall be safe no longer."
Dauntless Hildebrand had reached the height of anger.

2287 He struck the minstrel then a blow so hard
That rim of helm and shield both flew apart,
Scattered on every side to the walls of the room,
And thus it was that mighty Folker met his doom.

2288 Theoderich's warriors pressed to join the fray,
Striking so that rings spun far away,
And high in the air broken sword-tips shot.
They drew from under helmets rivers flowing hot.

2289   Hagen of Trony saw Lord Folker slain.
In all that festival this was the greatest pain
He suffered for loss of fellow knight or man.
Alas, what work of vengeance Hagen now began!

2290   "Old Hildebrand shall have from this no gain.
At hands of him my aid and help lies slain,
The best companion I have ever known."
He raised his shield and, lashing out with his sword,
    strode on.

2291   Dankwart fell to Helfrich, mighty thane—
To Gunther and Giselher most grievous pain,
Seeing how in bitter throes he fell.
He died, but for his death his hands had paid them well.

2292   Meanwhile Wolfhart, striding to and fro,
Dealt King Gunther's men blow after blow,
Making his third foray through the room.
There at his hands many champions met their doom.

2293   Now Giselher addressed Lord Wolfhart so:
"Alas that I ever gained so fierce a foe!
Bold and highborn knight, turn here to me,
And I shall help to end it; this can no longer be."

2294   So Wolfhart turned to him, in the battle-tide,
Each one leaving deep wounds gaping wide.
He pushed his way to the king—so hard he sped,
The blood beneath his feet splashed above his head.

2295   With fearsome savage blows, fair Uta's child
Met the hero Wolfhart. However wild
And strong this valiant knight, he could not save
His very life. No king so young could be so brave!

2296　He struck Theoderich's vassal then, a blow
　　　That cut through his byrnie, causing the blood to flow—
　　　A fatal wound for Wolfhart, such a one
　　　As no other man could strike, except this champion.

2297　When Wolfhart felt the wound he quickly slipped
　　　His shield to the ground, and with his hand he gripped
　　　A sharp and powerful sword. With a mighty swing
　　　He struck Lord Giselher, piercing helm and ring.

2298　Each had brought the other bitter death.
　　　Of all Theoderich's men, none drew breath.
　　　Old Hildebrand had seen Lord Wolfhart fall—
　　　It was, till his own death, his greatest pain of all.

2299　Theoderich's men were dead, Gunther's as well.
　　　Master Hildebrand came where Wolfhart fell
　　　And now lay deep in blood. He went to fold
　　　His arms about him—he was an excellent man and bold.

2300　He meant to carry him out, but he seemed to weigh
　　　Too much, he had to leave him where he lay.
　　　Then the dying man looked up from the blood
　　　And saw that his uncle would have helped him if he could.

2301　"Dear uncle," cried the doomed and wounded lord,
　　　"You can no longer help me. Be on guard
　　　Before Lord Hagen. This is wisdom's part.
　　　I tell you, he bears a fierce resolve within his heart.

2302　And if my best and closest kin incline
　　　To mourn my death, say this wish is mine:
　　　They should not weep for me, there is no call.
　　　In glory, at a king's own hand, in death I fall.

2303   And in this room I've so repaid my life
That tears are due from many a hero's wife.
If men should ask, let this be freely said:
At my own hand alone, a hundred men lie dead."

2304   Now Hagen thought of Folker, who was slain
By valiant Hildebrand, and cried to the thane:
"You shall pay me back my pain and sorrow.
You've here denied us joy of more than one proud hero."

2305   He struck at Hildebrand, and one could tell
The sound of Balmung, Sigfrid's blade that fell
To dauntless Hagen when he slew that knight.
But he was brave, the old man, and he fought with might.

2306   Theoderich's vassal swung on Trony's lord
A blow with his broad and fearsome cutting sword,
But could not wound King Gunther's man, whose blade
In turn struck through his byrnie, though it was skill-
fully made.

2307   Old Hildebrand felt the wound. In worried fear
That greater hurt at Hagen's hand was near,
He threw his shield across his back and ran
From Hagen, wounded as he was, Theoderich's man.

2308   Not one was living of all the warriors there
Except for Gunther and Hagen, this one pair.
Covered with blood, Hildebrand fled, to bring
Most painful tidings to Theoderich the king.

2309   He saw him sitting, sadly, unaware
That he had greater pain by far to bear.
When he saw Hildebrand, his byrnie red,
Moved by anxious fear, he asked the truth; he said:

2310 "Tell me, Master, why are you soaked through
With men's lifeblood? Or who did that to you?
You must have fought, it seems, with the guests inside.
What I forbid so strictly, you might well avoid!"

2311 He told his liege-lord, "Hagen did it all.
These wounds I got from him, inside the hall,
As I was trying to turn from him and go.
I fled that devil, still alive, but barely so."

2312 The lord of Verona cried, "That serves you right.
You heard me swear them friendship, knight to knight,
And you broke the peace I gave! Could I dismiss
From mind the long disgrace, you'd lose your life for this."

2313 "Theoderich, lord, do not be so irate!
The harm to me and my men is far too great.
We tried to carry Ruedeger away,
But royal Gunther's men were there, to answer nay."

2314 "Oh Lord, this pain! If Ruedeger has died
Then I am plunged in grief, and sorely tried,
For Gotelind is child of my father's sister.
Alas for all in Pöchlarn, orphaned and without master!"

2315 His death recalled true help in times of pain.
Bitterly he wept—the cause was plain.
"Oh, loyal help that will be mine no longer!
Oh, grief for Attila's man, which I shall never conquer.

2316 Can you tell me, Master Hildebrand,
The truth of this? Who is the knight whose hand
Has struck him down?" "Gernot did it," he said,
"Great is his strength. At Ruedeger's hand he too lies
dead."

2317 He said to Hildebrand, "Tell my men to get
Their armor on, and quickly; my mind is set,
I mean to go there. Have them bring to me
My shining gear. I'll question the men of Burgundy."

2318 He answered, "Who is to join your enterprise?
All who live you see before your eyes:
I alone am left. The rest are dead."
Theoderich was stunned, as well might be, at news so
  dread,

2319 For never had he suffered such great pain.
Theoderich cried, "If all my men are slain,
Then I am poor, and God has forgotten me.
I once was a glorious king, in power and property."

2320 He cried again, "How can this be so,
That all my worthy knights are thus laid low
By war-weary men, themselves in a perilous state?
They would be strangers to Death, but for my own ill fate.

2321 Since my unlucky star must work its will—
Tell me, are any Burgundians living still?"
Answered Hildebrand, "None, God knows,
But Hagen alone, and great King Gunther, of all our foes."

2322 "Alas, dear Wolfhart, losing you, I mourn
With the best of cause, the day that I was born.
Sigestab and Wolfwin, good Wolfbrand!
Who is there to help me back to Amelung land?

2323 Valiant Helfrich—what if he is killed?
And Gerbart, Wichart? When is my mourning stilled?
This is the last of all my days of joy!
Alas that grief is not enough to make men die."

✠ THIRTY-NINTH ADVENTURE

How Gunther and Hagen and Kriemhild Were Slain

2324   Theoderich went himself to get his gear,
And Hildebrand helped him arm. One could hear
The building echo with the sound of his voice,
This mighty man in mourning raised so great a noise.

2325   But then his true heroic will returned,
And as he armed, the warrior's temper burned.
Taking up a sturdy shield in hand,
He went his way, he and Master Hildebrand.

2326   "I see Theoderich coming," said Trony's knight.
"He means to seek us out and force the fight.
After all the pain that he has suffered.
Today we'll see to whom the prize of war is offered!

2327   My lord Theoderich here will scarely find
That he's so strong of frame, so fierce of mind—
Wanting to make us pay for the injury done him—
That I should ever feel compelled in war to shun him."

2328   Theoderich heard him, as did Hildebrand.
They came where they could see the champions stand
Outside the building, leaning against the wall.
Theoderich set his shield upon the ground, to call,

2329   In pain and sorrow: "Great King Gunther, say,
Why you have treated me in such a way,
A homeless man? What have I done to you?
I stand alone, deprived of help, my comfort through!

2330   You did not think unhappy fate fulfilled
        Enough when our lord Ruedeger was killed—
        You now begrudge me all my warriors slain.
        Truly, never have I caused you lords such pain.

2331   Think of your own case, the pain you feel,
        Death of friends, and all your great travail—
        Does this not leave your hearts weighed down with care?
        Alas, how harsh to me is the death of Ruedeger!

2332   In all this life, no man was stricken worse.
        Little you thought of the hurt, mine or yours.
        What joy I had lies slain by you, and the end
        Will never come of my lament for kin and friend."

2333   Hagen cried, "Our guilt is not so great!
        Your heroes entered this room in such a state
        Of readiness and with so vast a might—
        I do not think that you have heard the story right."

2334   "What else shall I believe? Hildebrand
        Has told me when my lords of Amelung land
        Asked that you let Ruedeger be borne
        From out the hall, you offered my men nothing but scorn."

2335   The king of the Rhine replied, "This was their word:
        They wanted to take him away. Not to hurt
        Men of yours but Attila did I refuse—
        Until Sir Wolfhart answered this with his abuse."

2336   The lord of Verona spoke, "So let it be.
        Great King Gunther, now make up to me,
        By your good breeding, the pain you caused, and harm,
        And give atonement, sir, that I may so affirm.

2337   Give yourself to me, along with your man,
As hostages. I'll see, as best I can,
That none among the Huns shall do you ill.
All you'll find in me is loyalty and good will."

2338   "God in Heaven forbid," came Hagen's words,
"That you should have surrender of two lords
Who in good defense, and armed, oppose
Your hand and walk untrammeled here before their foes!"

2339   "You should not refuse," Theoderich cried.
"Gunther and Hagen, both of you have tried
My spirit sorely, in heart as well as mind.
Well might you make amends, and well be so inclined!

2340   I pledge to you my faith and certain hand
That I will ride with you, home to your land,
Escorting you in honor—if not so,
To die—and for your sake forgetting all my woe."

2341   "Stop asking that!" said Hagen. "It would not do
To have the story told of us that two,
Both valiant men, surrendered to your hand.
I see no one beside you but Master Hildebrand."

2342   "Hagen," cried Master Hildebrand, "God knows,
A man has offered you peace, to go as you chose—
Of which the time has come to make good use.
You may as well agree to take my master's truce."

2343   "I'd probably take truce," Lord Hagen said,
"Before, in shame and plain disgrace, I fled
A room as you did here, Sir Hildebrand.

I thought you could better face your foes and make your
    stand."

2344   Cried Hildebrand, "Why give me that reproach?
Who was it sat on his shield at Mountain Vosges
While Walter of Spain destroyed his friends and slew
So many kin? There's enough to point to, sir, in you."

2345   Theoderich spoke, "It suits a hero ill
To shriek abuse the way old women will.
I forbid you, Hildebrand, to speak again.
I am a homeless man, hard oppressed by pain."

2346   And he went on, "Hagen, let us hear
What both of you were saying as I came near
And you saw that I was armed. You professed
That singlehanded you would put me to the test."

2347   Hagen answered, "You hear no denial.
I'll trade you heavy blows in such a trial,
Unless the sword of Nibelung breaks apart.
Your wanting us as hostage brings fury to my heart."

2348   Hearing Hagen's fierceness thus revealed,
Bold Theoderich quickly snatched his shield.
Straight at him from the stairway Hagen bounded.
The blade of Nibelung fell on Theoderich—how it re-
    sounded!

2349   Then Theoderich knew the valiant man
Was fierce at heart indeed, and he began
To guard himself against his furious blows.
Well did he know Hagen, most glorious of foes.

416

2350   At Balmung, too, that vicious sword, he quailed,
But often countering skillfully, prevailed;
And Theoderich conquered Hagen. As they fought
He had opened up a wound, deep and long. He thought:

2351   "Fighting wore you out. I'd gain no shred
Of honor here if I should leave you dead.
Rather I shall try to capture you
As hostage first." (A thing most dangerous to do!)

2352   He dropped his shield. Theoderich's strength was vast;
In his arms he seized Lord Hagen fast,
And so the gallant man was overcome.
Noble Gunther mourned to see him thus succumb.

2353   Theoderich carried Hagen to Kriemhild's side,
Into her hand delivering bound and tied
The bravest knight who ever drew a sword.
After her bitter pain, her joy was now restored.

2354   Delighted, Kriemhild bowed to him and said,
"Good Fortune descend upon your heart and head!
You've made up all my hurt. My gratitude
Shall ever again reward you, unless my death preclude."

2355   Theoderich said, "Grant to him his life!
And if you do this, oh great Attila's wife,
The injury he brought you he'll repay,
But you must not make him suffer for being bound this
    way."

2356   She ordered Hagen led where he would find
But prison comfort. There he lay confined,

Seen by no one. Shouting, Gunther said,
"The lord of Verona caused me this pain—where has he
    fled?"

2357   Theoderich went to Gunther—the king was a man
       Much praised for strength and valor; Gunther ran
       Out in front of the hall, waiting no longer
       The swords in both men's hands raised a fearful clangor.

2358   For all Theoderich's fame, from time long past,
       Gunther's rage and fury were so vast—
       Sworn foe of his, for the hurt he suffered under—
       That still they tell of his escape as of a wonder.

2359   Both were so great in valor and in power,
       That with the force of their blows palace and tower
       Echoed with swords on helmets hacking down.
       In royal Gunther's heart lay glory and renown.

2360   Yet Theoderich conquered him, as was before
       The lot of Hagen, causing his blood to pour
       From corselet rings, by the sharp sword in his hand.
       For his fatigue, King Gunther made a worthy stand.

2361   But now Theoderich bound him hand and foot,
       Though in such bonds no king should ever be put.
       Theoderich wondered then if he should try
       To free them both, but any who met them would surely
           die.

2362   The lord of Verona took him by the arm
       And led him to the queen. And through the harm
       That came to him, her great anxiety
       Was stilled. She cried, "Welcome, Gunther of Burgundy!"

2363   "Dear sister, before you I should bow my face
        If in your greeting there had been more grace.
        I know you, queen, to be so filled with hate,
        Your welcome to me and Hagen will be both little and
            late."

2364   Theoderich cried, "Wife of a noble king!
        Never were such heroes as I bring
        To you, milady, taken hostage yet.
        Let my good offices gain these men some benefit,

2365   So far from home." She said she would, and gladly.
        Theoderich left the heroes, weeping sadly.
        In grim and fearsome vengeance afterwards
        She took the very lives of both these excellent lords.

2366   She prisoned the two apart, to cause them pain.
        Neither would see the other one again,
        Until she brought to Hagen her brother's head—
        Kriemhild's revenge on both of them, a cause for dread.

2367   And then she went to Hagen—hostile and grim
        The tone of voice in which she spoke to him!
        "If you will give me back what you took from me,
        You may yet return alive, home to Burgundy."

2368   Fierce Hagen answered her, "You waste your breath,
        Highborn queen! I have sworn an oath
        Not to reveal the treasure, and to give
        No part away, while any of my lords shall live."

2369   "I'll bring an end to that," cried Attila's wife.
        She gave the word to take her brother's life.

They struck off his head; she carried it by the hair
To show to Hagen, lord of Trony, to his despair.

2370   When, sick at heart, he saw his master's head,
Hagen the warrior, turning to Kriemhild, said,
"And so your will is done, and you have brought
An end to things, and all has turned out as I thought.

2371   Now the noble king of Burgundy's gone,
Young Giselher, and Gernot, leaving none
Who knows where the treasure is, but God and me.
Discover, fiend of evil, how secret that will be!"

2372   "You rob me foully of my due redress,"
Cried the queen, "but I shall still possess
The sword my darling Sigfrid took to wear
When I saw him last—the pain is mine, the guilt you
    bear!"

2373   She took it from the sheath—what could he do?
She wanted the warrior's life. And so she drew,
And lifting high her hands, struck off his head.
Great King Attila saw it all; and his heart bled.

2374   "God help us!" cried the king. "Here lies slain
At a woman's hands, alas, the finest thane
Who ever carried shield or went to war.
My heart is sad, for all the enmity I bore."

2375   "She dared to kill him—little good will it be!"
Old Hildebrand cried. "Whatever happens to me—
And though he left me, too, in desperate plight—
I shall avenge the death of Trony's gallant knight."

2376   In wrath he sprang at the queen and cruelly swung
His sword upon her. Kriemhild, now unstrung
By fear of Hildebrand, began to wail
And scream most terribly, but all to no avail.

2377   Now all whose fate it was to lose their life
Lay slain, and cut to bits the great king's wife.
Attila and Theoderich now began
To mourn most pitifully the death of kin and man.

2378   All their glory and splendor now lay dead,
And people were in grief, beset with dread.
Sorrow ended the feast of Attila the Hun—
As ever pleasure turns to pain when all is done.

2379   I cannot say what afterwards occurred,
Except that ladies, knights, and squires were heard
Lamenting for the death of kin and friend.
This is the fall of the Nibelungs, and of this tale the end.

This manuscript was prepared for publication by Christine Colditz. The book was designed by Richard Kinney. The text type face is Granjon based on a design by Claude Garamond and redesigned under the supervision of George W. Jones for the Linotype Corporation. Various styles of Lydian type face designed by Warren Chappell for American Type Founders, 1938, are used for display.

The book is printed on Hammermill's Lock Haven antique offset paper, and is bound in Riegal's Foldcote Cover. Manufactured in the United States of America.

This manuscript was prepared for publication by Christine
Cedzo. The book was designed by Richard Kinney. The text
type face is Garamon based on a design by Claude Garamond,
and it is composed under the supervision of George W. James for
_____ Composition. With a mix of Ludlow type The display type is Weiss designed and Zenith by Type Founders is
_____ various forms of _____ _____.

The book is printed on Glatfelter B. Lock, Wove antique
_____ paper and is bound in Kingsli Holliston Cloth, Manufactured by _____ _____ _____ _____.